ISBN 978-1-332-02254-0
PIBN 10270423

1 MONTH OF
FREE
READING

at

www.ForgottenBooks.com

By purchasing this book you are eligible for one month membership to ForgottenBooks.com, giving you unlimited access to our entire collection of over 700,000 titles via our web site and mobile apps.

To claim your free month visit:
www.forgottenbooks.com/free270423

MEMORIALS

OF THE

FAMILY OF SKENE OF SKENE

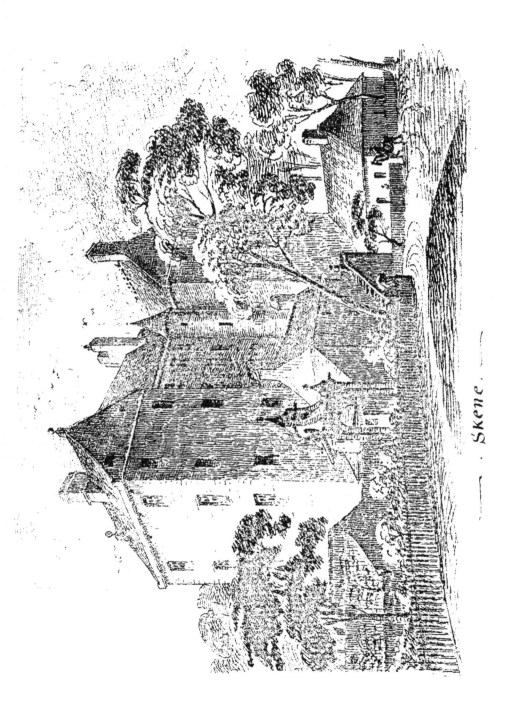

Skene.

FROM THE FAMILY PAPERS

WITH OTHER ILLUSTRATIVE DOCUMENTS

EDITED BY

WILLIAM FORBES SKENE, D.C.L., LL.D.

HER MAJESTY'S HISTORIOGRAPHER FOR SCOTLAND

ABERDEEN

1887

The New Spalding Club.

Founded 11th November, 1886.

Patroness:

HER MAJESTY THE QUEEN.

OFFICE BEARERS for 1886-87.

President:

THE EARL OF ABERDEEN.

1235083

Vice-Presidents:

THE DUKE OF RICHMOND AND GORDON, K.G.
THE EARL OF STRATHMORE.
THE EARL OF KINTORE.
THE EARL OF FIFE, K.T.
THE LORD FORBES.
THE LORD PROVOST OF ABERDEEN.

THE PRINCIPAL OF THE UNIVERSITY OF ABERDEEN.
CHARLES ELPHINSTONE-DALRYMPLE, of Kinellar Lodge.
GEORGE GRUB, LL.D.
ALEXANDER FORBES IRVINE, of Drum, LL.D.
JOHN WEBSTER, of Edgehill, LL.D.

Members of Council:

The Earl of Southesk, K.T.
The Lord Saltoun.
The Bishop of Aberdeen and Orkney.
Sir Francis W. Grant, Bart. of Monymusk.
Sir George Macpherson-Grant, Bart. of Ballindalloch.
Sir William C. Brooks, Bart., Glentanar, M.P.
Sir Mountstuart Elphinstone Grant-Duff, of Eden, K.C.S.I.
William Alexander, LL.D., Aberdeen.
Colonel James Allardyce, Aberdeen.
Alexander Baird, of Urie.
George Burnett, LL.D., Lyon King of Arms.
James A. Campbell, of Stracathro, LL.D., M.P.
The Rev. James Cooper, Aberdeen.
Peter M. Cran, Aberdeen.
John Crombie, of Balgownie Lodge.
Alexander Davidson, of Desswood.
Charles B. Davidson, Aberdeen.
The Rev. John Davidson, D.D., Inverurie.
Thomas Dickson, LL.D., H.M. General Register House.
Francis Edmond, of Kingswells, LL.D.
John Philip Edmond, Aberdeen.
Robert F. O. Farquharson, of Haughton.
William Ferguson, of Kinmundy.
The Rev. James Gammack, LL.D., Aberdeen.
James Murray Garden, Aberdeen.

Henry Wolrige-Gordon, of Esslemont.
The Rev. Walter Gregor, LL.D., Pitsligo.
Alexander Kemlo, Aberdeen.
Colonel William Ross King, of Tertowie.
The Rev. James Forbes-Leith, S.J., Paris.
George Arbuthnot-Leslie, of Warthill.
David Littlejohn, Sheriff-Clerk, Aberdeen.
Charles Fraser-Mackintosh, of Drummond, M.P.
Hugh Gordon Lumsden, of Clova.
James Matthews, of Springhill.
The Rev. John G. Michie, Dinnet.
James Moir, Rector of the Grammar School, Aberdeen.
Arthur D. Morice, Aberdeen.
Charles Rampini, Sheriff-Substitute, Elgin.
Alexander Ramsay, Banff.
Major John Ramsay, of Barra.
Alexander W. Robertson, Aberdeen.
Hercules Scott, of Brotherton.
William Forbes Skene, D.C.L., LL.D., H.M. Historiographer for Scotland.
The Rev. William Temple, Forgue.
Alexander Walker, Aberdeen.
George Walker, Aberdeen.
Robert Walker, Aberdeen.
John Dove Wilson, LL.D., Sheriff-Substitute, Aberdeen.

Secretary:

PETER JOHN ANDERSON, 2 East Craibstone Street, Aberdeen.

Treasurer:

PATRICK HENDERSON CHALMERS, 13 Union Terrace, Aberdeen.

PREFACE.

WHEN the Council of the New Spalding Club asked me to undertake to compile a history of the ancient Aberdeenshire family of Skene of Skene, which they proposed to issue as the first of a series of histories of ancient northern families, I willingly undertook the task, as I had ample materials at my disposal, the result of researches made by my late father into the Family History. I felt, however, that there might be a disadvantage in selecting one for this task who was himself among the few remaining male descendants of the family, from a natural tendency to over-estimate the importance of the Skene family, and the consideration in which it was held, fostered as it was in some degree by the language of previous family historians; but I have endeavoured to avoid this tendency, and to present a plain historical narrative of the history of the family, so far as it is based on authentic documents.

If there had existed only one manuscript history of the family of Skene of Skene, I would have been disposed to follow the example of my late much esteemed friend—Mr. Cosmo Innes— in the family histories edited by him for the original Spalding Club, and to print the family history entire, adding such authentic documents as tended to illustrate it; but I had no fewer than five manuscript histories of the family, written at different dates, at my disposal, and I therefore thought it better simply to insert extracts from them when it was desirable to present the narrative in their language instead of my own, and to add a reference to such authentic .documents as confirmed or corrected it.

The fact that I was able to refer to so many family histories, written at different periods, has, however, enabled me to shew the gradual growth and development of the traditionary history of the origin of the family.

The curious circumstance that in 1296 John de Skene, the first historic person of the name, bore as a cognizance the head of John the Baptist, while Patrick de Skene, the *Clericus,* bore on his Seal three Skenes or dirks, and that the Kirktown of Skene belonged to the family, rather indicates that the name of Skene was primarily connected with the Church, and extended from thence to the barony, while the wolves' heads do not then appear as forming part of the cognizance of the family. A circumstance, however, connected with the arms of an ancient English family, throws some light upon this fact. The Plumptons of Plumpton Hall were Hereditary Foresters of the Ancient Royal Forest of Knaresborough, in the West Riding of Yorkshire. In Wharf-dale, which formed part of the Forest, and was anciently covered with wood, still stands Plumpton Hall, a tower very similar to the old tower of Skene; and there is still preserved in it an old stone coat-of-arms of the Plumptons, shewing three wolves heads in *fesse,* a cognizance indicating, according to tradition, their connection with the Forest, which was infested by wolves, a certain number of which they were bound to kill each year. The only family in Scotland which bore three wolves' heads, besides the Skenes, was that of the Robertsons of Strowan, and they too were connected with a Forest, for their principal pos-session was the great north-west Forest of Atholl, called the Forest of Glengarry. The position of this family in the earlier generations was an exact counterpart of that of the Skenes. They possessed the Kirktown of Strowan, took their designation from it—though the smallest of their possessions—and when their lands were erected into a Barony the name of Strowan was given to the Barony. In like manner the Skene lands were originally part of a Forest. The family, too, possessed the Kirktown of Skene, took their designation from it, and when the lands were erected into a Barony it was termed the Barony of Skene. The Seal of Patrick the *Clericus* of Skene shews that the cognizance of the name was three Skenes or dirks, and the three wolves' heads borne upon them were no doubt derived from their original connection with the Forest. The combination of the two may have given rise to the tradition of the first Skene having saved the King from a wolf, and presented his head upon a Skene or dirk.

In the narrative which I have given of the different generations of the family of Skene of Skene, with its branches, I have not thought it necessary to print at length the Charters and Retours which I have referred to in support of it, but have merely quoted them from the originals in the Charter Chests, or from the Public Records, as they do not in fact possess any interest beyond the proof they afford of the succession of the different heads of the family. The chief value of such family histories lies much more in the pictures they afford of the social position and habits of life of such families at different periods, thus illustrating the social development of the country ; and these I have endeavoured to bring out as much as possible, both in the principal narrative and in the documents in the Appendix, which were selected with that view. Thus we can see these ancient Scottish Barons living in a tower "built of three arches or stories, and entered by a ladder on the second story." We can see the younger sons having no other resource than either to enter the Church, or to have their names inscribed in the rental books of the family as kindly tenants of some outlying farm, which their descendants, if the laird was embarrassed, acquired as property, or else descended to the condition of ordinary farmers. Then some generations later we see the increasing trade of the country, and the new ideas and new life infused into society by the Reformation, sending the younger sons of such families to seek their subsistence in other fields. We see them now obtaining a better education in the newly founded Colleges, some of them taking a University degree, and distinguished from their less cultivated brothers by the title of "Mr.," a designation at that time exclusively confined to Masters of Arts ; and then sometimes teaching for some years in their College as Regents. We can see those who would have entered the Church becoming Notaries Public, adopting learned professions, or becoming Professors in these Colleges. We can see others breaking through the aristocratic line of demarcation between land and Burgh, and, becoming burgesses of the County town, whence, if they were prosperous in trade, they again emerged and founded new County families by purchasing land. Add to this the foundation of the College of Justice, and the increasing trade between Scotland and the Netherlands and Poland, in which Aberdeen took a large share, and we can see the scions of County families resorting to one or other as an outlet for their energies, and a means of acquiring fame and fortune.

We can thus see the sons of one obscure Notary Public on Deeside furnishing a Professor of Medicine, who became Physician to the King, and a learned Advocate, who was "a good, trew, stout man, like a Dutche man, and culd mak them lang harangues in Latin," sent as Ambassador to Foreign Courts, and occupying the high position of Lord Clerk Register, receiving letters from learned persons abroad (App. ii.), and laudatory verses at home (App. iii.), while his last years are embittered by disputes among his sons, and the efforts which the Archbishop of St. Andrews narrates in such quaint language

to bring them to a settlement are defeated by the influence of
the puritan mother-in-law of the eldest son (App. IV.) We can
see a member of another branch occupying the position of
Conservator of Scotch privileges at Campvere, in the Netherlands (App. I.); the younger son of a Midmar farmer of the Halyards in Fife branch settling at Venloo, in the same country, and
founding a family, now occupying an important and influential
position in Austria; and the younger son of a Belhelvie farmer
of the Westercorse branch acquiring a fortune in Poland,
returning home, and founding a County family. We can see
a younger son of the Halyards in Midlothian family in the
army, serving in the Netherlands, marrying a young Dutch girl,
and dying at Tournay, and we can read the touching letters
written by himself from his deathbed, and by his young widow
(App. VII.) We can see a specimen of the intolerance exercised
by Charles I. in Scotland, under the auspices of Archbishop Laud,
when a Judge of the Court of Session was in danger of losing his
position because he had not communicated kneeling at Easter
in St. Giles (App. V.); while some years after we find him
President of the Court of Session, and rewarded by a Nova
Scotia Baronetcy, his patent, like other early patents, containing
the grant of a Barony, with almost regal jurisdiction, in Nova
Scotia, where the grantees were expected to settle, but which
grants were rendered nugatory by the entire district being
possessed by the French in 1638 (App. VI.) We can see, too,
the remarkable current of religious feeling which soon after
spread over Scotland, when a Magistrate of Aberdeen, and
his family, became Quakers, and a Provost of Aberdeen made
a solemn renunciation of his sins (App. IX.)

The History of the Skenes of Skene, and the families
whose descent from them can be traced, terminates with that
family to which I belong, two families whose connection with
the chief family has not been traced being placed in the

Appendix (No. i.) When I approached the present generation of my own family I felt myself treading on delicate ground, as I naturally desired to do justice to the members of it, and especially to the character and accomplishments so generally recognised of my late father, but was afraid that I might be led into over laudation. I was therefore glad, in the case of my father, to be able to substitute for my own account the obituary notice of him addressed to the Royal Society of Edinburgh, by so distinguished a man as Sir David Brewster, and to conclude the Appendix by adding the well-known lines addressed to him by his life-long friend, Sir Walter Scott (App. x.)

I was also glad to be able to supply the full-page illustrations to this volume from the collection of my father's drawings, part of which had already appeared in the edition of Spalding's Troubles, printed for the Bannatyne Club.

I have, in conclusion, to record my thanks to my friend, Charles Elphinstone-Dalrymple, Esq., for the kind interest he has taken in the work, and the judicious advice I have received from him ; and also to the Secretary of the New Spalding Club, P. J. Anderson, Esq., who has kindly revised my proof sheets, and given me many valuable suggestions from time to time.

I have only to add, that in compiling the history of so many branches of the family, I may occasionally have been led into inaccuracies of date or statement, for which I hope to meet with indulgence.

WILLIAM F. SKENE.

27 Inverleith Row,
Edinburgh, *December, 1887.*

TABLE OF CONTENTS.

APPENDIX OF ILLUSTRATIVE DOCUMENTS.

LIST OF ILLUSTRATIONS.

9
S

MEMORIALS OF THE FAMILY OF SKENE OF SKENE.

INTRODUCTION.

THE materials for a history of the ancient Aberdeenshire Family of Skene of Skene are more than usually abundant. They consist of the family papers in the charter chest of Skene of Skene, in the possession of the Earl of Fife, now the heir of line of the family; those in the charter chest of the family of Rubislaw, and in that of the family of Curriehill and Halyards, which fell to the late James Skene of Rubislaw, on the failure of that branch ; and five manuscript histories, compiled at different times.

The oldest of these (MS.A) is a manuscript bearing the following title, " Origo nominis necnon familiæ de Skein," and concluding with the following docquet, " Thir presents are exhibited by a wellwisher of both the families, viz., the Laird of Glenbervie, called Douglas, whose draught thereof is wrytten by Mr. Alexander Skene, Aberdeen, 22 January, 1678." This Mr. Alexander Skene is obviously also the compiler of another manuscript, containing coats of arms of all the principal Scottish families. The Skene families among them are—" Skene of that ilk, G. 3 wolfe-heads couped O., on the poynts of as many swords paleways A. hilted and pomelled of the 2d. ; Skene of Halȝards in Lothian ; Skene of Halȝards in Fyfe ; Skene of Fintrie ; Skene of Remore ; Skene of Dyce; Skene of Bandodle ; Skene of Dumbreck ; Skene of Corrihill ; Skene of Tillibirlach ; Skene of Newtyle ; Gilbert Skene [his own ancestor], bears the principall armes of the house, and for his cognisance

Adjuvante Jehovah

Hunc librum Pinxit
ALEX^{R.} SKENE
Scoto-Abredonensis
A.Æ.C. 1678
cui 25to Julij coronidem
Imposuit πάντοτε δόξα θεῷ.
O si possem pingere Æternitati
Duce Deo quidvis potest quivis.

כי ארני לך הוחלהי

* על-כן שמח אני בחלקי

Sors mihi grata cadet.

This is followed by an alphabetical Index, and by some Notes on Heraldry.

There can, I think, be little difficulty in identifying the compiler of these two manuscripts with a Mr. Alexander Skene, a man of some note and culture at the time, in Aberdeen, whose brother James, about the same time, held the office of Lyon Depute. They were, as will afterwards appear, sons of a Robert Skene, merchant burgess of Aberdeen, and treasurer of the burgh. Alexander, his eldest son, was born in 1621, and admitted a burgess in 1625, when only four years old—"jure paternitatis et dispens. cum jurejurando quia pupillus est et infra aetatem." In 1648 he was a Master of Arts, as appears from a sasine in favour "probi et discreti adolescentis magistri Alexandri Skene." In 1656 he became a magistrate of the town, and in the same year was chosen, as one of the nearest of kin, curator of John Skene of that ilk, whom he addresses, in 1675, in a letter in the same charter chest, as his "beloved friend."

---

* I am indebted to the Reverend Walter MacLeod for the following explanation of the Hebrew—" The Hebrew lines are not from any particular text, so far as I can discover, but the phraseology is Scriptural. They may be thus rendered :—

For in Thee, O Lord, is my hope ;
Therefore I rejoice in my portion."

In 1685 there appeared in Aberdeen a work with the title of "Memorialls for the Government of the Royall-Burghs in Scotland. By ΦΙΛΟΠΟΛΙΤΕΙΟΥΣ, or a lover of the Publick wellfare"; and, in the same year, "A Succinct Survey of the famous City of Aberdeen. By a Zealous Lover of Bon-Accord, ΦΙΛΟΠΟΛΙΤΕΙΟΥΣ." That Baillie Alexander Skene was the author appears from an entry in the Council Register in the same year—"the little book latlie emitted be Mr Alex^r Skene late bailie dedicat to the Mag^{rats} and Counsell . . . . to get tuentie thereof for the touns vse" (vol. lvii, p. 198).

His position, his literary character, and his connection with the family of Skene of Skene necessarily give great weight to his account of the family, and especially to that period when he must have been personally cognisant of the facts he narrates.

The second manuscript history, in point of date (MS.B), is unfortunately anonymous. Its title is "Some special Accounts concerning the house of Skene," and it belonged to the late Andrew Skene, advocate, Solicitor-General for Scotland. This account, however, must have been written between the years 1680 and 1724, as the writer mentions, "John Skene of that ilk, who was father to the present Laird of Skene, whose name is Alexander," and Alexander succeeded his father in 1680, and died in 1724. From its silence as to later events, it was probably written not long after the former date.

Of the third manuscript (MS.C) we can give a more distinct account. Its title is "Ane account of Sir John Skene, Lord Curriehill, Clerk Register, his Predecessors and Successors"; and there is this docquet—"This account was written by Mr. Robert Cowpar, brother to Sir John Cowpar of Gogar, who died in the 90th year of his age in the year 1726, at Balherton, in Midlothian, near Edinburgh. Sir John Cowpar's father was married (as per the account) to Mr. John Skene of Halyards, one of the principal Clerks of Session, his eldest daughter, Helen Skene; and Mr. John Skene of Halyards was Sir John's second son, who was a son of Skene of Raemoir's, the eldest cadet of the family of Skene of that ilk, now gone into the name of Hog, by the heiress marrying this Raemoir's father, who was first of that name. This is copied out of the original manuscript by John Ramsay of Menies, lineally descended of the family of Dalhousie, Anno 1727." This account, therefore, belongs to the same period with the previous manuscript.

The fourth manuscript account of the family (MS.D) consists of separate "accounts of the families of Skene of Skene, of Skene of Halyards (in Fife), and of Skene of Curriehill and Halyards, in Lothian ; to which is added some accounts concerning the family of Skene of that ilk ; an account of Sir George Skene of Wester Fintray, his predecessors, and account of some of the predecessors of Giles Adie, wife of Alexander Skene, who died at Skene, 20th January, 1724." These formed part of "The account of the families of Scotland, in the possession of the late George Chalmers, F.R.S.S.A.," and may be dated about 1770.

The last manuscript account (MS.E) is a volume with the title "Parentalia, or Genealogical Notes with reference to the different families of the name of Skene and others allied to the family of Skene of Rubislaw, collected from various sources by James Skene, 1820." This manuscript is chiefly valuable from recording many of the floating traditions regarding the family history, which were still current at the date at which it was compiled, and which the author lost no opportunity of obtaining from those old persons in whose memory they were still preserved.

The following memorials are compiled partly from these manuscript histories, and partly from documents among the family papers, or extracted from the public records. Where no references are added, they are from documents in the various charter chests.

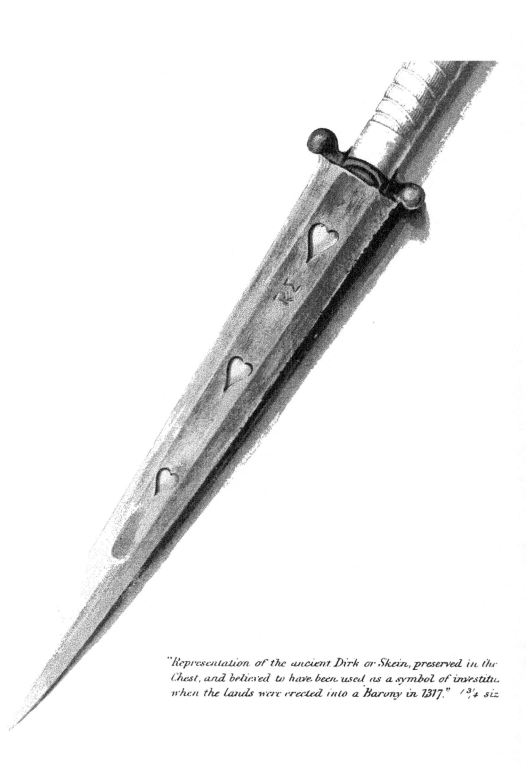

"Representation of the ancient Dirk or Skein, preserved in the
Chest, and believed to have been used as a symbol of investitu
when the lands were erected into a Barony in 1317." ¾ siz

CHAPTER I.

SKENE OF SKENE.

ABOUT ten miles due west from Aberdeen is the Loch of Skene, a considerable sheet of water, and on the north side of it extends the ancient barony of Skene, co-extensive with the more modern parish of the same name. It is bounded on the north by the parishes of Kinellar and Kintore, on the west by the parishes of Kinnernie, now annexed to Cluny, and Echt, and on the east by the freedom lands of Aberdeen. The barony consisted of two distinct portions. The western and larger portion contained the lands of the Maynes or Dominical lands of Skene, Hattown, Broomhill, Newton, Tearavell, Over and Nether Auchinlech, Craigdarg, Letter, Bervie, Easter and Wester Kinmundie, Easter and Wester Carney, Fiddie, Mill of Keir, Ord, Blackhill, Graystone, Rodgerhill, and Broadiach. The eastern and smaller portion, usually termed the lands of Easter Skene, consisted of the Kirkton of Skene, Liddach, Garlogie, and Millbuie. On the former was situated the old tower of Skene, said by tradition to be the first built stone house in Mar. It now forms the west wing of the House of Skene. On Easter Skene was the Church of Skene, now a parish church, but formerly a vicarage, dependent upon the mother church of Kinkell.

These lands were erected into a barony by King Robert Bruce, in the year 1317, and have from time immemorial been in the possession of the baronial family of Skene of Skene. Mr. Robert Cowpar tells the following anecdote with reference to the antiquity of the family. He says—" This present Laird of Skene's father being in Edinburgh, and desirous to see his relations, Sir John Cowpar of Gogar being in company with him at the Cross of Edinburgh, asked him if he desired to see and be acquainted with my Lady Dundonald, being ane relation of his, he was very well pleased, and they went together to her lodging. Sir John Cowpar, intro-ducing him to the Countess of Dundonald, told her he had brought her Chief the Laird of Skene to wait upon her. She received him with great joy and kindness, being the person in the world she longed to see, being her chief, and hearing that he was ane old family—' But, Skene, I would gladly know what you can produce to instruct your antiquity?' 'I can instruct, in my charter-chest, one-and-thirty services and retours, from father to son, and not a daughter intervening;' whereupon she called upon the Earl of Dundonald, and gave him account of what Skene told her; the Earl being so well pleased that he embraced him and carried him to his foreroom, where there were several noblemen in company with the Earl, and desired them to take his Lady's chief by the hand, who could say that which, he believed, none of them could say the like. 'This Laird of Skene can produce, lying in his charter chest, thirty-one services and retours, from father to son, and not a daughter intervening;' which all of them declared there was none of them could say the like, and that it was both ane honest and old evidence of his family; so this present old laird's son is thirty-third from father to son" (MS.C)—and no doubt none of them could say the like, and it would have been "ane honest and old evidence" if the retours could have been produced; but that the old laird's son was the thirty-third from father to son, was simply a matter of traditionary belief, evidently derived from the legendary origin of the family. Taking the average length of a generation in the Skene family, which, from the early marriages of the lairds, is unusually small, thirty-one generations would take us back to the eleventh century, and through a period when there were no such documents as services and retours.

The traditionary origin of the family is thus given by Mr. Alexander Skene, in 1678 :—

"Ane old tradition yr is that the tribe and family of Skein had their origin from Struan Robertson of Athole, and they from McDonald, and yt our first author was a son of the Laird of Struans, and had his first donation immediately from the king, for killing ane devouring wolfe in the forest, near the freddom land of Aberdeen, for which he got ye confirmation of East and Wester Skein, to the freedom of Abdn, and that with ane coat of arms helmed and flurished, relating to the valorous act, viz., 3 wolf's heads crazed upon the points of 3 Skeens, triumphant in a field of Gules; above the helmet ane naked hand holding a laurel branch, w^t this motto, ' Virtutis Regia merces,' which arms are registered in ye booke of Heraldry. Under the reign of what king y^t happened I am not certainly informed. But sure I am that there was lately in the charter chest of the House of Skein a restauration from a forfauture granted by K. W. the Lion. This is now amissing." (MS.A).

Sir George Mackenzie, in his "Science of Heraldry," published two years after, in 1680, gives the same account. He says—"Some also derive their names as well as their arms from some considerable action ; and thus a second son of Struan Robertson, for killing of a wolf in Stocket Forrest by a durk in the king's presence, got the name of Skein, which signifies a durk in Irish, and three durk-points in pale for his armes." (p. 5.)

The next manuscript account, written not very long after, gives us the king's name. It says—"King Malcolm Kenmore, having defeat the Danes at Mortlich, which was then the Bishop's see, and killed the King of Denmark there, on his road south from the Buttoch of Mortlich, being fiercely purshewed by a devouring woulfe in the wood of Culbleun, which then stretched itself from Breymar to the forest of the Stocket of Aberdeen,

miles abov that town, a second son of Donald of the Isles, perceiving the fierceness of the woulfe with his open mouth coming upon the king, wrapt his plaid about his left arme, and thrust in his mouth, and interposed himselfe to the furie of the wyld beast rather than have his prince in hazard, and then, with his right hand, drew his Skene, and under his arme that was in the mouth of the woulfe, struck in his Skein at his head, and cut of his head and delivered to King Malcombe, for the quhilk Malcome gave him the lands of Skene, and caused him to be called Skene of y^t ilk, as lykways the great Laik or Loch of Skene, being sax myles of circuit, well plenished with fresh water fishes, Elk Bulls and Croched Cows on the sydes thereof, who have but on ear or lug, and gives exceeding mutch milk, and are said never seen to Bule, but its vulgarly reported that these Elfe Bulls comes out in the night season and returne with a great Bulying in the Watter.

" The armes given for this noble atchievement and act of valour was Gules, three Skeines palewayes, in fess argent, pomelled or, surmounted of alse many woolfe heads couped of the third ; above the shield ane helmit befitting his degree, mantled gules, doubled argent ; supported on the dexter by a Dunewassell in highland habit, viz., a blue bonnet, pinched up on the left syde with a bon pin, a slashed out coat or doublet, enveloped with a plaid over his left shoulder, and girded in his sword, and his left hand curving up the shield, and in his right hand a Skene or dagger guarding it, and on the sinister syd a Gillieweetfoot, with his master's target on his left arme, and his doorlach pendant to his heels, with short hoise, and rullions on his foot ; and for his Crest a Crowne of Lawrell, with this motto over it, in a scroll, '*virtutis regia merces.*'   This Coat was *donum Regis*, and not the douyer of a Herauld. . . .

"John Skene of y^t ilk, who was father to the present Laird of Skene, whose name is Alexander, was the Twentie-sevent Laird of Skene served and retoured, as the breves and services by the Monsars [Macers] and Sheriffe Court Books of Aberdene can witness."   (MS.B.)

The third manuscript (MS.C) repeats the traditional origin given by Mr. Alexander Skene in 1678 ; but Sir John Cowpar, in introducing this John Skene of that ilk to Lady Dundonald, adds four generations to the twenty-seven given in the previous manuscript, and credits him with thirty-one services and retours.

In the next manuscript history (MS.D) we find a still further development of the story, extending, in the same manner, the antiquity of the family.   The author repeats the story in MS.B, but substitutes Malcolm the Second as the King, and gives 1014 as the date, and then adds to it this further account :—" The first of this family we have now upon record is John de Skeen, who lived in the reign of King Malcolm Canmore, after whose death he had the misfortune to join Donald Bain, the usurper, who was his near relative, for which he was most justly forfeited by King Edgar.   But afterwards, in the reign of King Alexander 1st., when that monarch was marching against the Rebels in the North, the Laird of Skeen joined the Royal army, did them singular service in assisting them to pass the rivers, and in short behaved with such courage and magnanimity against the King's Enemies upon every occasion, that his Majesty was graciously pleased to rehabilitate him, and restored unto him his Estate of Skene, Anno 1118 (in the charter chest of the family), which has been enjoyed by his posterity ever since."

In another edition of this manuscript the story is thus told :—

" The family, by the troublesome times which afterwards prevailed, lost many of their charters and principal papers, so that there is very little accounts of thirteen Lairds of Skene who succeeded one another, from King Malcolm the second to the time of King Robert the Bruce ;

only there is still extant a Restoraution from a forfaulture of the Lands of Skene, granted by King Alexander the first to John de Skene, An. 1118.; and the tradition of the forfaulture is, that upon Donald Bane usurping the Crown of Scotland, after the death of King Malcolm the Third, surnamed Keanmore, the then Laird of Skene joined with Donald as his relation, for which he was forfeited ; and upon King Alexander succeeding to the Crown, and going north to Murray, to subdue the Rebells, who had attacked him in his Castle of Luff, in the Carse of Gowrie, the Laird of Skene followed the king north, and by his valour and conduct was the principal mean of passing the king and his army over the water of Spey, in spite of the Rebells who had taken possession of the Foords, and did the king many other remarkable services in that campaign, for which· he was restored by him to his Estate."

It is no wonder that the writer could find little account of the supposed thirteen early Lairds of Skene, but he makes up for the want of records, by transposing the restoration from forfeiture, which Mr. Alexander Skene said was granted by King William the Lion, to the reign of Alexander I. in 1118, and attaches to it a fanciful tale, in which he appropriates to his imaginary Laird of Skene the valiant actions which Hector Boece attributes to Alexander Carron, the king's standard bearer.

The first appearance of the surname of Skene, in any authentic document, is in 1296, when " Johan de Skene del counte de Edneburh," and " Johan de Skene, Patrick de Skene del counte de Aberdene," did homage to King Edward the First (Calendar of Documents relating to Scotland, pp. 203-208). The seals attached to these homages are preserved, and show that Johan de Skene del counte de Edneburh and del counte de Aberdene was the same person. His seal bears the device of a head of John the Baptist upon a charger, with a hand pointing down, and the inscription " S. Ioh'is de Sceyn." The Seal of Patrick de Skene has the device of a small shield within quatrefoil, bearing three Skenes or dirks paleways, "S. Patricii de Sken Cl'ici." It is probable that Johan de Skene did homage as holding the lands of Skene, with the Tower, of the Crown, and Patrick as holding the lands of Easter Skene, containing the Kirktown of Skene, and that he was himself the vicar of Skene. The name of Skene is thus plainly territorial. And as these Church lands always formed part of the subsequent barony, we may infer that, like other families, the Skenes were hereditary possessors of the vicarage of Skene, and took their name from it. · What lands Johan de Skene possessed in the county of Edinburgh it is difficult to say, but they may have been the lands of Halyards, in the parish of Kirkliston, which were afterwards acquired by the family, and were connected with the possessions of the Hospitallers or Knights of St. John of Jerusalem ; and so may have given rise to the device upon his seal. This is the more probable as his successor, in 1358, as we shall afterwards see, bore the name of Gilian, which means the servant of St. John.

Seals of Johan de Skene and Patrick de Skene.

There are some documents, however, which bear upon the territorial history of the lands. In the Chartulary of the Bishopric of Aberdeen is the following:—"Conventio inter Petrum episcopum et Alanum Hostiarium." "Hec est conuentio facta inter venerabilem patrem episcopum Aberdonensem ex parte vna et dominum Alanum hostiarium justiciarium Scotie ex altera. Videlicet quod dictus dominus Alanus hostiarius dedit et concessit Deo et ecclesie beate Marie et sancte Machorij de Aberdon et episcopo Petro eiusque successoribus viginti duos solidos sterlingorum legalium de terra sua de Schene ad duos terminos imperpetuum percipiendos medietatem videlicet ad Penthecosten et aliam medietatem ad festum sancti Martini in yeme pro decimis de Onele quas sui antecessores Episcopi ex collatione illustris regis Dauid et regum successorum eiusdem actenus percipere debuerunt. quas quidem decimas predictus Petrus episcopus prefato Alano hostiario et heredibus suis pro dictis xxij solidis annuatim soluendis imperpetuum dimisit ct quieteclamauit. Ita tamen quod dicta terra de Schen pro prefata quantitate pecunie dictis terminis soluenda Episcopo Aberdonensi qui pro tempore fuerit in perpetuum remaneat obligata. In cujus rei testimonium parti hujus scripture in modum cirograffi confecte penes dictum dominum Alanum remanenti sigillum dicti domini Episcopi vna cum sigillo capitull ecclesie sue Aberdonensis est appositum. alteri vero parti penes dominum Episcopum residenti sigillum prefati domini Alani est appensum. Hiis testibus domino Willelmo de Brechyne. W. Byset. Colmero hostiario. Johanne de vallibus. Gregorio de maleuile. R. Flandrensi. magistro W. officiali Aberdonensi. domino Gilberto de Strivelyng. et Hugone de Bennam canonicis ecclesie Aberdonensis et alijs."—(I. 17).

In a Rental of the Bishopric, in the reign of Alexander III., there is this entry—" De terris de Skyen dentur domino Episcopo Aberdonensi pro secundis decimis de Onele xxij. s. ex conuentione inter episcopum et capitulum Aberdonense et Alanum Hostiarum dominum earundem."— (I. 57).

Alan Hostiarius or Durward died in 1275, so that this agreement must have been entered into before that date. What his precise connection with the lands of Skene was, at this time, is not very clear, but it may be inferred that he possessed only the superiority of the lands from the following circumstance.

The Church of Skene was undoubtedly a vicarage dependent upon the Church of Kinkell. In the same Register there is the following:—"Carta domini comitis mariscalli facta magistro Alexandro Gallouay rectori a Kinkell de et super concessione vnius crofte iuxta ecclesiam de Skein pro mansione construenda vicario dicte ecclesie. Celebrando missam hebdomadatim omni secunda feria. Data apud Castrum de Kyntor xij Decembris A.D. MDXXXIX."—(I. 416). What the Earl Marischall's connection with the lands was will after appear. In 1613 there is in the Register of the Privy Seal " ane letter maid makand mention that umquhile Mr. Thomas Lumsden, parson of Kinkell, had, by tack, to Alexander Skene of that ilk, set to him the teind Sheaves of the lands of Wester Skene, &c." And by an Act of the Scotch Parliament, in 1649, the kirks of Drumblate, Skeene, Kintore, Kynnellar, Dyce, and Kemnay, " as being kirks and pendicles of the kirke of Kinkell of auld erected in ane benefice and parsonage, quhairof the kirkis aboue writtin were proper parts and pendicles," are dissolved, disunited, and separated, "with the right of patronage and title of the teynds rexue of the samen kirks from the forsaid kirk and benefice of Kinkell," and declared "to be severall and distinct paroche kirkis and parochines be thameselffis, and nowayes to be parts and pendicles of the said kirk of Kinkell, benefice and personage theirof, in all tyme comeing."—(Acts of Parl. vi., pt. ii., 183).

This parsonage of Kinkell was, as its name implies, the *plebania* or mother church of the great Thanage of Kintore ; and the lands attached to the other dependent vicarages all belonged to the Thanage. It is therefore probable that the lands of Skene originally formed part of the Thanage of Kintore ; and the narrative is probably correct which describes it as forming part of an extended forest, for that part of the parish of Kintore which bounds it on the north, was the "foresta de Kintore," and at the northern extremity of the forest was the old tower of Hall Forest, believed to have been a hunting seat of the Scottish kings. It is thus described—" Hall Forest [a royal castle], according to tradition, was built by King Robert Bruce for a hunting hall. It consisted of four stories, having battlements, besides what is called a Capehouse, with a moveable ladder, by which those who occasionally lodged in it, entered to the first floor. The Earl Marischall, having acquired a right to it from the Crown, presented it to his son, the first Earl of Kintore."—(Kennedy's "Annals of Aberdeen," vol. ii., p. 323). That the old tower of Skene was an analogous structure, will appear from the description of it given in one of the MS. histories of the family—" The Tower, or old house, still stands, which was originally built of three arches or stories, and entered by a ladder on the second story. It was covered with a mound of earth upon the top of the third arch, and is all built with lime, quite run together or vitrified, and the walls about ten feet thick. It continued in its original state till about the year 1680, that the arches being taken out, it was roofed and floored by Jean Burnet, Lady Skene, Relict of John Skene of that ilk, in her widowhood, and makes now a part of the accommodation of the present house"—(MS.D). Both towers, however, belong, from the style of their architecture, to a much earlier period than the reign of King Robert Bruce, and were probably erected not later than in the twelfth century.

The Thanage of Kintore was in the possession of the Crown in the reign of Alexander the Third, as appears from a Rental preserved in the

Chartulary of the Bishopric of Aberdeen (i. 57), but in the same reign Alan Durward undoubtedly possessed extensive lands in the Earldom of Mar. These lands were acquired in consequence of a claim made by his father, Thomas Durward, before 1228, to the Earldom of Mar, and renewed by his son Alan, in 1257. This claim seems to have been compromised by the Durwards obtaining possession of three hundred pound land, partly in domain (*dominiis*) and partly in holdings (*homagiis*), or more, in the Earldom (Palgrave Records, p. 22). Part, if not the whole, of the Thanage of Kintore, including the lands of Skene, may thus, for the time, have been in his possession. The tenure on which Thanage lands were held was analogous to that of lands held in *feodofirma*, that is, for an annual money payment. Alan Durward is termed, in connection with Skene, "Dominus earundem," and therefore held it probably as "a holding," that is, the superiority only, and his grant of xxij shillings to the Bishop was probably from the feu rent due to him as overlord. Fordun tells us that Alan Durward died in 1275, and that his three daughters succeeded to him in his lands, but these acquisitions to the Earldom of Mar appear not to have fallen under his succession, but to have reverted to the Crown. The Thanage, afterwards the Barony, of Oneill, one of his principal possessions, appears to have been granted to the Earls of Fife, and the possessions of the lands of Skene would now come to be held of the Crown, as we find was the case with John de Skene and Patrick de Skene in 1296.

It is quite possible that the family of Skene is at least as old as the reign of William the Lion, and that Mr. Alexander Skene may be correct in saying that there had been in the charter chest a restoration from forfeiture by that monarch, for in 1174 there broke out in the north an insurrection in favour of a Donald Bane MacWilliam, who held possession of the northern counties till 1181, when it was suppressed, and the ancestor of the Skenes may have been among those who supported him. The confusion between the Donald Bane of King William's time and the Donald Bane, brother of Malcolm Canmore, who usurped the throne in the eleventh century, would at once account for the earlier tradition. The name of Skene, signifying in Gaelic a dirk, would give rise, by the canting heraldry of the time, to the arms, and, if Skene was a forest, to the addition of the wolves' heads, and thus lead to the traditionary origin of the name.

The history of the family, so far as it is really based on services and retours, commences in the reign of King Robert Bruce, and is as follows:—

I.—ROBERT DE SKENE.

In 1317 he received the following charter from King Robert the Bruce :—

"Robertus Dei gracia Rex Scotorum Omnibus probis hominibus totius terrae suæ Salutem. Sciatis nos dedisse, concessisse et hac presenti carta nostra confirmasse Roberto Skene dilecto et fideli nostro pro homagio et seruicio suo, omnes et singulas terras nostras del Skene et lacum ejusdem cum pertinenciis infra Vicecomitatum del Aberdene. Tenendas et Habendas dicto Roberto et heredibus suis de nobis et heredibus nostris in vnam integram et liberam Baroniam in feodo et hereditate in perpetuum cum furca et fossa soc et sac thol et theme infangandthef et outfangandthef et per omnes rectas antiquas metas et divisas suas in longitudine et latitudine in boscis planis pratis pascuis et pasturis silvis moris et maresiis viis semitis aquis et stagnis in mollendinis multuris et corum sequelis in aucupationibus venationibus et piscariis et cum omnibus aliis libertatibus commoditatibus aisiamentis ac justis pertinentibus quibuscunque tam non nominatis quam nominatis ad dictas terras et lacum cum pertinentibus spectantibus seu quoquomodo juste spectare valentibus in futurum. Faciendo inde nobis et heredibus nostris dictus Robertus et heredes sui quolibet anno imperpetuum communem sectam curie ad placita nostra vicecomitatus del Aberdene et in exercitu nostro Scoticanum servicium pro omni alio servicio consuetudine actione seu demanda quae de dictis terris et lacu cum pertinentibus per nos vel heredes nostros exigi poterit vel requiri. In cujus rei testimonium presenti carte nostre sigillum nostrum precepimus apponi. Testibus Bernardo abbate del Aberbrothoc cancellario nostro, Thoma Ranulphi comite Moravie et domino vallis Anandie et Mannie nepote nostro, Waltero senescallo Scocie, Jacobo domino Douglas, Alexandro Fraser, Dauid Berclay et Roberto de Lawider militibus. Apud Sconam primo die Iunij anno regni nostri duodecimo."

"This Robert married Marion Mercer, daughter of the Baron of Adie and Meiklure, then provost of Perth" (MS.D). In a retour, dated 10 April, 1629, afterwards quoted, he is said to have died at the peace of David II., that is between 1329 and 1370.

His successor appears to have been—

II.—GILIAN DE SKENE.

There is in 1358 the following entry in the Exchequer Rolls, in the accounts of " Thomas comes de Marr camerarius Scocie " :—

" Item, in solucione facta Giliane de Skene, vt patet per literam ipsius comitis de Marr, camerarii, de precepto et ipsius Giliane de recepto, ostensas super compotum iij li. vj s. et viij d., de quibus idem comes, camerarius, respondebit "—(Exch. Rolls, Vol. I., p. 552).

Nothing more is known of him ; but his name Gilian, a servant of St. John, suggests a descent from the John de Skene who bore the head of St. John the Baptist on his seal.

III.—ADAM DE SKENE.

He is mentioned in the retour of 1629 as grandson of Robert de Skene, and ancestor of the subsequent lairds of Skene. He is followed by another

IV.—ADAM DE SKENE,

and he by a third

V.—ADAM DE SKENE,

" who before the battle of Harlaw married Janet Keith daughter of Earl Marischal of Scotland. About this time, when Donald Lord of the Isles had invaded that part of the country, Skene raised his friends and followers and joined the Royal army to oppose them and raised 300 merks from his father-in-law, Lord Marischal to equip himself and men : he mortgaged a part of his estate for it which afterwards brought great trouble upon the family all which appears in the family writs which we have seen. He was killed at the battle of Harlaw in the year 1411 and his lady being with child brought forth a son William Skene who died in 1445 leaving a son James Skene of that ilk" (MS.D). This account is confirmed, as we shall see by the family papers, except that James was the son of Adam, and there was no William intervening. By him Gilian is probably meant, who preceded Adam, instead of following him.

VI.—JAMES DE SKENE—1411-1461.

We now come upon firmer ground in the history of the family.

In the year 1428 there is the following entry in the Exchequer Rolls:—

"Et in liberacione facta Jacobo de Skene, pro firmis terrarum suarum de Corntoun, existentibus in manu regis de terminis Pentecostes et Sancti Martini ultimo preteritis, ut patet per literas regis de precepto et dicti Jacobi de recepto ostensas super computum vj li. xiij s. iiij d."—(Exch. Rolls, Vol. iv., p. 444) ; and in the following year among the payments —"Et Jacobo Skene, pro firma sua tercie partis de Corntoun per assedacionem in manibus regis existente de anno computi, ut patet per literas domini regis de mandato pro voluntate duraturas, et dicti Jacobi de recepto, ostensas super computum vj li. xiij s. iiij d."—(Ib., p. 483).

Again, in 1434, it is more distinctly given, and the king's letter of authority is endorsed :—

"Et Jacobo Skene, pro firmis tercie partis terre de Corntoun spectantis uxori ejusdem, de duobus terminis hujus computi vj li. xiij s. iiij d. Et eidem ex causa xiij s. iiij d., de mandato regis, ut patet per literas suas de precepto ostensas super computum et registratas in dorso hujus rotuli. . . .

"James, be the grace of God king of Scottis, to the custumaris of oure gret custome of Abreden greting. We charge yhu and commandeʒ that yhe content and pay yherly to James of Skene of that ilk ten markkis of usuale mone of oure realme at two termes of the yheir proporcionaly qubil yhe have contremandment of us, the first term begynnand at the fest of Saynt Martin last passit, takkin his lettres of ressayt to schaw to us, and to be alowit to yhu yherly in ʒour comptis, this presentis enduring for our will. Gevin under our signet at Edynburch the xxj. dai of Februar the yhere of our reigne xxj "—(Ib., p. 567).

The learned editor gives the following explanation of these entries :—

"Corntoun, in the first half of the fifteenth century, belonged to a branch of the Fraser family, and was occupied by the king, who paid a rent for it. But by an excambion of date 1455 it became Crown property, Fraser getting in exchange for it Muchal (afterwards called Castle Fraser), in Mar, and Stoneywood, near Aberdeen." He adds in a note—"From 1428 to 1435, James I. paid annually £6 13s. 4d. to James Skene of Skene, for his occupation of terce lands of Corntoun, belonging to Skene's wife, widow of a Fraser of Corntoun. From 1438 to 1450, Thomas Fraser of Corntoun got £20 yearly out of the king's fermes north of Dee, or the customs of Aberdeen, in compensation for the king's occupancy of Corntoun "—(Ib., vi., pref, p. lxxvi).

James Skene of Skene was thus married to the widow of Fraser of Corntoun as early at least as the year 1428, and had, by his wife, a son, Alexander, who succeeded him, and who was marriageable in 1438, as on the 12th of May in that year, Egidia de Moravia, domina de Culbin, in her widowhood, with consent of Alan of Kynnarde, her son and heir, grants to Alexander Skene, son and heir of James Skene of that ilk, on account of the marriage to be contracted between him and Mariot of Kinarde her daughter, the lands of Dulpoty, Estertown, and Mill of Dulpoty, in the Barony of Culbin, and Sheriffdom of Forres, in security of the sum of £100 Scots, James Skene must therefore have been born long before the year 1411, when his father was killed at Harlaw, and the statement in MS.D that Adam's successor was a posthumous child is plainly apocryphal.

‚ The family seems now to have spread somewhat, as we find others of the same name appearing for the first time. In 1430 a Jacobus Skene appears as Notarius Publicus. In 1440 a Fergusius de Skene is admitted a burgess of Aberdeen, and in 1443 a John Skene. In the same year Robertus Skene is "vicarius de Logymar," and is again mentioned in 1477; and in 1461 an Alexander Skène appears in the Town Council of Aberdeen. These scions of the family probably belonged to an old branch of the family, the Skenes of Auchtererne, in the parish of Logie Coldstone.

It was in the time of this James of Skene that the family entered into an arduous struggle with the more powerful family of the Earls Marischal, to regain possession of the lands of Easter Skene, which had been pledged to them, as has been previously adverted to.

The family appears to have lost the original deed of impignoration or wadset, and commenced the contest by instructing by the evidence of witnesses, that such a deed had existed. There are still preserved, in the Skene charter chest, two official reports, by a Commissioner appointed for the purpose, of the evidence then taken. They are printed at length in the third volume of the "Antiquities of the Shires of Aberdeen and Banff," p. 318; but a short abstract may here be given :—

The first is dated 22nd September, 1446, and reports the evidence of three witnesses before a Court held in the Cathedral of Aberdeen. The first witness, John Petkarne, being sworn and examined, states that he read a deed, written on parchment, concerning the impignoration *seu fornalyn* of the lands of Ester Skene, in favour of the late Lord William

D

de Keth, Marischal of Scotland, by Adam de Skene, Lord of the same, father of James de Skene of that ilk, and that said lands were impig-norated *seu fornalyt* for two or three hundred merks Scots, and this was about 21 years ago, and that it was shown to him by Mariota, then "Domina de Keth." The second witness, William de Sancto Michaele, depones that he was present when the previous witness saw a charter or evidence made in favour of William Lord Keith, by Adam de Skene, of the lands of Ester Skene, sealed with two seals, a round one of the said Adam, and an oval one of the Bishop of Aberdeen, and that John Pet-karne told him that it was a deed made by Adam de Skene, *super for-nalyn*, of Ester Skene, for 304 marks. A third witness, William Norvele, depones that he was present in the house of Lord William de Keth, Marischal of Scotland, in the town of Aberdeen, before the battle of Harlaw, when Lord John Stewart of Invermey, and David Berkley of Mernys, instigated the said Lord William de Keth to found two chaplain-ries, for the souls of himself and the Lady Margaret, his wife ; and that Lord William agreed to assign twenty merks of the lands of Ester Skene, with its pertinents, for two chaplains, in the Cathedral of Aberdeen, but the said Lady Margaret declared, in a loud and clear voice, that she never would consent to the chaplainries being founded out of the lands of Ester Skene, because they had no right to the said lands ; upon which the Earl Marischal said, in a rage, that he would not found a single chap-lainric for their souls, but at length, after consulting with the said Lord John Stewart and David Berkley, assigned an annual payment of twenty-two merks for two chaplains, to celebrate for ever in the Cathedral of Aberdeen, out of the lands of Ester Skene, with warrandice from the lands of Kyntor, should the lands of Ester Skene fail them ; and the Lady Margaret consented to this warrandice : the Earl then sent for Sir John Yoill, priest, and Thomas Spryng, Burgess of Aberdeen, who read, among other documents, the deed by Adam de Skene, regarding the lands of Ester Skene, by which they were *fornalit* for three hundred merks, and which deed was sealed with two seals, the round seal of Adam, and the oval seal of the Bishop of Aberdeen. Interrogated whether he deponed these things from party or prejudice, hatred or love, he replied, that it was not so, but for the safety of his soul, to avoid the excommunication which he heard widely published, with sounding bells, lighted and extinguished candles, by the reverend fathers in Christ the Bishops of St. Andrews and Aberdeen, against all persons detaining or concealing said deed, and not revealing it to the said James de Skene. This public instrument was issued at the instance of the said James de Skene, in presence of Ranald Chene of Crechie, John Burnet of Leyis, David Scrymgeour, Andrew Buchan of Auchmacoy, and Thomas Beset, witnesses.

This proceeding, however, seems to have led to nothing, and James of Skene appears, after a time, to have committed the conduct of the struggle to his son and heir, Alexander Skene, at whose instance a second examination of witnesses was made. This inquiry took place in the parish church of Kincardine, on the ninth day of November, 1456, when a discreet man, John Yoill, was examined, and deponed that eight days before the death of the late Sir John Yoill, vicar of Peterculter, the late Lady of Keth, mother of the Lord William de Keth, now Marischal of Scotland, came to the said Sir John Yoill, at Culter, when grievously sick in bed, and interrogated him regarding the lands of Ester Skene, Ledach,— Kirktoun of Skene, Milboy, Garlogy, with the mill thereof, whether his Lord, the Lord William de Keth Marischal, had a real right to the said lands, or whether, as she had often heard asserted, James Skene of that ilk had the right of reclaiming said lands, as belonging, by hereditary right, to the Barony of Skene ; to which Sir John Yoill answered, as he should answer at the great day of judgment, that the Earl Marischal had the said lands *in formalyn*, made by Adam de Skene for three hundred merks, as contained in a certain deed ; and further stated on oath, that the said Earl Marischal had no other rights from the said Adam to these lands : whereupon the said Lady said, that the Lord Marischal possessed these letters of *formalyng* of the said lands of Skene, granted by the said Adam de Skene, and nothing else. Interrogated who were then present, said only the Lady of Keth and Sir John Yoill, with himself. Interrogated how it came there were not more, stated, on oath, that the said Lady caused several others to leave the room, and retained him to serve at mass in the room, asserting him to be hereafter a native man to his Lord, the said Marischal ; and that he made this deposition without party or prejudice, hatred or love, in presence of Master William of Coultis, vicar of Tarlane, Alexander Yrwin of Stradie,   of Strathachyn, and Kennocht of Cragmyle, with many others.

The right which the Keith family claimed to the lands of Ester Skene

seems now to have passed to Janet de Keith, only daughter of Robert de
Keith, who was eldest son of William, first Earl Marischal, and brother
of William, second Earl Marischal, and was thus heir of line of the
family ; and on 26th April, 1457, she obtained a decreit from the Sheriff,
upon a brief of richt, dated 21st February, 1456, between " Jacobus de
Skene de eodem et Joneta de Keth cum patruo suo nobili Domino
Willelmo domino de Keth Mariscallo Scocie de et super terris de ly
Ledach de Skene de ly Kirktoun de Skene de Mulboy et de Garlogy,"
on which the Jury, after hearing evidence " antiquorum virorum," gave
their verdict " quod Jacobus de Skene supradictus habet majus jus
quam habet dicta Joneta de Keith in et ad dictas terras ; " and on 30th
April, Jacobus Skene de eodem is infeft in these lands.

The Keith family did not, however, notwithstanding these proceedings,
relax their grasp of them, and the scene of litigation was now transferred
to Parliament, and a declaration was obtained, on 7th November, 1457,
from the King, through the Chancellor of the Kingdom, that James de
Skene was to refrain from retaining the rents of these lands till the fourth
day of the meeting of Parliament, in the month of March next.   Before
this Parliament the following protestation was made by his son and heir,
Alexander, whose position was strengthened by his taking infeftment on
a charter confirming " Alexandro Skene filio et haeredi apparenti Jacobi
Skene de eodem," the charter of King Robert the First to Robert Skene
of the Barony of Skene :—

" Reuerendis nobille and worschipfull lordis of Parliament, I yhour
serviter Alexander of Skene procuratour to my fader Jamys of Skene of
that ilke humbli protestis in my fader name that qubat euer be saide
done reformyt decretit or adjugit ony maner of way agayn Alexander of
Douglas depute to the Shira of Aberdene, now befor yhour lordschippis
that hes the force of parliament, or in tym to cume, for the execucioune
of his office, made to my fader upoun a briefe of rycht purchast be hym
agayn Jonet of Keth for hir unrychtwise deforsing him of the landis of
the Ledache of Skeyn, the Kyrktoune of Skeyn, Moylboy, and Garlogy,
with the myln of that ilke, with the pertinentis lyaud in the Barouny of
Skeyne wythin the Shiradome of Aberdene, turne nocht my fader na
his ayris to prejudice of the said landis and mylne with the pertinentis
in tyme cuming, for sa mekell as my fader hes be the saide briefe recouerit
the said landis and mylne with the pertinentis fra the saide Jouet be

decret and deliuerance of a gret assise of rycht and dome giffin thar-apoun and thareftir hes tane sesing of thaim, quhilke assise procedit be uertu of the said briefe and be compromise made betuix my fader and the said Jonet and my Lorde of Keithe chosin be thair avise of four shiradomes to determin the saide cause, but ony excepcioune dilatour or peremptour proponit in the entrance, suppose the saide shirefe wald graunt he had done amys owthir for aid or lufe of the said Lord or Jonet, considering that the said Lorde and Jonet ar bundyn be lettir and seel, and be thar bodely athis sworne on the Haly Ewangelis, for till underly the finale determinacioune of the said assise irreuocabli for euermare."

This was followed on 5th October, 1458, by a petition by Alexander Skene, that his father might be preferred to the possession and rights of said lands, and protestation that no decree to the contrary might prejudge his undoubted right thereto ; which appears to have been granted and the grant again recalled, as on 12th October, 1459, there is again a protesta-tion by Alexander Skene, as procurator for his father, James Skene of that ilk, before the Parliament held at Perth, which narrates that after the king had recognised his right, he had recalled his recognition, at the in-stance of Jouet de Kethe, and given her the lands " *ad plegium*," contrary, the said Alexander maintained, to the laws, rights, and statutes of the realme, and to the hurt, loss, and prejudice of the said James Skene, and on the part of the said James humbly pressed the king to replace him in possession of the said lands, according to the rights, customs, and ancient laws of the kingdom, and protested that the demising of the said lands to the said Jonet de Kethe *ad plegium*, should not prejudice his rights in future, and that he should have free regress to these lands.

A similar protestation was made on 7th March, 1460. In the mean-time, while his son and heir was carrying on this contest with their powerful neighbours, the Keiths, his mother, the widow of Fraser of Corutoun, had died, and his father had married a second time Giles Murray of Cowbin, widow of Thomas Kinnaird of that ilk, in 1458, for we find an obligation by Alane of Kynnarde of that ilk, narrating that "forasmeikle as my tender fader James Skene of that ilk and Giles of Murrane of Skelbo, his spouse, has set to me all and sundrie the lands of Skelbo, in the Earldom of Sutherland and Sheriffdom, &c."

James Skene of Skene appears to have died in the year 1461.

⋏ VII.—ALEXANDER DE SKENE—1461-1470.

There is, on 1st June, 1461, a sasine in favour of Alexander Skene of
that ilk, as heir to the said James, his father, of the lands and barony of
Skene, following upon a retour and precept of Chancery.

Soon after, his contest with the Keith family seems to have been
brought to a conclusion, at least for the time, in his favour, a result to
which the marriage of his half-brother, Alan of Kinnarde, with his
antagonist, Janet of Keith, may have contributed; for, on 18th May, 1464,
there is a sasine in favour of Alexander Skene de eodem, on a charter
from William Earl Marischall, of the lands of "Leddach de Skene Kirkton
de Skene Milbuy et Garlogy in Baronia de Skene ;" and the close connection with the Kinnards is still further evinced from a charter of
Balerdmund, in the Skene charter chest, granted in 1467 by Alanus de
Kynnarde "dilecto fratri nostro naturali Alexandro Skene de eodem.
Testibus Gilberto Skene nepote meo Magistro Roberto Skene."

The term *naturalis* did not at that time imply bastardy but the
reverse.   It was opposed to the terms *carnalis* and *bastardus*.

VIII.—GILBERT DE SKENE—1470-1485.

In May, 1470, Gilbert Skene is infeft as heir, served and retoured, to
Alexander Skene, his father, in the lands and barony of Skene.

In 1481 he married Cristina Mercer; and settled two farms in Wester
Skene as her jointure lands, as appears from a Crown charter granted in
23rd May, 1481—"Gilberto Skene de eodem et Cristine Mersare sponse sue
in conjuncta infeodatione et post corum decessum legitimis et propinquiori-
bus heredibus dicti Gilberti quibuscunque de terris de Adloche et Tulivale
cum pertinentiis jacentibus infra vicecomitatum de Aberdene super
resignationem dicti Gilberti. Tenendas de Rege. Reddendo jura et
servitia debita et consueta."

⋎ IX.—ALEXANDER DE SKENE—1485-1507.

On the 19th of March, 1485, Alexander Skene is infeft as heir, served
and retoured, to Gilbert Skene, his father, in the lands and barony of
Skene.

In 1504 he acquired, from David Strathaquhyn of Carmyle, certain lands in the parish of Kinnernie, which bounds the lands of Skene on the west, as appears by charter granted on 16th April in that year, by " David Strathaquhyn de Carmyle et Dominus de Tulibrochloch dilecto meo Alexandro Skene de Eodem terras meas de Tullibrochloch Tulyna-hiltis Balnadodill cum le Cumeris Auchquhory et molendino ejusdem ; " and among the witnesses is Johannes Skeyne. This charter is confirmed on 17th April by Johannes Comes Crawfurdiae et Dominus de Lyndesay, the Superior ; and on the 22nd April he was infeft in these lands. The lands thus conveyed to him, consisting of five separate possessions adjoining the lands of Skene, formed what were called Tanistry lands, in order to make a provision for the younger sons of the family, who occupied them during their lives as kindlie tenants.

Alexander appears to have died in the year 1507, as towards the end of that year, on 12th February, 1507-8, there is in the Privy Seal Record a letter to Sir Alexander Irving of Drum and Duncan Forbes of the ward of the lands of the late Alexander Skene of that ilk, and of the marriage of Alexander Skene, his son and heir ; and on the third day of October, 1508, Agnes Forbes is served by a jury assembled at Aberdeen, before John, Earl of Crawfurd, and Lord Lyndesay, " qui jurati dicunt quod Agnes Forbes relicta Alexandri Skene de eodem tenetur habere racionabilem terciam omnium terrarum baronie de Skene exceptis duabus partibus terrarum de Lattir que attigit habere suam terciam in solari parte hujusmodi terrarum."

This Agnes Forbes, according to MS. authority, was a daughter of Lord Forbes, probably of James, second Baron Forbes, by Egidia de Keith, daughter of William, First Earl Marischal, and was thus sister of that Duncan Forbes who was one of the guardians of her infant son. By her Alexander Skene had two sons—

I. Alexander Skene, who succeeded him.

II. James Skene, kindlie tenant of Bandodill, ancestor of the families of Skene of Ramore, Curriehill, Halyards in Midlothian, and Rubislaw.

X.—ALEXANDER DE SKENE—1507-1517.

With this laird Mr. Alexander Skene begins his genealogical account of the family. He says—" After many generations succeeded Alexander

Skene of yat ilke. At that tyme the family being weak and under burdens, he married Elizabeth Black, daughter to a burgess of Aberdeen, with whom he got in dott and tocher good all that tract of land called *the round table* ;" and MS.D adds—"being that part of the town of Aberdeen bounded on the east with the Castle Street or present Exchange, on the south with the Exchequer Row, and on the west with the Rotten Row, and on the north with the Narrow Wynd. Besides these houses, he got a considerable sum of money with her." No doubt the protracted struggle with the principal family of the Keiths Marischal would, in some degree, account for the depressed state of the family. Alexander Skene was, as we have seen, in pupillarity when his father died in 1507, and attained majority in 1514, as in that year he obtains, on 8th May, a charter of the Tanistry lands, from "Alexander Comes Crawfordiae et Dominus de Lindesay et dominus omnium et singularum terrarum de Tulibroloch, Tullynahiltis, Balnadodill, le Comeris, Auchorye, Auchmor et molendini ejusdem Alexandro Skeyne filio et heredi quondam Alexandri Skeyne de eodem ;" and among the witnesses is "Johannes Skeyne de Auchterarnane."

On 17th July, in the same year, he is infeft as heir, served and retoured, to Alexander Skene, his father, in the lands and barony of Skene.

In 1516 he married Elizabeth Black, as on 20th May in that year he receives a Crown charter to himself and Elizabeth Black, his spouse, of the lands of Newton in Skein and Letter, in Baronia de Skene, by his own resignation, as her jointure lands. He seems to have died in 1517.

XI.—ALEXANDER DE SKENE—1517-1604.

Mr. Alexander Skene says of him—"Alexander Skene, commonly designed the little laird, who was left a child in his mother's womb when his father, fighting for his king and country, was slain in the battle of Pinkey. Therefore, he being the only child of his umquhill father, his land fell ward in the king's hands. The laird of Drum being at that time at Court, got the gift of his ward, which he gave to the laird of Corsenday for a horse ; and the said Corsenday took the tutilage of the child, till such tyme as he was for marriage, and then gave him 10,000 merks of tocher, with his own daughter in marriage, called Margaret Forbes." This is a good specimen of the character of such family traditions. They state facts which are or may be true enough, but attribute them to wrong persons and dates. It seems true that he was a posthumous child, and the account given by MS.D of the reason why he was called "the little laird," bears all the appearance of probability. "He was killed at the battle of Pinkie in 1547, and wâs called the little laird from his being hunchbacked from a fall he got out of his nurse's arms when going up the ladder to the old house of Skene." But it errs in saying that he was killed at the battle of Pinkie, as Mr. Alexander Skene does in saying his father was killed in that battle.

Mr. Alexander Skene is also mistaken in saying that the gift of his ward was given to the laird of Drum, and by him transferred to the laird of Corsinday, for, as we have seen, it was his father whose ward was given to Sir Alexander Irving of Drum and Duncan Forbes of Corsinday, and "the little laird," as he was called, was under the guardianship of his uncle, James Skene, for we find, on 2nd November, 1538, in a mutual agreement between Alexander Skeyne of that ilk and Mr. Walter Styvart, regarding the marches of the lands of Tullibroloch, belonging to the former, and Tullocht belonging to the latter, that Alexander Skeyne becomes bound, with the consent of his uncle and curator, James Skeyne (Protocol Book of John Christisone), and he came of age in the following year, as on 22nd March, 1539, he is infeft in the lands and barony of Skene, as heir served and retoured, to Alexander Skene of that ilk, his father.

Neither was he ever at the battle of Pinkie, for when the trumpet call to this great national conflict resounded over all Scotland, and caused many a quiet laird to buckle on his armour, we find in the record of the Privy Seal—"Ane brieve maid to Alexander Skeyne of yat ilk, giving leave to him to remain fra ustin al ye days of his life, because he is wake of complexion and inhabill for travel, vexit with infirmities and sikness, provided alwayis that the said Alexander sends ane habill furnished man, with his household and servants, to the said oistis at St. Andrews, penult October, 1546." The "habill furnished man" was his uncle, James Skeyne in Bandodle, and he it was, as we shall afterwards see, who, with other Skeynes, was slain at the fatal battle of Pinkie.

It is true, however, that he married a daughter of Duncan Forbes of Corsinday, for on 18th March, 1541, there is a charter " Alexandro Skene de eodem et Elizabethe Forbes ejus spouse terrarum de Auchloche et

E

Cragydarg jacen. in Baronia de Skene in conjuncta infeodatione super resignationem dicti Alexandri.'

Notwithstanding Alexander Skeyne being " vexit with infirmities and sikness," he was longer in possession of the barony than any other laird, was twice married, had a large family of children, lived to see his eldest son and heir and *his* son and heir both married, was predeceased by his grandson, saw his great-grandchildren, and died in the year 1604, at the age of 87.

The author of MS.B refers to this period when he says—" There were foyve lairdes at on tym, with from father, son, grandchyld, gryt-grand-chyld, and gryt-great-grandchyld, designed by the laird of Skene elder, the laird of Skene younger, the laird of the Letter, &c., being parcel of the Barronie of Skene ; and each succeeded another in a short space."

On 27th August, 1557, "Alexander Skene de eodem fecit constituit et creavit proles suos sequentes suos assignatos irrevocabiles in et ad summam mille mercarum monetae Scotiae quam habuit in deposito vizt Gulielmum Skene ejus filium ad 300 merks, Patricium Skene ejus fr. filium ad 300 merks et deficien. dicto Patricio Alexandrum Skene ejus fr. filium et Agnetem Skene ejus filiam ad 400 merks " (Ab. Sas. Regr.), no doubt part of the tocher he got with Elizabeth Forbes.

In the following year Agnes was married evidently to a relation of his mother, as we find in the Burgh Sasine Register, on 16th February, 1558 —" Possessio of John Black and Agnes Skene, his future spouse, of Auchmoir, in Baronia de Tillibrohloch, on precept of sasine from Alex-ander Skene of Skene."

On 10th January, 1566, Alexander Skene de eodem is infeft in the Burgh Suburbs belonging to the family, and one of the witnesses is Gilbert Skene, his son.

His mother, Elizabeth Black, appears to have died in 1573, as on 4th March in that year " Alexander Skene de eodem haeres Alexandri Skene de eodem," serves heir "in terris de Newton de Skeyne, et Letter de Skeyne," which were his mother's jointure lands.

There seems to have been some quarrelling about the burgh lands, as, in the Register of the Privy Council, the following entry occurs on 9th February, 1566 :—" Registration by Mr. Robert Irving, as procurator of Band, by Alexander Skein of that ilk, for James Skein of Bandodill, Gilbert Skein, Mr. Patrick Skene, and Alexander Skene, ' my lawful sons,' £500 each, not to harm Thomas Buk, burgess of Aberdeen. Subscribed at Aberdeen 5th February, before Mr. Duncan Forbes of the Letter, Mr. William Skeyne, Johnne Forbes, servitor to the parson of Kinkell ; Andro Skeyne, in the Glak ; William Forbes, son of Johnne Forbes of Tolquhon ; and Mr. Patrick Skeyne, burgess of Aberdene, writer hereof ; William Reid and John Nicolsoun, notaries, subscribing for Alexander Skein of that ilk "—(V., p. 673).

Alexander Skene was twice married, and by his first wife, Elizabeth Forbes, he had—

I. James Skene, his heir, designed, during his father's life, as James Skene of Bandodill.

II. Gilbert Skene in Tillibirloch, ancestor of the families of Dumbreck and Newtyle.

III. Mr. William Skene, burgess of Aberdeen, married, in 1563, Elizabeth Lesly, and had by her a son, William Skene, also a burgess of Aberdeen, who served heir to his father, William Skene, on 10th June, 1586, and married Janet Donaldson, only daughter of John Donaldson. In 1602 he was ruined, from having been cautioner for Duncan Leslie, son to the laird of Wardes, and probably his mother's brother, who fled the country. He complained of being starved, and unable to maintain a wife and sundry young infants. He died before 1605, when Janet Donaldson, relict of William Skene, burgess, is buried ; and no more is heard of that family.

IV. Mr. Patrick Skene, burgess of Aberdeen, ancestor of the family of Dyce.

V. Mr. Alexander Skene. "As for Alexander, the fifth son to the little laird, he died unmarried " (MS.A). He died in 1601, and was buried on 1st January, 1601. In 1602, Mr. Patrick Skene, burgess of Aberdeen, appears for Barbara, natural daughter to umquhile Alexander Skene, his brother.

VI. Agnes Skene, married, in 1558, to John Black.

By his second wife, Katharine Stewart, he had three daughters—

VII. Elspeth Skene, married to John Forbes of Boquharm, in Millboy, 17th July, 1576.

VIII. Beatrix Skene married James Forbes of Tilliboy.—(Burgh Prop. Book.)

IX. Isobel Skene died unmarried 5th September, 1604.
The "little laird" died in 1604, at the age of 87.

XII.—JAMES SKENE OF SKENE—1604-1605.

During his father's life he appears sometimes as James Skene of Bandodill, one of the tanistry lands, and at others as James Skene apparent
of that ilk. In a sasine of the Manor Place of Monymusk, in favour of
William Forbes, in March, 1688, the witnesses are James Skeyn apparen.
de eodem, Patrick and Alexander Skeyns, his brothers, James Forbes of
Tilliboy, and John Forbes of Camphill.

On 7th August, 1541, there is an action, at the instance of Alexander
Skene of that ilk, against James Strachan of Carmylie, concerning the
alienation made by umquhile David Strachan of Carmylie, guidsir to the
said James Strachan to umquhile Alexander Skene of that ilk, guidsir to
the said Alexander Skene, now of that ilk, in the year 1485, or thereby,
of all and haill the lands of Tulliebreloche, Tullnahilt, Auchorie, Ban-
dodell, Auchmore, Commoris, with the miln of the same and their
pertinents, lying in the Barony of Auchterellon and Newpark and Sheriffdom of Aberdeen, as the infeftments thereupon bear, &c. ; the defender
alleging that there was a reversion granted by the pursuer's umquhile
guidsir for redemption of the said lands, containing the sum of 840 merks,
and which the pursuer attests is false and forged, &c. ; and in August,
1591, there is a counter action, at the instance of James Strauchan, now
of Carmylie, and Mr. David McGill of Cranston Riddell, king's advocate,
against James Skene, apperand of that ilk, Alexander Skene, elder, of
that ilk, and Alexander Skene, younger, his nevvy—mentions that where
the said James, as abnevvy and heir male to umquhile Sir David
Strachan of Carmylie, his foir grandsir, has action of redemption
depending befoir the Lords against the said Alexander Skene, elder, of
that ilk, oy and heir, at least apparent heir to umquhile Alexander Skene
of that ilk, his guidsir James Skene, apparent of that ilk, and Alexander
Skene, his son, and apparent heir, for redemption of all and haill the
lands of Tillibrolloche and others lying in the Barony of Auchterellon and
Newpark, and Sheriffdom of Aberdene, conform to a reversion granted
be the said umquhile Alexander Skene to the said umquhile David
Strachan of Carmylie, for eluding of which action the defenders have
lately fabricated and forged certain discharges, contracts, &c., alleged

made by the said umquhile David Strachan, since the date of the said reversion, which is dated 16th May, 15— ; therefore the said defenders ought to be punished, their persons, goods, &c. The case was submitted to arbitration on 22nd January, 1591-2, and it is probable the deeds referred to on both sides were found to be genuine, as on 2nd October, 1604, there is a special service, " Jacobus Skene de eodem hares Alexandri Skene de eodem patris in terris et Baronia de Skene terris de Tillibriloch Tilnahiltis Balnadodill Auchinmoir Auchorie et Comaris infra Baronium de Ochterellone." On the same day there is the service of Katherine Stewart, "relicte dict. quondam Alexandri Skene suam vitalem redditum et Margarete Skene relicte quondam Alexandri Skene de Letter."

On the 8th November, in the same year, James Skene is infeft in the lands and barony of Skene, as heir served and retoured to Alexander Skene of that ilk, his father, his procurator being "Honorabilis vir Robertus Skeyne de Tillibroloch actornatus pro Jacobo Skene de eodem sui patris."

James Skene of that ilk was upwards of sixty years old when he succeeded his father, and appears to have died within the year, as in 1605 Johanna Skene or Douglas, widow of James Skene of that ilk, is served to her terce. She was daughter of Sir Archibald Douglas of Glenbervie, and sister of the ninth Earl of Angus ; married to him about 1563 ; and it was through this marriage that the connection between the families of Glenbervie and Skene arose which led to MS.A being compiled in 1678.

.This James Skene of Skene had the following children :—

I. Alexander Skene, called " Barron of the Letter " (MS.A). There is among the Skene papers a contract of marriage in the year 1584, between Alexander Skene of that ilk, younger, with consent of his father, James, then liferenter of Bandodle, and his grandfather, Alexander Skene of that ilk ; and Margaret Johnston, daughter of Sir George Johnston of Caskieben, with whom he got 5000 merks of tocher. Mr. Patrick Skene, sone lawful of Alexander Skene of that ilk, is a witness, but he predeceased both his father and grandfather, dying before 1599, as appears from a discharge by Margaret. Skeyne, eldest lawful daughter to umquhile Alexander Skeyne, fiar of that ilk, with assent of Maister Duncan Forbes in Letter, and Robert and Alexander Skeyne,

his curators, for their interest, to John Forbes of Camphill and
Andrew Skeyne in Aberdeen, executors of said umquhile
Alexander (Council Regr., Abdn.).

Alexander Skene left by his wife, Margaret Johnston, three children—

1. Alexander Skene, who succeeded his grandfather.
2. Mr. Andrew Skene. In 1620 Mr. Andrew Skene, frater germanus Alexandri Skene de eodem, is admitted a burgess.
   In 1628 he receives a tack, from James Skene of that ilk, of
   the lands of Newton of Skene. In 1633 we find him in
   Kirkton of Dyce, where he and Margaret Forbes, his spouse,
   are infeft in the lands of Overtown of Dyce.

   " Mr. Andrew Skene, Alexander's second son, married
   Margaret Forbes, daughter to Mr. John Forbes, minister of
   Delft, in Holland, on whom he begat seven daughters—
   (1) Christian, married to David Drummond, factor in Campvere, in Holland, to whom he had but one daughter, Mar.
   Drummond. David Drummond dying, she married the
   second time Andrew Skein of Rudrestoun, Dean of Guild
   of Aberdeen, to whom she had Robert and John, and two
   daughters ; (2) Margaret Skene, second daughter to Mr.
   Andrew Skene, married John Anderson of Standingstones ;
   (3) Katherine married Mr. William Cheyne, minister of
   Dyce ; (4) Jannet married David Anderson, Provost of
   Kintoir.; (5) Isobel married David Warrand, Town Clerk of
   Forres ; (6) Jean married David Dunbar, Bailyie of Forres ;
   (7) Bessie married Captain James Ross " (MS.A).
3. Margaret, only daughter of Alexander Skene, married, in 1599,
   Duncan Forbes in Letter ; and in 1604 there is a contract
   of marriage between her and Mr. Robert Irving of Mincoffer.
   She married, thirdly, John Forbes of Leslie.

II. Andrew Skene of Auchorie, ancestor of the family of Halyards in
Fife, and Pitlour.

III. Robert Skene in Tilliebirloch. There is recorded in the Register
of Deeds in 1610, a contract between Alexander Skene of that
ilk and Mr. James Skene, Clerk of Register and others, the said
Alexander's curators on the one part, and Robert Skene of
Tillibrolocht, for himself, and taking burden upon him for Jeane

Douglas, relict of Mr. James Skene of that ilk, his mother, on the
other part, at Edinburgh and Aberdeen, 24th April and 22nd
May, 1605. Robert appears to have been appointed tutor to his
nephew, Alexander Skene of that ilk, on his grandfather's death,
as in 1606 he appears as "Robert Skene in Tillibroloche, called
the tutor" (Forbes papers), and on 22nd April, 1636, there is an
obligation by Robert Skene of Tillibury, and Christiane Johnstone,
his spouse, to Alexander Black, elder burgess of Aberdeen.
"Robert Skein of Tillibirloch, son to James Skein of that ilk,
married, 1st, Christian Irving, sister to Captain Irving of Mon-
durch, on whom he begat Alexander, and ane daughter, named
Jean, who both died unmarried. After her death he married
Christian Johnston, daughter of the laird of Crimond, on whom
he begat Mr. Robert Skene, schoolmaster at Banchorie, and
thereafter of the Grammar School of Aberdeen, which Mr. Robert
Skene married Elizabeth Reid, daughter to
and sister to Mr. Robert Reid, minister of Banchorie-ternan'
(MS.A); and had by her Robert Skene, who went to Poland, and
two daughters, the eldest of whom married Mr. George Skene,
parson of Kinkell.

IV. Mr. William Skene. "He lived most part of his days at Court,
and was schoolmaster of the Music School of Aberdeen" (MS.A).
In 1591 Mr. William Skene was appointed master of the Song
School of Aberdeen; and in 1597 "Alexander Skene de Eodem"
resigns two annual rents, payable out of Angelscroft and Cullinges,
in Futtie, "nepoti suo Magistro Willielmo Skene Schole Musice
dicti Burgi preceptori." "He married Janet Preston, daughter
to Mr. John Preston, Merchant Burgess of Aberdeen, on whom
he begat Alexander, who died a child, and a daughter, Isobell,
unmarried" (MS.A).

V. Patrick Skene appears, on his father's succeeding to the barony of
Skene, to have obtained the Tanistry lands of Bandodle, having
previously been a tenant of Forbes of Corsinday, with whom he
was connected through his grandmother; as in 1606 Patrick
Skene, sometime in the Muirtown of Corsinday, and now in Bandodle, discharges the tocher of Bessie Alshenor, sister of Robert
Alshenor, burgess, and now spouse of Patrick. Contract of

marriage, dated 9th January, 1605 : John Forbes of Camphill, cautioner for Patrick and Robert Alshenor, and Gilbert Skeyne of Westercorse, for Bessie, umquhile William Alshenor, and Bessie Skene, his spouse, her parents. By her he appears to have had two sons, Gilbert Skene, burgess of Aberdeen, who married, in 1688, Elizabeth Cordiner, daughter of William Cordiner, Notary Public, and died in 1669 ; and Alexander. He married, a second time, Jeane Cushney, by whom he had a son, John ; as on 29th April, 1653, there is an obligation by Walter Forbes of Tolquhone, principal, and Master William Forbes, Advocat in Edinburgh, his brother-german, as cautioner to Patrick Skene in Bandodle, for himself, and in name and behalf of Jeane Cushney, his spouse ; and on 7th November, 1673, John Skene, in Wester Kinmundie (in the Barony of Skene), serves heir of provision to Patrick Skene of Bandodle, his father, by Jean Cushney, his wife.

VI. Mr. John Skene " died unmarried " (MS.A).

VII. Jean Skene married John Forbes of Camphill.

VIII. Margaret Skene. There is, on 25th May, 1590, Renunciation by Elizabeth Lumsden, spouse of Alexander Cullen, Burgess of Aberdeen, in favor of Margaret Skene, dochter lawful to James Skene of Badindodill, future spouse to Andrew Cullen, sone eldest to the said Alexander Cullen and Elizabeth Lumsden, of the town and land of Cottoun. Either this marriage did not take place, or she became soon a widow, for we find her, in 1600, wife of William Forbes of Pittalochie, and she was soon again a widow, for there is, in 1620, an action of Removing against Margaret Skene, relict of William Forbes of Pittalochie, from the lands of Kinaldie.

IX. Katharine Skene " married, 1st, John Leith of Likliehead, and 2nd, to Arthur Forbes, sometime Baillie of Old Aberdeen, who had no succession by any of them " (MS.A). Action at the instance of Katharine Skeyne, relict of umquhile Robert Leith of Likliehead, and Arthur Forbes, now her spouse, against Patrick Leith, now of Likliehead, relative to contract, dated 16th September, 1621 (Acts and Decreets).

X. Christian Skene " married James Fraser of Balbrydie " (MS.A).

XIII.—ALEXANDER SKENE OF SKENE—1605-1634.

On 5th May, 1605, there is a sasine in favor of Alexander Skene, proceeding upon precept by the Earl of Crawford to him as " pronepos et legitimus haeres quondam Alexandri Skene de eodem sui proavi " of the lands of Tillibirloch, &c., and on 27th February, 1611, when he attained majority, there is a retour " Alexander Skene de eodem haeres Jacobi Skene avi in terris et baronia de Skene cum lacu," followed by infeftment on 27th April, 1612.

In 1623 he obtained a crown charter of the lands and barony of Skene to himself, and failing him to James Skene, his son and heir apparent, whom failing, to return to himself and other heirs male of his body, whom failing, " Magistro Andree Skene fratri germano dicti Alexandri et heredibus masculis de corpore suo," whom failing " Magistro Andree Skene de Chappelton et heredibus masculis de corpore suo," whom failing, to return to him and his heirs male whomsoever. He was infeft on 3rd September, 1623.

Soon after, and perhaps in consequence of this, the old controversy broke out again between the Skenes of Skene and the Keiths, with regard to the possession of the lands of Ester Skene, which ended this time to the disadvantage of the former.

On 10th April, 1629, Alexander Skene de eodem served heir in general to Robert Skeyne " de eodem avi quondam Adami Skeyne de eodem *attavi tritavi*," and on the same day, by a separate service, he serves heir to Adam Skene " de eodem *proavi* Jacobi Skeyne de eodem *avi tritavi*."

The question seems to have been submitted to the arbitration of the Lords of Council and Session, as on 1st December, 1629, we find the Lords of Session assigning to William, Earl Marischall, of his own consent, the eighth of December next, to exhibit and produce the writs and evidents of the lands, barony, and loch of Skene, libelled in the action of improbation pursued at the instance of Sir Thomas Hope of Craighall, King's Advocate, and Alexander Skene of that ilk, proprietor of said lands, against the said Earl and others ; and on 26th March, 1631, there is a Decreet Arbitral in the process at the instance of Alexander Skene of that ilk and Sir Thomas Hope, King's Advocate, against William Earl

Marischall and others, touching the exhibition of all infeftments, charters, &c., alleged made and granted to the said Earl or his predecessors (of whom a long line is enumerated), "be the said Alexander Skene, now of that ilk ; umquhile James Skene of that ilk, *his guidsir ;* umquhile Alexander Skene of that ilk, *his grandsir ;* umquhile Alexander Skene of that ilk, *his foir grandsir ;* umquhile Alexander Skene of that ilk, *his foir grandsir's father ;* umquhile Gilbert Skene of that ilk, *his foir grandsir's guidsir ;* umquhile Alexander Skene of that ilk, *his foir grandsir's grandsir ;* umquhile James Skene of that ilk, *his foir grandsir's foir grandsir ;* umquhile Adam Skene of that ilk, the said umquhile James Skene of that ilk, *his grandsir ;* and umquhile Adam Skene of that ilk, the said umquhile Adam *his guidsir ;* or by any or other of them ; or in a decreet granted by any sovereign back to King Robert Bruce, of and concerning the lands and barony of Skene, and loch of Skene, to be considered by the said Lords, and to have the same lawfully improvin, &c., the parties compeiring by their procurators, and compeiring also Mr. Andro Skene of Halyairds, taking burden on him for the said laird of Skene." Submission being entered into for amicable settlement of matters, the Lords "decree and ordain the said Alexander Skene to resign in favour of the Earl Marischal, all claim to the lands of Kirktown of Skene, Ledach, Mylnebowie, and Garlogie, with the pertinents, to be bruikit be the said Earl in his own proper lands in all time coming. Lyke as the saide Lords arbitrators declairit that the loch of Skene, nor no pairt thairof, is naways comprehendit under the decreet arbitral."

These documents are interesting, as showing both the Latin and the corresponding Scotch technical names designating the steps in a pedigree ; and if the lairds of Skene failed eventually to redeem these lands under the clause of reversion in the impignoration of them, they had at all events the satisfaction of having successfully resisted a similar attempt, on the part of the Strachans of Carmylie, to redeem the lands of Tillibirloch and others, forming the Tanistry lands of the family.

Alexander married Janet Burnet, daughter of Sir Thomas Burnet of Leyes, and had by her—

I. James Skene, who succeeded him.

II. Jean Skene married " Alexander Innes of Pethenick."

III. Margaret Skene married, 1st, " Mr. John Garrie," and 2nd, Mr. John Skene in Knowheade. 1646. Sasine Margaret Skene, future

spouse of Mr. John Garioch, son to William Garioch of Tillie-
bethie, in the lands of Auchballoch.* 1675. Carta per Willelmum
dominum de Forbes concessa Margarete Skene relicte Magistri
Johannis Skene in Knowheade in vitali redditu et post ejus
decessum Willelmo Gareoch de terris de Auchballoch in parochia
de Awfurde.

IV. Janet Skene married "Mr. Adam Barclay, minister of Nigg" (MS.A).
Ratification, by Oliver Cromwell, of contract between James
Skene of Skene and Mr. Adam Barclay, minister of Tarvie, and
Janet Skene, his wife, at Edinburgh, 14th August, 1656. Sasine
Mr. Adam Barclay, younger of Towie, and Janet Skene, his spouse.

V. Isobell Skene married " the laird of Aswanlie " (Calder).

VI. Katharine Skene married, 1st, " to a younger son of Sir Alexander
Cumming of Coulder ; and 2nd, to Robert Cheyne " (MS.A).

VII. Mary Skene married "George Mackenzie of Kincardine, second
brother to the Earl of Seaforth" (MS.A). 1653. Sasine Isobell,
Katharine, and Maria Skene, lawful daughters to umquhile
Alexander Skene of that ilk, with consent of Gilbert Skene of
Dyce, and Mr. Andrew Skene of Overdyce. 1692. Discharge
Robert Cheyne, son to Mr. William Cheyne, minister of Dyce,
and Katharine Skene, his spouse, sister to James Skeyne of that
ilk. Assignation and Disposition Mary Skene, youngest sister of
James Skene of that ilk, with consent of George Mackenzie of
Kintowdie, brother-german to Kenneth, Earl of Seaforth, her
husband.

XIV.—JAMES SKENE OF SKENE—1634-1656

succeeded his father in 1634, and was infeft in that year in the lands and
barony of Skene as heir served and retoured to Alexander Skene of
Skene, his father.

He married Elizabeth Forbes, daughter of Arthur Lord Forbes, in
1637, as on 14th July, in that year, there is a sasine in her favour in his
jointure lands of Letter and Broomhill.

On 17th October, 1639, there is a sasine in favour of James Skene de
eodem, upon letters of four forms, dated 6th April, in a tenement in
Aberdeen, " ex boreali parte ly Keyhead," in payment of 4000 merks,

contained in an obligation by Alexander, Master of Forbes, to Elizabeth Forbes, his sister, " nunc sponse dicti Jacobi Skene de eodem," dated 20th December, 1629, and assigned by the said Elizabeth Forbes, with consent of Arthur Lord Forbes, to James Skene, on 5th July, 1637.

" This James of Skene was a great loyalist, and suffered many hardships on account of his attachment to the interest of the Royal Family."

" In that copy of the covenant subscribed before the Sheriff of Aberdeen, still extant, this James Skene of that ilk subscribes, along with the Marquis of Montrose. However, afterwards he was a great companion of the Marquis of Montrose, and got a protection from him for saving his estate from being pillaged in Charles the 1st time. He had the misfortune, soon after his marriage, to be bitten by a swine in the knee, and his lady, who liked gadeing abroad, and had an expensive turn, persuaded him, for his cure, to go to the wells in Germany. They stayed there a year or two, with a brother of his, a merchant there, and by his wife's expensive turn, brought the estate under a great load of debt. He died young, and was greatly esteemed for his capacity in every respect, while he lived. The said Elspet Forbes lived a widow on the estate till the year 1695 " (MS.D). By her he had two sons and one daughter.

I. John Skene, who succeeded him.

II. James Skene, " called the martyr, had the misfortune to associate with the Covenanters at Queensferry, Rutherglen, &c., when he was taken prisoner, tried, and executed in the Gressmerceat " (MS.D). " He was hanged, with two others, at the Cross of Edinburgh, on the 1st December, 1680, Skeen being all cloathed in white linnen, to his very shues and stockings, in affectation of puritie and innocence, and I wish it might be a praelibation and type of a white robe to be given him in heaven." (Fountainhall Historical Observes, p. 10.) His trial and last speech are recorded in the " Cloud of Witnesses."

III. Barbara Skene married her cousin, Calder of Aswanlie.

XV.—JOHN SKENE OF SKENE—1656-1680.

On 31st October, 1656, an edict of curatory was issued, charging William, Master of Forbes ; Andrew, Master of Fraser ; Sir Alexander Cumming of Cults ; John Urquhart of Craigstone ; Alexander Urquhart of Dunlugus; John Skeen of Auchtertoill; Richard Maitland of Pitrichie; Gilbert Skene of Dyce; Mr. Andrew Skene of Overdyce; *Mr. Alexander Skene, baillie burgess of Aberdeen ;* Mr. Robert Burnet of Crimond, advocate, as " friends and nearest of kyn on the father and mother's syde, to John Skene of that ilk" (Sheriff Register of Deeds) ; and on 24th July, 1657, John Skene of that ilk, served heir in special to James Skene of that ilk, his father, in the lands and barony of Skene, with the loch thereof, the lands of Tillibriloch, Tulnahilt, Bandodle, Auchmoir, Auchorrie, with the myles and burghar lands of Comers, unite into the barony of Skene, the lands and mains of Aslowne in the parish of Alford, the lands of Dorrsoilt, Muchills, Badinapettis, and Drumnalunda (Index Retours).

On 25th January, 1658, he was infeft on this retour, among the witnesses being Mr. Andrew Skene of Overtown, and Robert Skene, pedagogue to the said John Skene—no doubt the Robert Skene, son of Robert Skene in Tillibirloch, who was schoolmaster at Banchorie, and afterwards of the Grammar School of Aberdeen.

The Tanistry lands seem now to have finally left the family, as on 5th May, 1659, there is a ratification, by John Skene of that ilk, with consent of William, Master of Forbes ; Gilbert Skene of Dyce ; Mr. Alexander Skene, baillie burgess of Aberdeen ; and Mr. Andrew Skene of Overdyce, his curators, of a procuratory of resignation granted by the deceased James Skene of that ilk, dated 30th June, 1641, to John Forbes of Corsinday, of the lands of Tillibirloch, Tilnahilt, Bandodle, Auchmore, Auchorrie, &c.

On the 14th February, 1678, he obtained a crown charter of the lands and barony of Skene, on which he was infeft on 30th June, 1679 ; but died in the following year.

He married Jean, daughter of Alexander Burnet, eldest son and apparent heir of Sir Thomas Burnet of Leys.

In the end of a small bible are the following notes in his handwriting:—

" Nott of my childrens ages—

"Junii 24 166⅔ my eldest daughter Elizabeth was born. August 4 166⅔ my second daughter Anna was born. Sept. 12 166⁴⁄₃ my eldest sone Alexʳ was borne. May 2 1666 my second son George was born 1666.

"Junii 4 1667 my third daughter Margret was born. Apryll 16 1670 my third sone Andrew was born. July 1 1671 my fourt sone John was born. February 1 1673 my fourt daughter Jean was born.

"July 4 1676 my fuivt daughter Barbara was born. On August 19
1678 my sext daughter Catren was born.   July 24 1679 my fift sone
Thomas was born."

In a later hand there is added—

" In the end of October after the dear father Jo. Skene of .that ilk in
death he departit the 9th of May 1680. his sone James was born.   He
died the 3d day after his birth.

" Jean Burnett mother of the above writtin children grandaunt to
the present Sir Al. Burnett of Leyes wife to John Skene of that ilk died
at Crathes in harvest 1688 somewhat more than eight years after her
husband's death.   This is writt 1745.

" Jean Burnett aforesaid wife to John Skene of that ilk built the new
midle part of the house of Skene in her widowhood and put the roof upon
the old tower.   This is writt by her grandchild George Skene of that
ilk at Skene the 7th of July 1745.   The above built by Jean Burnett is
the main or middle part, the south wing was built by her said grandchild.
The old tower makes the north wing " (Old Bible).

" The said Jean Burnet, Lady Skene, was a woman of uncommon
conduct and frugality, and altho' she got things in the greatest disorder
from the former lady's mismanagement, yet she kept the family together
and lived in a very decent way, and after her husband's death, from her
savings of her jointure, she floored and roofed the old tower, after taking
out the vaults, and also built a large addition to it, which is at present the
main body of the house of Skene ; the family having always lived before
that in low thatch houses, like the better kind of their common farm
houses " (MS.D).

John Skene of Skene had the following children by Jean Burnett,
who survived him, the others mentioned by her having died young :—

  I. Alexander Skene, who succeeded him.
 II. George Skene, "who served under the Duke of Marlborough in
     Queen Anne's wars, and afterwards acquired a considerable sum
     in the Mississippi Stock, in France, with which he bought the
     estate of Caraldstone, An. 1720 " (MS.D).   He married Elizabeth
     Baird, widow of Francis White, coffee merchant in London, by
     whom he had two daughters—

     1. Elizabeth married her cousin, George Skene of Skene.
     2. Jean married Sir Alexander Forbes of Foveran, Baronet.   He
        died in London, 3rd August, 1724.

III. Thomas Skene "was a lieutenant in the army, and was among the troops sent by Queen Anne into Spain, where he was killed" (MS.D).
IV. Elizabeth Skene married William Livingstone, merchant, Aberdeen.
V. Ann Skene married James Barclay, son to the minister of Keig.
VI. Jean Skene married Donald Farquharson, son of Charles Farquharson.
VII. Barbara Skene married John Tytler, merchant, Aberdeen.

XVI.—ALEXANDER SKENE OF SKENE—1680-1724.

On the 19th March, 1686, when he had attained majority, he was served heir to John Skene of that ilk, his father, in the lands and barony of Skene, with the lake and mills of the same, and was infeft in the same on 13th May, 1686.

Four years after, he made a marriage, which brought to the family the lands of Wester Fintray. This was with "Giles Adie, daughter of Mr. David Adie of Newark and Easter Echt, Baillie and Burgess of Aberdeen, and Guild Brother of Edinburgh" (MS.D). Her mother was Katherine Skene, niece of Sir George Skene of Wester Fintray and Rubislaw, who was unmarried, and settled the estate of Wester Fintray on his grandniece, by the contract of marriage between her and Alexander Skene, to which he was a party, and which may be given at length—

Contract of marriage between Alexander Skene of that ilk, on the one part; and Sir George Skene of Wester Fintray, late Provost of Aberdeen, and David Adie of Newark, late Bailie of the said burgh, for themselves, and taking burden upon them for Giles Adie, daughter to the said David Adie, procreate betwixt him and the deceased Katharine Skene, his spouse, who was niece to the said Sir George Skene, and the said Giles Adie for herself, on the other part: Whereby the said Alexander Skene and the said Giles Adie agree to enter into the bonds of matrimony with each other, and thereafter love, cherish, treat, and entertain each other as becometh Christian married persons of their estate and rank: .And narrating that the said Sir George Skene stands infeft, in virtue of a charter granted by King Charles II., in the lands of Wester Fintrayes, and that by his disposition, dated 15th September, 1658, he disponed the said lands to the deceased George Skene, his nephew, eldest

son of the deceased David Skene, merchant burgess of Zamosky, in the
kingdom of Poland, and the heirs male of his body ; whom failing, to
Alexander Skene, youngest son of the said David Skene, and the heirs
male of his body ; whom failing, to Mr. George Skene, eldest son of
Robert Skene, late treasurer burgess of Aberdeen, and the heirs male of
his body ; whom failing, to the deceased John Skene of that ilk, his heirs
and assignees whatsomever, bearing the arms and surname of Skene ;
reserving power to himself to dispone the said lands during his lifetime,
or to set the same in tack, and also to redeem from the said George and
Alexander Skenes and others above mentioned, by payment of the sum
of £3 Scots, in the Tolbooth of Aberdeen, on any day between the hours
of twelve and two, intimation having been given to them twenty-four
hours previously, with various other provisions : And that having resolved,
from various reasons, to revoke said disposition, and having paid the said
sum of £3 Scots to the said disponees, and being most zealous and
desirous to contribute his endeavours and assistance for the flourishing
and standing of the family of Skene, which had stood in a prosperous
and flourishing condition for some hundreds of years, in the person of
the said Alexander Skene of that ilk and his predecessors, of the surname of Skene, and of which the said Sir George Skene is duly descended,
and for the special love and respect which the said Sir George Skene
bears to the said Alexander Skene of that ilk and Giles Adie, his
apparent spouse :   Therefore, in view of the said marriage between them,
he dispones to them in liferent, and to the heirs male to be gotten between them ; whom failing, to the other heirs male of the said Alexander's
body ; whom failing, to his heirs male whatsoever ; whom all failing, to
the said Alexander's heirs and assignees whatsoever ; the said lands of
Wester Fintrayes, with all their pertinents.   Dated at Aberdeen the
eighth February, 1690.   Witnesses, John Skene, younger of Dyce ;
George Adie ; Robert Skene, late treasurer of Aberdeen ; and Mr. George
Skene, his son.

Among the letters in the Skene charter chest is one dated 15th
August, 1694, from George Skene of Rubislaw, grand-nephew of Sir
George Skene, and his successor in that estate, to the laird of Skene,
" with five guineas to buy a pony for Lady Skene ;" and another written
on 7th April, 1715, which led to a still more important addition to the
family estates.   This was a letter from George Skene to his brother, the

laird of Skene, asking advice as to the marriage of his eldest daughter, Elizabeth, and acknowledging the advice received from Andrew Skene of Hilton. Dated at London, 7th April, 1715.

What this correspondence led to, the following document shows :—

Post-nuptial contract of marriage between Alexander Skene of that ilk and George Skene, his eldest son, on the one part, and Major George Skene of St. James's, London, and Elizabeth Skene, his eldest daughter, on the other part, for the marriage of the said George and Elizabeth, which took place at York, in August, 1719. The contract is dated 26th February, 1723.

Giles Adie adds her quota to the family Bible thus :—

I. My eldest son, George, was born at Aberdeen the 23° of February, being Saturday, betwixt four and five in the afternoon, in the year of God, 1695.

II. My daughter Jeane was born at Skene the twa of November, 1696 years; married to George Forbes of Alford; died in March, 1723, at Skene.

III. My second daughter, Keatren (married Moncoffer), was born at Skene the sixtint of January, one thousand seven hundred and one, being Thursday, in the forenoon, at 11 o'clocke or thereby; died in Feby., 1744, at Banff; married their to Dr. Fotheringham.

IV. My third daughter, Elizabeth, was born at Skene 24 Maye, being Monday, at eleven o'clock or thereby, in the year of God, 1703 years; died a child.

V. My fourt daughter, Margret, was born on Monday, 24 Dec^r., in the year of God, 1704 years; died a child.

VI. My second sone, Alexander, on Tuesday, the nint of July, was born in the year of God, 1706; died in Jamaica, 1732.

VII. My third son, David, was born on Saturday, 24 of Aprill, in the year of God, 1708 years, at Skene; died coming from the East Indies, 1733, at sea.

VIII. I had a fourt sone dead-borne on the first day of April, in the year of God, 1711 years.

IX. My 5 son, John, was born the 6 October, being Tuesday, betwixt 8 & nine in the afternoon, in the year of God, 1713.

Her eldest son adds to this—

" John, the said Alexander's fifth son, was born 1713, was a lieutenant

G

in Colonel Murray's regiment, and was killed under Sir John Cope, at the battle of Preston, near Edinburgh, by some called the battle of Glads-muir, fought the 21st September, 1745, being the first fought in that rebellion, so that he wanted only a little of being 32 years of age, so that none of the children are now alive but one, the writer, and eldest."

Alexander Skene of that ilk, the father, died at Skene the 20th January, 1724 ; his brother, Major George Skene of Caraldstone, died at London, the 18th of August said year, 1724—(old Bible).

XVII.—George Skene of Skene—1724-1756

succeeded his father and uncle in 1724, and on 10th June, 1725, he took infeftment upon a disposition by the late Major George Skene of Carald-stone, with consent of Elizabeth Baird, his spouse, in favour of himself and her, and the heirs male between them ; whom failing, to the heirs male of his body, by any other marriage ; which failing, to Elizabeth Skene, his eldest daughter, now spouse to George Skene, now of that ilk, eldest son. of the late Alexander Skene of that ilk, who was brother-german to the said Major George Skene, and to the heirs male between them ; which failing, to the other heirs of entail of the granter ; of his lands and barony of Balnamoon and others contained in said disposition, and in the disposi-tion thereof by Sir John Stuart of Grandtully, baronet, to the said Major George Skene, of date 15th August, 1721, now disponing an annuity of £600 sterling, in trust, for behoof of the said Elizabeth Skene, his eldest daughter, and her heirs, the said George Skene of that ilk, and Andrew Skene of Lethenty, being of the trustees.

The deed of entail of the lands and barony of Balnamoon, compre-hending the lands and barony of Caraldstone, Little Watterston, Brocklaw, and Berrytullich haugh, on the west side of the South Esk, executed by Major George Skene on the 24th October, 1721, was recorded in the Register of Entails on 6th January, 1725.

On 20th August, 1725, the testament dative and inventory of the goods gear debts and sums of money pertaining to the deceased Major George Skene of Caraldstone, residenter in the City of London, who died there upon the 13th of August, 1724, was given up by George Skene of that ilk, husband to, and in name and behalf of, Elizabeth Skene, his spouse, and by Sir Alexander Forbes of Foveran, Bart., husband to, and in name and behalf of, Dame Jean Skene, his spouse ; which Elizabeth and Dame Jean Skene, lawful daughters to the said Major George Skene, are only executrixes, dative decerned as nearest in heir to him, and the said George Skene of that ilk, husband to the said Elizabeth, and the said Sir Alexander Forbes, husband to the said Dame Jean Skene, for their interests, and that by decreet of the Commissaries of Edinburgh, of date 10th March, 1725. Amount of the inventory, £10,791 14s.

Among the moneys owing to the deceased is the following, viz., Item, the said defunct, his four shares in the capital stock of the Governor and Company of the Bank of Scotland, being £4000 Scots subscription, of which three was paid in by the defunct (designed in the said company's books Captain George Skene, in the Royal Regiment of Dragoons). Amount of inventory and debts, £17,065 15s. 9d.

Among the Skene papers are a number of letters relating to the death of Elizabeth, the wife of George Skene of Skene, which happened at Montrose on 30th March, 1730, her husband being then in London. In one of these, from Sir Alexander Burnet of Leyes, his brother-in-law, mention is made of the welfare of the " two pretty boys," the sons of the said George Skene, then staying at Leyes. He married a second time his cousin, Sarah, daughter of Baillie Simpson of Aberdeen, by whom he had no children. She died 28th November, 1789.

George Skene of Skene was, on nine successive occasions (1737-45), elected Lord Rector of Marischal College and University. The following notice of his death appeared in the *Aberdeen Journal* of September 7th, 1756 :—" On Friday morning [September 3rd], about 10 o'clock, died at Skene (the seat of this ancient Family), in the sixty-second Year of his Age, much and justly lamented, George Skene of that Ilk, a Man of superior Capacity ; fitted for Business ; remarkable for doing good, and making up Differences amongst his Friends and Neighbours. He was a sincere and steady Friend, a dutiful Son, a tender and affectionate Husband, a fond indulgent Parent, a kind and encouraging Master. His Humanity and Benevolence was extensive, especially to the poor ; and those in Distress were sure of a Friend in him. He was a Father to the Fatherless, and a Husband to the Widow ; a sincere good Christian, without Ostentation or Show. These substantial Qualities being accompanied with great Knowledge, true Taste, and an inimitable Turn of Humour, make the Tears of his Friends flow unbidden o'er his grave."

He had two sons by his first wife, Elizabeth, daughter of Major George Skene of Caraldstone, viz. :—

I. George Skene, who succeeded him.

II. James Skene, who was a captain in the army, and married a Miss Allan, by whom he had seven sons and three daughters.

　1. George Skene, who was executed in London for forgery.

　2. Alexander Skene, captain in the Navy (well known as a beautiful musician), married Miss Fordyce of Ayton, and died at Edinburgh on the 14th September, 1823, leaving no issue.

　3. David Skene, died young.

　4. Andrew Skene, died young.

　5. James Skene, died in India, leaving a natural son, James, an officer in the army.

　6. John Skene, died in India.

　7. Another son died.

　8. Elizabeth Skene, married the Reverend Dr. Munroe, and had issue.

　9. Sarah Skene, married 　　　　 Lynch of Jamaica, and had issue.

　10. Barbara Skene, married 　　　　 Sturgeon, and had issue (MS.E).

XVIII.—GEORGE SKENE OF SKENE—1756-1781.

On 27th July, 1757, there is a sasine on a charter under the great seal, in favour of George Skéne of that ilk, eldest lawful son of the deceased George Skene of that ilk, procreated between him and the also deceased Elizabeth Skene, his spouse, eldest lawful daughter of the deceased Major George Skene of Caraldstone ; and to the heirs male of his body ; whom failing, to James Skéne, only other son now in life of the said George Skene of that ilk, senior, procreated between him and the said Elizabeth Skene, his spouse, and the heirs male of the body of the said James Skene ; whom failing, to the heirs male procreated between Sir Alexander Forbes of Foveran, baronet, and Lady Jane Skene, second daughter of the said Major George Skene ; whom failing, to Alexander Skene, second lawful son of the deceased Alexander Skene of that ilk, and the heirs male of his body ; whom failing, to David Skene, third lawful son of the said Alexander Skene of that ilk, and the heirs male lawfully procreated of his body ; whom failing, to John Skene, fourth son of the said deceased Alexander Skene, and the heirs male lawfully procreated by his body ; whom failing, to the heirs male of the body of the said Alexander Skene, brother of the said Major George Skene ; whom all failing, to the heirs female of the substitutes above mentioned, without division.

In the same year there is a discharge by Sarah Simpson, widow of George Skene of that ilk, of various sums of money contained in bonds granted by her late husband, now paid by George Skene, also of that ilk. Dated at Skene, 8th November, 1757.

George Skene of Skene married his cousin Mary, daughter of George Forbes of Alford, by Jane, daughter of Alexander Skene, his grandfather. She is said to have been exceedingly handsome, but had the misfortune to be dumb. She died 15th March, 1786.

- By her he had the following children :—
  I. George Skene, who succeeded him.
  II. James Skene, who died unmarried.
  III. David Skene, was a burgess of Aberdeen, and died at Croydon in March, 1817.
  IV. Andrew Skene, died unmarried.
  V. Alexander Skene, was born deaf and dumb.
  VI. Mary Skene, married, 17th August, 1775, the Honourable Alexander Duff, afterwards third Earl Fife, by whom she had two sons.
    1. James, fourth Earl Fife, who died without issue 9th March, 1857.
    2. General the Honourable Sir Alexander Duff died 21st March, 1857, leaving by Anne, daughter of James Stein of Kilboagie, two sons and two daughters :—
      (1) James succeeded as fifth Earl.
      (2) George Skene.
      (3) Catharine.
      (4) Louisa Tollemache.
  VII. Sarah Skene, married, 12th June, 1780, Thomas Macdonald, W.S., and had issue.

George Skene of Skene died in 1781, and was succeeded by his eldest son.

XIX.—George Skene of Skene—1781-1825.

" He was educated for the Scotch bar, and passed advocate, but never practised. He afterwards entered the army, and served for some years in General Gordon of Fyvie's regiment of infantry, as captain. He was afterwards elected member of Parliament for the county of Aberdeen, but being subsequently opposed by Mr. Ferguson of Pitfour, did not succeed in a second canvass. He was an ardent admirer of the Ministry of Mr. Fox, and a firm adherent of the Whig side of politics to the termination of his life. Had it not been for the violence of his political opinions, and the dissipated life to which he was addicted, he was a man of talents and dispositions calculated to have made a figure in the corner of the country where his fortune and the antiquity of his family entitled him to take a lead. But in spite of these disadvantageous circumstances, his acuteness in the public affairs of the county, and remarkably conciliatory manner, continued, during the course of his life, to give great weight to his opinion at the meetings of the Freeholders. He never married ; and having lived to see every member of his family of the name of Skene disappear, save one unfortunate remnant, he executed, towards the end of his life, a deed of entail of the whole of his property, movable as well as heritable, upon the line of heirs contained in the entail of the estate of Caraldstone, and thus, notwithstanding his pride in the antiquity of his name and family, and the strong interest he was in use to express in the duration of the clan of which he was the chief, he voluntarily extinguished almost, in his own demise, the name of Skene of Skene " (MS.E).

The editor well remembers having seen this laird of Skene when visiting his father at Inverie House, on the Feuch, near Banchory. The editor was then only six years old, but a circumstance connected with the visit made an impression upon his mind, and corroborates the sketch above given of the convivial habits into which the laird had fallen in the later years of his life. The editor's father and he used to exchange an annual visit, but their habits were very different, Mr. Skene of Rubislaw being sobriety itself. He was known, on one of his visits to Skene— when detained till early in the morning at the laird's convivial table—when at length he was allowed to escape to his bedroom, to have jumped out of the window and walked 17 miles home to Inverie. On the occasion of a return visit of the laird to Inverie, the editor—then a little boy— had been promised by his father that he would take him out next morning with him, when he proposed to fish for salmon ; but when he was detained till a late hour at the dinner table, seeing that the laird had drunk himself into such a state that he could not see the difference, he quietly slipped out and substituted his Swiss servant, a man of good appearance and manner, to sit with the laird. The editor recollects being in his father's dressing-room at six o'clock, A.M., and seeing the laird with the Swiss servant walking round the court, the former clamouring for another bottle, while the latter was vainly advising him to go to bed.

George Skene of Skene died at Skene on the 28th April, 1825, and was succeeded by his brother.

XX.—Alexander Skene of Skene—1825-1827.

He was "upwards of sixty years of age, and having the misfortune to have been born deaf and dumb, and now (1826) for many years nearly blind, by reason of a disease in his eyes, his mind, though not absolutely in a state of imbecility, has been so little cultivated, as to render him quite unfit to take charge of his own affairs in any respect. Application was accordingly made to the Court of Session by his three nearest relatives, Earl Fife, General Duff, and the Reverend Mr. Macdonald, his nephews, to appoint a factor *loco tutoris*, which has been done. Upon his decease the family may be considered extinct, as the whole of the properties merge in the extensive entailed territories of the Earl of Fife, thus giving a singular confirmation to a traditional malediction reported to have been pronounced against the race of Skene of Skene. With what degree of truth I cannot say, but I have heard it narrated that the grandfather of the present laird, who married the dumb lady, Mary Forbes of Alford, who was very handsome, had had the baseness previously to seduce her, and was compelled by the family to fulfil the marriage, having previously fought with and wounded her brother. Upon which occasion the aged father of the lady is said to have imprecated the judgment of Heaven upon the family, that they might be cursed in their generation and come to a speedy termination. I have known in my time eleven males of the family, and seen nine of them swept off in the full vigour of life, one by an ignominious death; the last laird remarkable for a dissolute life ; his only sisters both divorced from their husbands, abandoned in their conduct, the one accidentally burnt to death, the other dying in misery a prostitute in a foreign land ; and now the only remnant left a poor helpless object, unconscious of the affluence and honors to which he has succeeded, vegetating in the old mansion of Skene, bereft nearly of all the attributes which distinguish man from the brute creation, and wearing out in humiliating obscurity the last dregs of his ancient race" (MS.E). He died of an attack of apoplexy on Sunday the 29th of April, 1827, and with him terminated the line of Skene of Skene. One exception to this melancholy picture of the younger members of the family appears to be "Miss Betty Skene,

eldest daughter to the Laird of Skene," who died at Carreston on the
16th February, 1766, and who is said, in the *Aberdeen Journal*, to have
been "much regretted, as she was a most amiable, virtuous young lady."

The succession to his estates fell under the deed of entail executed by
his great grand uncle, Major George Skene of Caraldstone, and by his
elder brother, George Skene of Skene, to his nephew, James, Earl Fife;
while the male representation of the family devolved upon the Skenes
of Halyards, in Fife.

James, fifth Earl Fife, who succeeded his uncle in 1857, was in the
same year created a British Peer, by the title of

BARON SKENE OF SKENE.

Arms of Alexander, XVI. of Skene, and Giles Adie his Spouse, from a Stone at Skene House.

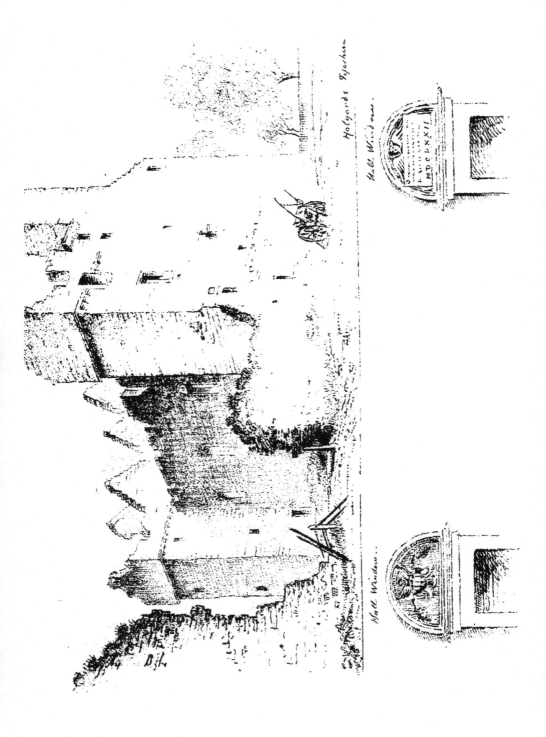

Halyards Ryerhus

Hall Window.

Hall Window.

MDCLXXII

CHAPTER II.

SKENE OF HALYARDS IN FIFE.

I.—Andrew Skene in Auchorie

is erroneously called, in MS.A, second son of "the little laird," but correctly, in MS.D, second son of James Skene XII. of that ilk, by Jean Douglas, his wife, and grandson of "the little laird," a filiation which his son's being called to the barony of Skene in the deed of 1623, immediately after Mr. Andrew Skene of Overdyce, shows to be correct.

He appears, in 1598, as burgess of Aberdeen ; and in 1599 Andrew Skene in Aberdeen (the brother), and John Forbes of Camphill (the brother-in-law), appear as executors to umquhile Alexander Skene, sometime fiar of that ilk ; and again, in the same year, on 3rd November, as executors, lawfully confirmed, to umquhile Alexander Skene, fiar of that ilk.

He appears, after his father's death in 1605, to have obtained possession of the Tanistry lands of Auchorie, as we find him so designed in a service in 1610 ; and, in 1613, Andrew Skene in Auchorie is baillie of the barony of Skene.

He married " Bessie Cadell or Calder, daughter of the laird of Asloun, by whom he begat three sons—

I. Sir Andrew Skene, thereafter laird of Halyards, in Fife.

II. Patrick Skene [ancestor of the Skenes in Austria].

III. William Skene, died unmarried.

IV. Jean Skene, married Mr. Robert   , Professor of Divinity at St. Andrews.

V. Isobell Skene, died unmarried " (MS.A).

He appears to have died in 1619.

H

II.—SIR ANDREW SKENE OF HALYARDS—1619-1653.

He appears, during his father's life, to have filled the lucrative office of servitor to Sir John Skene, the Lord Clerk Register, and to have been a Master of Arts.

In the Register of the Privy Seal we find, on 17th December, 1608, "Ane letter maid to Mr. Andro Skene, servitor to Sir John Skene of Curriehill, knight, Clerk of Register, of the gift of the escheit of John Irving, in Quhytrigis, at the instance of David Ramsay of Balmain, for payment to the said David, as cautioner for Arthur Stratoun of Canterland, of certain sums"; and again, on 28th June, 1610, "Ane letter maid to Maister Andro Skene, servitor to Sir John Skene of Curriehill, knight, Clerk of the Register, of the gift of the escheit, whilk is pertenit of befor to Alexander Skene, lawful sone to umquhile Gilbert Skene of Tillebirloche, at the instance of Robert Forbes, portioner of Findrossie."

On 8th December, in the same year, there is a precept "Jacobus &c dedimus &c dilecto nostro Magistro Andreæ Skene servitori Clerici nostri registri heredibus suis et assignatis quibuscunque hereditarie totas et integras terras et Baroniam de Leslie specialiter in se comprehenden. villas terras et alias suprascriptas."

On 22nd August, 1612, there is another precept which shows his identity with the son of Andrew Skene of Auchorie—"Jacobus &c dedimus &c dilecto nostro Magistro Andreæ Skene filio natu maximo Andreæ Skene de Auchorie heredibus et assignatis quibuscunque terras de Cammo et Chappelton."

When Sir John Skene resigned his office of Clerk Register in 1612, he appears to have become servitor to the Earl of Crawford, as there is recorded in the Register of Deeds, on 9th June, 1613, a bond, by David, Earl of Crawford, to his servitor, Mr. Andro Skene, eldest son to Andro Skene of Auchorie, dated at the castle of Edinburgh, 2nd January, 1612.

In the year 1628, we find him in possession of the lands and barony of Auchtertule. The whole parish of Auchtertule was the property of the bishops of Dunkeld, and they were in the habit of granting their lands, as was the usual custom with church lands, to lay proprietors, in feu-farm. We find that Auchtertule had been granted, in this manner, to Sir William Forbes of Craigievar, in 1617, and subsequently to Mr. John Skene, Clerk of Session, second son of Sir John Skene, from whom it passed to Mr. Andrew Skene, who received a crown charter confirming these grants, and thus came to hold it of the crown. This charter, granted on 18th January, 1628, confirms "duas cartas feudifirmæ subscriptas unam quarum factam per reverendum in Christo patrem Alexandrum Dunkelden. episcopum superiorem terrarum &c dilecto nostro Magistro Joanni Skene uni clericorum nostri concilii et heredibus suis et assignatis de omnibus et singulis terris et baroniæ de Auchtertule jacen. infra vic. de Fife et alteram dictarum cartarum factam per dictum reverendum in Christo patrem dilecto nostro Magistro Andreæ Skene tunc de Chappeltown nunc de Auchtertule heredibus suis et assignatis de omnibus et singulis terris et baronia de Auchtertule."

The barony of Auchtertule contained within it the old castle of Halyards, situated on the lake of Halyards, and Mr. Andrew Skene appears to have made it his residence, and eventually taken his title from it, as we find him designed in 1633 "Mr. Andro Skene of Halyards," in an assignation by Thomas Bruce in Parkhill, and Elspet Skene, his spouse, with his consent, to William Leslie, in Ley of Tulliebardie.

Sir Andrew Skene was knighted by King Charles the First, in Parliament assembled at Edinburgh, 6th November, 1641, along with three others who served as esquires upon the installation of General Leslie as Earl of Leven—(Balfour's Annals, III., p. 140).

He married Barbara Forbes, daughter of William Forbes of Craigievar, and had the following children :—

I. John Skene, who succeeded him.

II. James Skene of Wester Bogie, who married Elizabeth Orrock, and was, in 1662, infeft in the lands of Watstoun, in Cambusnethan, in which he is designed lawful son of the deceased Sir Andrew Skene of Auchtertule, knight, and Mr. Andrew Skene, his brother, is attorney ; and, in 1673, James Skene of Wester Bogie, brother-german to John Skene of Halyards, and Elizabeth Orrock, his spouse, are infeft in the town and lands of Bogie Wester, in the constabulary of Kinghorn. He had by her—

1. Andrew Skene, younger of Wester Bogie, mentioned in 1693.

2. John Skene of Wester Bogie, who receives, in 1708, a Renunciation, by Michael Malcolm of Balbeadie, of an annual rent of £19 4s. 6d., out of the lands of Wester Bogie. He had a son, John Skene, mentioned by Sibbald as in possession of Wester Bogie in 1710. He seems to have been the last of the family.

III. Mr. Andrew Skene appears, in 1665, as indweller in Edinburgh. He married Christian Wardlaw, and had three, sons—Henry, Andrew, and John.

IV. Mr. Alexander Skene. In 1663, on 1st, July, Mr. Alexander Skene, Halyards' brother, is admitted Regent of St Leonard's College, St. Andrews, and became Provost of St. Salvador's. Appended to one of the maces is this inscription—"Dr. Alexander Skene Collegii Sancti Salvatoris nostri prepositus me temporis injuria laesum et mutilatum publicis dicti Collegii sumptibus reparandum curavit An. Dom. 1685." On 24th April, 1718, the testament dative and inventory of the debts and sum of money pertaining to the deceased Doctor Alexander Skene, residenter in the Canongate, sometime Provost of the Old College of St. Andrews, who died in the Canongate in the month of , 1707, is given up by executors dative as creditors.

V. William Skene.

VI. Patrick Skene. 20th September, 1693, Mr. Andrew Skene and Patrick Skene, sons of deceased Sir Andrew Skene of Halyards, are mentioned.

VII. Robert Skene in Lamington. John Skene of Halyards, and James Skene, his brother, tutors to Robert Skene, our brother-german. Disposition John Skene of Halyards, and Robert Skene, his brother-german, to James Skene of Wester Bogie, their brother-german, of an annual rent of £20 Scots, dated at Lamington, 20th October, 1668.

VIII. Barbara Skene married, 1st, David Ramsay of Grangemuir. "1657, December 15, David Ramsay, by way of rapt, took away Barbara Skeyne, Halyards' eldest sister, out of her mother's house at Kingorne, and went and married her at the Border" (Chron. of Fife). She married, 2nd, Sir David Mores, advocate.

IX. Katharine Skene married William Lindsay, afterwards Bishop of
Dunkeld, son of James Lindsay of Dowhill, by contract, dated
in 1666.

"January, 1653—The old laird of Halyards (surnamed Skene)
departed this life at Halyards, and was interred at Auchtertoole church.
In November, 1653, his lady left Halyards, and went and dwelt in Dun-
fermling. All her children went with her "—(Chron. of Fife).

III.—JOHN SKENE OF HALYARDS—1653-1707.

On 24th May, 1653, John Skein of Halyards served heir to Sir Andro
Skeene of Halyards, his father, in the lands and barony of Auchtertule,
viz., the lands of Newtoune and Craigtoune of Auchtertule ; the lands of
Weltoun ; the lands of Milnetoun and Milne of Auchtertule ; the lands
and loch of Halyairds ; the lands of Easter and Wester Clintrayes, with
the loch of Lochorishburne, unite into the barronie of Auchtertule ; the
burgh of barronie of the Milnetoun of Auchtertule with the weiklie and
yierlie faires ; the lands of Shepletoune, with the commonties of White-
hills, Greenmyre, and Pilmure, within the parochin and barronie of Meigle,
with the advocatione of the kirk of Auchtertule, within the diocie of
Dunkeld and Sheriffdom of Fyff—(Ind. Ret.).

John Skene's arms are recorded in the Lyon Register : "Gules three
Daggers Argent, hilted and pomelled Or, surmounted of as many woolfs
heads couped of the third, a crescent for difference." Crest : "A dexter
hand proper holding a dagger as the former." Motto : "Virtutis regia
merces."

He was twice married, 1st, on 4th February, 1653, to "Margaret,
daughter of David McGill of Rankeillor, by whom he had two sons and
two daughters" (MS.D).

I. John Skene, who succeeded him.

II. James Skene, "who got from his father the lands of Grange and
Kirkcaldy" (MS.D).

6th December, 1684—Sasine on crown charter in favour of John
Skene of Halyards, in liferent, and James Skene, his second son,
in fee, of the lands and barony of New Grange. "He married
on 12th January, 1688, Anna Drummond, 2nd daughter of James

Drummond, Cultmalundie, by whom he had two daughters "
(MS.D).

1. Margaret Skene married to John Carnegie of Boysach.

2. Katharine Skene died unmarried.

James died without issue male, in 1698 ; and on 29th November, 1699, John Skene, senior, of Halyards, was served heir of provision to James Skene, his second son, in the lands of Mains of Grange and Banchrie.

III. Elizabeth Skene married Sir Henry Wardlaw of Pitreavie, bart.

23rd May, 1691—Disposition by John Skene, elder, of Halyards, to Dame Elizabeth Skene, his eldest lawful daughter, spouse to Sir Henry Wardlaw of Pitreavie, of an annual rent of £120. out of the lands of Milnehills.

IV. Katharine Skene was three times married, 1st, to Sir James Anstruther of Airdrie; 2nd, to Major Andrew Quhyt ; and 3rd, to Lord Edward Murray ; and had issue by them all. It is said that she obtained her three husbands from the extreme beauty of her hand ; and there is a portrait of her by Sir Peter Lely, formerly in the possession of the editor, and now in that of H. J. Trotter, Esq., M.P., a descendant of the family, in which the hands are prominently displayed, so as to show the back of one, and the palm of the other.

28th February, 1688—Charter under the great seal, in favour of Dame Katharine Skene, relict of Major Andrew Whyt and Philip Anstruther, only lawful son, procreat between her and the deceased Sir James Anstruther of Airdrie, of the lands and barony of Airdrie.

4th June, 1744—Testament dative of the deceased Dame Katharine Skene, relict of Lord Edward Murray, who died in the Canongate of Edinburgh, given up by John Murray, son lawful procreated between the deceased Lord Edward Murray and the defunct, his spouse.

John Skene of Halyards married, 2nd, Helen, daughter of Patrick Pitcairn, sometime of Pitlour, from whom he had, in 1683, bought that estate, and by her he had a son.

V. David Skene, born 17th January, 1696, ancestor of the Skenes of Pitlour.

On 23rd April, 1684, there is a sasine on a disposition by Henry Pitcairn, elder of Pitlour, and Patrick Pitcairn, fiar thereof, his eldest lawful son, in favour of John Skene elder of Halyards, John, Charles, and Thomas Skene, his grandchildren, of the town and lands of Wester and Easter Pitloures, in the barony of Strathmiglo, dated at Edinburgh, 22nd November, 1683, and at Balmuill, 24th November, 1683.

On 29th July, 1700, John Skene of Halyards grants a disposition in favour of David Skene, his lawful son procreat betwixt him and Helen Pitcairn, lawful daughter to Patrick Pitcairn, sometime of Pitlour, his present spouse, and the heirs male to be procreat of his body ; which failing, to the eldest for the time, of John, Charles, Thomas, William, David, and Edward Skenes, lawful sons to John Skene, younger of Halyards, eldest son to the said John Skene, elder and so forth, of the lands of Wester and Easter Pitloures, in the Lordship of Balmerino, dated at Grange.

And on 18th July, 1706, there is a sasine on a royal charter in favour of David Skene, lawful son to John Skene, senior of Halyards, and the heirs male to be lawfully procreat of his body; whom failing, James Skene, lawful son of John Skene of Halyards and the heirs male to be lawfully procreat of his body; whom failing, Andrew Skene, lawful son of the said John Skene and the heirs male to be lawfully procreat of his body; whom failing, David Skene, lawful son of the said John Skene, junior, and the heirs male to be lawfully procreat of his body; whom failing, Edward Skene, also lawful son of the said John Skene and the heirs male of his body; whom all failing, to the said John Skene, senior, and his nearest heirs and assignees whomsoever, of the lands of Easter and Wester Pitloures, and the town and lands of Friermilne, in the parish of Strathmiglo. Dated at the Palace of St. James, 19th January, 1706.

1707, December 10—Upon the 10th instant, John Skene of Halyards departed this life (Par. Reg.).

IV.—JOHN SKENE OF HALYARDS—1707-1709

succeeded his father, and is infeft on 11th December, 1708, on a charter under the great seal in favour of John Skene of Halyards and the heirs male, lawfully to be procreat of his body ; whom failing, the heirs male, procreat of the body of the deceased John Skene of Halyards, his father, and whom failing, his heirs male whomsoever ; whom all failing, his nearest and lawful heirs and assignees whomsoever, of the lands and baronie of Auchtertoole, at Edinburgh, 29th November, 1708.

He married Elizabeth, second daughter of Sir Thomas Wallace of Craigie, Baronet.

1680, August 28—John Skene, younger of Halyards, in Fife, Mrs. Elizabeth Wallace, lawful daughter to the deceased Lord Craigie, married by Dr. Alexander Skene, Provost of St. Salvators College, in St. Andrews—(Edin. Session Records).

22nd January, 1690—Sasine on contract of marriage, of date, at Edinburgh, 11th August, 1680, entered into between John Skene, elder of Halyards, John Skene, younger thereof, his eldest lawful son, and Margaret McGill, spouse to the said John Skene, elder; and Mistress Elizabeth Wallace, then promised, and present spouse to the said John Skene, younger of Halyards, therein designed, lawful daughter to the deceased Sir Thomas Wallace of Craigie, Knight, Baronet, Lord-Justice Clerk, with advice and consent of Sir William Wallace of Craigie, Knight, and Baronet, her brother-german: whereby the said John Skene, elder, with consent of his said spouse, bound him to infeft and seize the said John Skene, younger, his eldest lawful son, and the heirs male, to be procreat between him and the said Elizabeth Wallace, in the lands, barony, and whole parish of Auchtertool.

By Elizabeth Wallace he had the following children :—

I. John Skene, who succeeded him.

II. Charles Skene, who was a lieutenant in Lord Dalrymple's regiment, "was married and had a son, who died 1741, and two daughters living in 1788" (MS.E).

III. Thomas Skene died unmarried before 29th June, 1706, when his Testament is confirmed in Edinburgh Commissary Court.

IV. William Skene died unmarried.

V. James Skene, who carried on the line of this family.

VI. Andrew Skene, lieutenant in Earl of Orkney's regiment.

19th April, 1710—Renunciation by Andrew Skene, lieutenant in the Earl of Orkney's regiment of foot, and sixth lawful son of the deceased John Skene of Halyards, in Fife, in favour of John Skene, now of Halyards, his eldest lawful brother, now served and retoured, and infeft, to the said deceased John Skene, their father, of an annual sub-rent of the lands, barony, and parish of Auchtertool.

VII. David Skene died unmarried.

VIII. Edward Skene died unmarried.

IX. Margaret Skene.

X. Elizabeth Skene married Calderwood of Pittedie.

John Skene appears to have married a second time Mrs. Anne Stuart.

On 19th January, 1709, there is a sasine on a bond of provision by the deceased John Skene, younger of Halyards, in favour of Charles, William, James, Andrew, David, and Edward, Margaret and Elizabeth, his lawful children, whereby he bound himself and his heirs to pay to his said children the sums of money following, viz., to each of his sons, 5000 merks Scots, to his eldest daughter Margaret, 10,000 merks Scots, and to his youngest daughter Elizabeth, 9000 merks Scots, and bound himself to infeft them in an annual rent of £2120, or any other rent corresponding to the principal sum of 53,000 merks forsaid out of the land and barony of Auchtertool, reserving the liferent interest of Mrs. Anne Stuart, lady of the said John Skene. It is dated at Halyards, 10th July, 1705.

" John Skene, fiar of Halyards, having married Elizabeth, second daughter of Sir Thomas Wallace of Craigie, Baronet, his third daughter having married John Drummond, brother to the Duke of Perth, and himself Duke of Melfort, in France, John Skene and his lady accompanied them to France, where he ran through his estate" (MS.E). He survived his father only two years, and died in 1709.

V.—JOHN SKENE OF HALYARDS—1709-1717

succeeded to an encumbered estate on his father's death, and on 29th August, 1713, is infeft on a precept of clare constat by Charles, Earl of Murray, Lord Doune and Abernethy, as nearest heir male of the deceased John Skene of Auchtertool, his grandfather, of the kirklands of Auchtertool, dated at Donniebristle, 10th August, 1713, and on the 20th August, 1713, he resigns these lands to Charles, Earl of Murray.

Two years after, on 30th June, 1715, there is a resignation, by John Skene of Halyards, eldest lawful son and heir male, served and retoured to the deceased John Skene of Halyards, his father, procreat between him and the late Elizabeth Wallace, his spouse, to Charles, Earl of Moray, of the lands, barony, and whole parish of Auchtertool, with the manor place of Halyards, in Fife, 5th May, 1713.

John Skene died unmarried and the line of the family was carried on by his brother.

VI.—JAMES SKENE

" was engaged in the rebellion of 1715, and taken prisoner at Preston. On the 7th April, 1716, he was arraigned for high treason, condemned on 12th May, but afterwards pardoned. He again engaged in the attempt of 1719, and was taken at Glenshiel. He was examined for his share in Bishop Atterbury's treason in 1722 "—See " State Trials," vol. vi., pp. 389, 448, and 466).

" James Skene married Mary Ann Smith, daughter of the Reverend J. Smith of Battersea. He engaged in trade, but being unfortunate died of grief in 1736 " (MS.E).

He left two sons and one daughter—

I. Philip Wharton Skene, born 5th February, 1725.

II. James Skene, a surgeon in the East India Company's Service, died unmarried in London in 1780.

III. Elizabeth Skene died unmarried in June, 1799.

VII.—PHILIP WHARTON SKENE

" first joined the army under his uncle Andrew's charge, then a captain in the Royal Scots. He served in the same regiment in the West Indies, where Captain Andrew Skene died, 30th March, 1742, in Jamaica. He afterwards served in Flanders, at Dettingen, Fontenoy, and in 1745 at Culloden, and again in Flanders in 1747. After the peace he went to Ireland, where he married Katharine, only child of Samuel Heyden of Arklow. Colonel Philip Skene went upon service to North -America in 1756, and returned to Ireland in 1765, in order to take his family to North America, where he established them at Skeneborough, on Lake Champlain, a property obtained partly by purchase and partly by grant from the Crown. Mrs. Skene died there in 1771. In 1775

Colonel Skene was appointed lieutenant-governor of the forts at Crown Point and Ticonderoga, and surveyor of the forest of Lake Champlain. When the American war broke out, he and his family were arrested, and his estates confiscated. He served during the war, and came to England in 1778. In 1786 or 1787, the commissioners for the claims of American loyalists awarded him £20,000 for his personal losses, with which he purchased property in Northamptonshire and Buckinghamshire, and died at Hartwell, in June, 1810, in the 86th year of his age " (MS.E).

He married in 1752 Katherine, daughter of Samuel Heyden of Kilmacow, in Arklow, County Wicklow, and had by her—

I. Andrew Philip Skene, born 25th March, 1753.

II. Mary Ann Margaret Skene, born 1755, died unmarried.

III. Katharine Skene, born 1756, married Major de Piguet, and had issue.

VIII.—ANDREW PHILIP SKENE

"served along with his father in America, in the 27th, 72nd, and 43rd regiments, and was afterwards Major of Brigade in America, subsequently on the staff in Scotland " (MS.E).

He died 18th January, 1826, having had by his wife, Henrietta, only child of David James, of Serjeants Inn, London, whom he married on 20th December, 1792—

I. Philip Orkney Skene, born 14th October, 1793, first lieutenant Royal Engineers. He married Elizabeth, daughter of Richard Wood, Esquire, and died without issue in April, 1837.

II. David James Skene, born 13th October, 1794, lieutenant in the 68th regiment of foot, and afterwards in the 1st Light Dragoons, died without issue, 1st February, 1835.

III. Andrew Motz Skene, born 28th June, 1797 ; a captain in the navy, married Rachel Jemima, youngest daughter of James Walmesley, Esq., and died in July, 1849, having had the following children—

1. Andrew Philip Skene, born 6th September, 1832.

2. Elizabeth Rosa Skene, born 8th September, 1826, and died 10th September, 1846.

3. Augusta Maria Skene, born 22nd November, 1827 ; married Charles, son of Warren Maude, Esq.

4. Jemima Margaret Skene, born 3rd March, 1836 ; married George Edward, son of Reverend R. Booth.

IV. William Wallace Skene, born 4th February, 1800, died unmarried,
1st July, 1829.

V. George Robert Skene, born 11th April, 1802, died unmarried.

VI. Katherine Heyden Skene, born 8th April, 1805; married,' first,
Richard Smyth, Esq., by whom she had a daughter, Henrietta,
who married Canon Walter, and secondly, George Hutton
Wilkinson, Esq. of Harperley Park, Co. Durham, Recorder of
Newcastle-on-Tyne.

VII. Henrietta Skene, born 16th November, 1806 ; married William
Trotter, third son of Colonel John Trotter, of Haughton Hall,
near Darlington, and had by him eight children—

    1. William Dale Trotter, Colonel of the Durham Militia, died 1875.

    2. Henry John Trotter, of Byers Green Hall, Co. Durham, and the
Temple, London, M.P. for Colchester.

    3. Margaret Jane Trotter, married the Rev. J. E. W. Loft.

    4. Harriet Susannah Trotter married Rev. W. T. Tyrrwhitt Drake.

    5. Caroline Elizabeth Trotter married Rev. A. Williamson.

    6. Emily Katharine Trotter unmarried.

    7. Charles Vaughan Trotter, captain in the army.

    8. Catherine Francis Trotter married W. J. Walter, Esq.

"Died at his house in Durham, on the 18th instant [January, 1826],
highly respected, aged seventy-three, Andrew Philip Skene, B.A., of New
York, Esquire of Hallyards, in Fife, and Kilmacoe, Wicklow, Ireland,
only son of the late Colonel Philip Wharton Skene of Skenesborough,
United States, and of Hackleton, Northamptonshire, governor of Crown
Point and Ticonderoga, North America. This gentleman was a descendant of the famous Sir William Wallace, and traces his descent from the
year 1014, from the first Skene of Skene, according to tradition, a
younger son of the (Donalds) Lords of the Isles. He also held a military
commission in the British service above sixty years. His remains were
interred in the cathedral on the 21st instant, and were borne to his vault,
according to his request, by eight old soldiers. A few weeks before his
death he requested the following epitaph to be placed on his tomb :—
'Terræ filius in terram hic reposuit' "—(Newspaper notice).

IX.—ANDREW PHILIP SKENE,

his grandson, is now the male representative of the family of Skene.

SKENE OF PITLOUR.

I.—DAVID SKENE OF PITLOUR,

son of John Skene III., of Halyards, by his second wife, Helen Pit-cairn, succeeded to the estate of Pitlour, in terms of his father's settlement.

He married, on 25th July, 1718, Jean Douglas of Strathhenry, by whom he had three sons and three daughters—

I. Robert Skene, who succeeded him.

II. Philip Skene, who succeeded his brother.

III. David Skene, a captain in the 28th Regiment ; he died 11th May, 1788, leaving by his wife, Elizabeth Morrison, one son—
    1. David Skene, who succeeded his uncle, Philip.

IV. Helen Skene married, in 1746, to Colonel George Moncrieff of Reddie, by whom she had—
    1. Patrick Moncrieff, who succeeded his father, and had by his wife, Emily Raitt, a son—
        1. Patrick George Moncrieff, who eventually succeeded to the estate.
    2. George Moncrieff, youngest son.
    3. Jane Moncrieff.
    4. Ann Moncrieff married Dr. John Govan, physician in Cupar.
    5. Margaret Moncrieff.
    6. Catharine Moncrieff married John Hay Balfour, Esq. of Leys and Randerston.
    7. Helen Moncrieff married James Cheape of Strathtyrum.
    8. Christian Moncrieff.
    9. Douglas Moncrieff.

V. Jane Skene.

VI. Catharine Skene.

David Skene of Pitlour granted a disposition, dated at Pitlour, 29th January, 1747, in favour of himself, in liferent, and to Robert Skene, lieu-tenant in the Honourable Major-General Charles Howard's Regiment of Foot, his eldest lawful son, his heirs and assignees whomsoever, heritably and irredeemably, in fee, of all and whole the lands of Easter Pitlour, with the fortalice and manor place of Pitlour (*now and in all time here-after to be called Halyards*), Wester Pitlour, and Auchmorie, lying in the barony of Strathmiglo and Sheriffdom of Fife ; Steedmuirlands, in the Lordship of Balmerino and Sheriffdom aforesaid ; Friermilln, lying in the barony of Pitgarno ; West Mill of Strathmiglo, and others: but always with and under the burden of a liferent annuity of 1000 merks Scots, provided by the said David Skene to Jean Douglas, his spouse, conform to contract of marriage, dated 25th July, 1718, and that notwith-standing Helen Pitcairn, his mother, be alive, and with and under any burdens made, or to be made, for behoof of his younger children.

This disposition was followed by a royal charter of Resignation, dated at Edinburgh, 29th February, 1747, on which infeftment was taken on 17th March, 1747.

David Skene appears to have died soon after, and was succeeded by his eldest son.

II.—ROBERT SKENE OF PITLOUR (VI. OF HALYARDS).

As on 22nd April, 1748, there is a factory by Robert Skene of Halyards, lieutenant in the Honourable Major-General Charles Howard's Regiment of Foot, in favour of Mrs. Jean Douglas, relict of David Skene of Pitlour, his mother.

On 21st December, 1752, Robert Skene of Pitlour, then a lieutenant-general, made a settlement of his estates in favour of himself and the heirs of his body ; whom failing, to General Philip Skene and his heirs male. He died without issue, and was succeeded by his brother.

III.—PHILIP SKENE OF PITLOUR (VII. OF HALYARDS), 17 -1788,

who, on 14th August, 1752, was infeft, on a charter of resignation, under the great seal, in favour of Captain Philip Skene, of the regiment of foot commanded by General Philip Anstruther, of Airdrie, in the town and lands of Wester Pitlour, in the barony of Strathmiglo, at Edinburgh, 27th July, 1752.

He served heir to his brother in 1757.

On 10th August, 1787, he executed a deed of entail of the estate of Pitlour, in favour of himself and the heirs of his body ; whom failing, to Captain David Skene, of the 28th Regiment of Foot, then Inspector of Military Roads in Scotland, his brother-german ; whom failing, to David Skene, the said Captain David Skene's son procreat of the marriage betwixt him and Mrs. Elizabeth Morrison ; whom failing, to the other heirs of the body of the said Captain David Skene ; whom failing, to Mrs. Helen Skene, otherwise Moncrieff, relict of Colonel George Moncrieff of Reidie ; whom failing, to Patrick Moncreiff, then of Reidie, eldest son of the said Mrs. Helen Moncrieff and the heirs of his body; whom failing, to Captain George Moncrieff, youngest son of the said Mrs. Helen Moncrieff and the heirs of his body; whom failing, to their seven sisters in order, and their heirs ; whom failing, to his own two younger sisters.

General Philip Skene died on 22nd June, 1788, and was succeeded by his nephew.

IV.—David Skene of Pitlour (VIII. of Halyards), 1788-1803,

son of Captain David Skene, who was served heir to his uncle upon the 2nd October, 1788, and obtained a crown charter of the lands of Pitlour, &c., on 3rd February, 1789.

He died unmarried, in Paris, in 1803, upon which event Mrs. Moncrieff made up her titles to the estate, and died in 1826, aged 96 years. She was succeeded by her grandson, Patrick George Moncrieff, who changed his name to

V.—Patrick George Skene of Pitlour (IX. of Halyards),

and was twice married, 1st, to Emily, second daughter of James Rait of Anniston, by whom he had—

I. Moncrieff Patrick George Skene, who died unmarried in October, 1868.

He married, secondly, Jessie, daughter of Dugald John Campbell of Skerrington, by whom he had—

VI.—William Baillie Skene of Pitlour (X. of Halyards),

married, in 1874, Sarina Charlotte Liddell, daughter of the Very Reverend the Dean of Christchurch, Oxford, and has issue.

SKENE OF PRERAU, IN AUSTRIA.

I.—PATRICK SKENE,

second son of Andrew Skene of Auchorie, " married Jean Forbes, daughter of Robert Forbes, sometime of Drumlassie, on whom he begot—

I. Mr. Andrew Skene, parson of Turriff, who married Jean Coutts, daughter to the laird of Auchtertoull.

II. John Skene, yet unmarried " (MS.A.).

John Skene appears to have been settled, first, at Bridgend of Puttachy, in the parish of Keig, and afterwards at Mill of Turriff, and to have married, and had two sons—

1. Mr. Andrew Skene.

2. James Skene in Turriff.

11th January, 1666—John Skene of Bridgend of Puttachy, cautioner for Mr. Andrew Skene, parson of Turriff, at Turriff, 3rd June, 1666.

1666—Andrew Skene, rector, in Turriff, to William Lumsden of Leach, of tenement in Aberdeen. John Skene, witness.

1667—Disposition Rice Joans, in Turriff, of a tenement in favour of John Skene in Turriff. Andrew Skene, parson of Turriff, witness.

1672—John Skene at the Mill of Turriff, in favour of William Coutts in Caminter.

1688—Mr. Andrew Skene, lawful son to John Skene, in Turriff.

1704—Andrew Skene, eldest son to John Skene, in Turriff.

III. "Jean Skene married one John Skene" (MS.A). She seems to have married Richard Jones, in Turriff.

1688—Alexander Leask, rector, in Turriff. Joanna Skene, relict of Richard Jones, in Turriff.

Patrick Skene is mentioned, in 1633, as Patrick Skene in Auchorie, and probably died not long after.

II.—MR. ANDREW SKENE,

parson of Turriff, was, in 1665, infeft in the lands of Craigytocher, Over and Nether Bridgend, and with right to feal and divot from the lands of Fintry and Doorlathers, and any others belonging to late Patrick Forbes of Gask. He died in the year 1678.

A monument was erected to his memory, consisting of a mural tablet, still in a good state of preservation, built into the inside wall, on the north side of the old parish church of Turriff, with the following inscription :—

M. S.
MR ANDREAS SKEIN VIR CANDORE EXIMIVS
VERBO ET OPERE PRÆPOTENS
CATHEDRÆ TVRRIFENSIS DECVS EXVVIAS
MORTALITATIS PRÆTER QUAS NIHIL MORTALE
HABVIT POSVIT IN SPE
ANNO 1678 APRILIS.

He appears to have had a son,

III.—MR. ROBERT SKENE,

who had, by his wife, Barbara Douglas, as appears from parish register—
I. John Skene, born 28th December, 1671.
II. Anna Skene, born 9th August, 1673.
III. William Skene, born 14th June, 1676.

IV.—JOHN SKENE

occupied successively the farm of Doorlathers, Bogues of Lathers, Bogues of Raclach, all adjacent to each other, and in the parish of Turriff. He had, as appears from the parish records, the following children :—
I. John Skene, born in Doorlathers, 29th December, 1707.
II. James Skene, born in Doorlathers, 1st July, 1711.
III. Andrew Skene, born in Doorlathers, 11th April, 1713.
IV. George Skene, born in Bogues of Lathers, 24th April, 1715.
V. Agnes Skene, born in Bogues of Raclach, 13th June, 1717.
VI. Isabella Skene, born in Raclach, 24th May, 1719.

K

VII. Alexander Skene, born in Bogues of Raclach, 19th March, 1721.

VIII. Peter Skene, born in Bogues of Lathers, 31st May, 1723.

John Skene appears, after the birth of Peter, to have removed to Midmar.

V.—PETER SKENE,

the youngest son, left Midmar to seek his fortune in Holland, where a number of Scotchmen had settled as merchants, and became a burgess of the town of Venloo.

He married on 31st May, 1751, Sarah Catharine Landmeter, and is described in the marriage register as " Peter Skene from Midmar, in the province of Aberdeen."

He had by her four children—

I. Henry Skene, born in 1752, died at Venloo without issue.

II. Alexander Skene, born in 1755.

III. William Skene, born 10th November, 1757 ; lieutenant in the Navy, married Henrica Adela Guichenon de Chastillon, and had by her—

    1. Peter Skene, born 22nd June, 1788 ; married Helena Maria Daemen, and had an only son, Peter Ludwig William Max, born 24th June, 1843, officer in the Dutch Army, died December, 1885.

    2. Max Skene, born 20th March, 1791.

IV. Johanna Skene, born 1761 ; married Francis William Guichenon de Chastillon.

By two resolutions of the General Estates of the Netherlands, on 14th January and 8th April, 1755, Peter Skene was appointed a civil officer of the High Court of Justice, at Venloo. This office he retained till his death. He married, 2ndly, on 11th November, 1786, Elizabeth Passage, from Nymmegen. He died on the 24th December, 1787.

VI.—ALEXANDER SKENE

was made a Doctor of Laws of the University of Duisbourg, 29th July, 1778, and Secretary of the Dutch Embassy at Cologne. There he married, 1st March, 1790, Johanna Jacoba Theodora Hoffman, daughter of Geheimerath Hoffman of Prussia, by whom he had an only son, Philip William, and two daughters, Louisa Jacoba and Johanna Carolina.

VII.—PHILIP WILLIAM SKENE,

born at Cologne, 13th June, 1790, served in the army of the Netherlands ; married at Verviers, Belgium, Jeanne Catherine Hauseur, 13th April, 1812. He left Verviers, after the revolution, in 1830, and went to Brünn, the capital of Moravia, in Austria, where he settled with his family, and founded there a cloth manufactory. He had five sons—

X   I. William Skene died without issue, in America.

II. Alfred Skene, born at Verviers, 15th May, 1815.

III. Charles Skene died in 1855, leaving issue—
    1. Charles Skene married, and has issue.
    2. Jenny, married to Baron Kurt Gablenz.
    3. Mary married her cousin, Alfred Skene.

IV. Adolf Skene fell in the battle of St. Lucia in Italy, 1849.

V. August, born in 1829, knighted 1880, married Auguste von Schoeller, Vice-President of the "Banque des pays de l'Autriche," has issue four sons and two daughters.

VIII.—ALFRED SKENE

was an officer in the Austrian Imperial Dragoons; married, 1846, Francisca de Rosenbaum, daughter of Lieutenant-Colonel de Rosenbaum. He left the army, in 1847, to assist his father in the great business he had established in Brünn : was 1864-1866 Provost of the City of Brünn, and 1861-1885 member of the Austrian Reichsrath. He was proprietor of the estate and cloth manufactory of Alexavitz and the sugar refinery at Prerau, Moravia. He was a man of great energy and consummate ability. He attained a position of commanding influence in all matters connected with trade and manufactures, was recognised in the Austrian Parliament as the great authority in such matters, exercised much influence over the administration of the finances of the empire, and left a large fortune, entirely gained by honourable enterprise. The editor had the privilege of knowing him well at this time; and this account of him is consistent with his personal knowledge. He married, a second time, Louisa von Blumendorf, died 14th May, 1887, in his 72nd year, and left two sons and one daughter—

I. Alfred Skene.

II. Louis Skene married, in 1880, Janka, Countess Firmian.

III. Gabrielle Skene married, 1872, Baron de Widman, Imperial Governor of Tyrol, Austria.

IX.—ALFRED SKENE

married, in 1873, his cousin, Mary Skene, and is present proprietor of
Pawlowitz-Prerau, and member of the Landtag of Austria. He is now
the representative of this branch of the family.

Arms of Mr. Andrew Skene and Jean Coutts his Spouse, *from a Stone in
Turriff Churchyard.*

CHAPTER III.

SKENE OF DUMBRECK.

I.—Gilbert Skene in Tillibirloch,

second son of Alexander Skene XI. of Skene, commonly called "the little laird," married Barbara Forbes, daughter of Robert Forbes of Echt, by whom he had three sons and three daughters—

I. Alexander Skene in Dumbreck.

II. John Skene, died unmarried, in 1627, when Alexander Skene, in Dumbreck, is executor to umquhile John Skene, merchant burgess of Aberdeen.

III. Robert Skene, ancestor of the family of Newtyle.

IV. Margaret Skene married John Burnett.

V. Elspeth Skene married Andrew Gray.

VI. Agnes Skene married Thomas Spens.

John Forbes of Echt, the only son of Robert Forbes of Echt, and brother of Barbara, died without issue, in 1609, when the unentailed portion of the estate fell to Alexander Skene, consisting of Culquhorsie and Dumbreck, and the entailed portion to Robert Forbes of Finnersie, the heir male.

On 2nd January, 1610, there is an inhibition at the instance of John Forbes of Finnersie, against Alexander Skene, on contract made at Edinburgh on the 19th December, 1609, between the said Robert Forbes as only nearest and lawful heir of tailzie, to umquhile John Forbes of Echt, on the one part; and Alexander Skene, eldest lawful son of umquhile Gilbert Skene of Tillibirloche, procreated between him and umquhile Barbara Forbes, his spouse, who was only lawful sister to the said umquhile John Forbes of Echt, and so the said Alexander, as only nearest apparent heir of line to the said umquhile John Forbes of Echt, on the other part; by which contract the said Alexander, as apparent heir of line foresaid, for certain causes therein specified, became bound to have himself duly retoured as nearest heir of line foresaid, and by special provision has declared that he has no right nor title to the lands and barony of Echt, except the lands of Culquhorsie and Dumbreck, and pertinents thereof: and a corresponding inhibition by Alexander Skene against Robert Forbes.

On 27th July, 1610, there is an advocation to the Court of Session of an action pursued before the Commissary of Aberdeen, at the instance of Alexander Irving, advocate, and others, cautioners and sureties for Robert Forbes of Echt, against John and Robert Skene, Margaret Skene and John Burnet her spouse, Elspeth Skene and Andrew Gray, her spouse, and Agnes Skene and Thomas Spens, her spouse, decerning them to free and relieve the said parties of their cautionary obligation, &c.

Alexander Skene, the eldest son, was thus the heir of line to his uncle in heritage; his younger brothers and sisters representing him in the moveable estate.

On 24th October, 1610, there is an obligation to Robert Skene, son to umquhile Gilbert Skene, of Tilliebirloch, at Aberdeen, November 1688, before which date both Gilbert Skene and his wife were dead.

II.—ALEXANDER SKENE OF DUMBRECK.

Prior to his father's death, Alexander Skene had married Elizabeth Mercer, relict of John Deanes, and in his right possessed the Mylne of Hall Forest, also called the Mylne of Durno. In 1605 there is a Removing, by Elizabeth Merser, relict of John Deane and Alexander Skene, at Mylne of Hall of Forest, and her spouse; and again, on 14th June, 1606, Removing Elspet Mercer, relict of umquhile John Deanes, and now spouse of Alexander Skene, at Mylne of Durno.

On 27th February, 1611, there is a special retour—Alexander Skene filius legitimus primogenitus quondam Barbare Forbes sororis unice· germane quondam Johannis Forbes de Echt haeres dicti Johannis Forbes de Echt avunculi in terris de Culquhorsie cum outsett vocato Dumbreck de Kirkton de·Echt, terris de Hillside in Baronia de Clune.

And on 16th December, 1633, Alexander Skene, in Dumbreck, and his spouse, are infeft in the town and lands of Dumbreck.

He married 1st, Elizabeth Mercer, by whom he had one son—

I. Alexander Skene in Cairnday.

He married 2nd, " Agnes Keith, daughter of Mr. Gilbert Keith of Affrosk, on whom he begat—

II. Robert Skene of Dumbreck, who married Marjorie Mollyson, daughter of Thomas Mollyson, town-clerk of Aberdeen, by whom he had three daughters—

    1. Isobell Skene married William Tosh.

    2. Janet Skene married William Jobson.

    3. Margaret Skene married John Smyth.

III. Mr. Gilbert Skene, Minister at Cariston" (MS.A).

    16th April, 1656—Obligation Robert Skene in Dumbreck, sone lawful to umquhile Alexander Skene of Dumbreck and Alexander Skene in Cairnday, his brother. Witness, Gilbert Skene, student in the Old College of Aberdeen.

    14th December, 1653—Obligation Gilbert Skene of Dyce, to Mr. Gilbert Skene, sone lawful to umquhile Alexander Skene of Dumbreck,

" and six daughters—

IV. Janet Skene married Alexander Burnett of Sluie" (MS.A).

    1637—Contract of marriage between Mr. Andrew Burnett of Sluie, son of the minister of Strachan, and Janet Skene, daughter of umquhile Alexander Skene of Dumbreck, with consent of Anna Keith, her mother.

V. " Isobel Skene, married to John Keith, Chamberlain to the Countess Marischall.

VI. Elspett Skene married to Andrew Forbes, portioner of Kinellar.

VII. Jean Skene married William Bruce, Notary Public.

VIII. Helen Skene married to Alexander Fraser of Corskil.

IX. Katharine Skene married to one William Forbes " (MS.A).

III.—MR. ALEXANDER SKENE.

" The lands of Dumbreck and Culquhorsey, in the parish of Echt, continued in the family for several generations, until carried off by the Forbeses of Echt, by a comprising" (MS.D). It is in connection with this, probably, that we find, in 1638, a decreet of Mr. Alexander Skene, eldest son to deceased Alexander Skene of Dumbreck, against Arthur

Forbes, now of Echt, son and heir of deceased Robert Forbes of Echt, to implement a contract ; and on 21st May, 1656, he appears as Mr. Alexander Skene in Cairnday ; and again, on 12th April, 1676, there is a bond by Mr. Alexander Skene, eldest son to the deceased Alexander Skene of Dumbreck, now in Cocairdie.

"He was married to Jean Leslie, daughter of Patrick Leslie of Kincraigie, and was father to George Skene that was late minister of Kinkell, near Aberdeen" (MS.D).

IV.—George Skene, Minister of Kinkell.

He was twice married, 1st to Mary Gordon, daughter of Francis Gordon of Craig, by whom he had—

I. Francis Skene.

He married, secondly, Margaret Skene, daughter of Mr. Robert Skene, Rector of the Grammar School of Aberdeen, by whom he had—

II. Agnes Skene, married to Mr. John Burnett, minister at Cluny.

III. Mary Skene.

IV. Katharine Skene.

V. Helen Skene.

VI. John Skene, Librarian of Marischal College and University, 1736-1750.

There is a monument in the old church of Kinkell, bearing the following inscription :—

JACET HIC SEPVLTA DNA:
MARIA GORDON MRI: GEO:
SKENE PASTORIS VXOR
QVÆ OBIIT AUG. I 1712 ÆTATIS 32

Mr. George Skene, himself, died in April, 1724 ; and, on 12th August, 1724, the inventory of the goods, &c., of the deceased Mr. George Skene, minister at Kinkell, was given up by Margaret Skene, his relict, and confirmed to Francis, John, Mary, Katharine, and Helen Skene, his children, and Mr. John Burnett, minister at Cluny, husband to Agnes.

V.—Mr. Francis Skene

was admitted, 16th March, 1734, one of the regents in Marischal College; and on the classes being fixed in 1753, became Professor of Civil and Natural History. He taught altogether for 41 years.

In 1724 he served heir to George Skene, his father, minister of Kinkell.

He married, 15th May, 1740, Mary Reid of Mounie, by whom he had:

I. George Skene, born 14th April, 1741.

II. William Skene, born 19th November, 1743; died 13th Nov., 1769.

III. John Skene, born 2nd August, 1744.

IV. James Skene, born 25th August, 1746; took degree of M.D. in 1766, and settled in Charlestown, Carolina.

Mr. Francis Skene died on 13th February, 1775, aged 71; and his wife on 31st March, 1781, aged 60.

VI.—DR. GEORGE SKENE,

M.D., 1755, was a Physician in Aberdeen, and on 8th October, 1760, at the age of nineteen, was elected Professor of Natural Philosophy in Marischal College. On his father's death he was transferred to the Chair of Civil and Natural History, which he held until compelled by his increasing medical practice to resign in 1788. "He was a genuine scholar, of good ability, great shrewdness and sense, and witty" (Knight's Mar. Coll. Collections).

He married, on 26th October, 1769, Margaret, daughter of Charles Gordon of Abergeldie, and had by her the following children :—

I. John Skene, born 23rd August, 1770, died young.

II. Francis Skene, born 22nd November, 1771, died young.

III. Emilia Skene, born 30th May, 1773; married, 4th October, 1794, Captain Edmund Filmer, by whom she had Sir Edm. Filmer, Bart.

IV. Mary Skene, born 20th January, 1775, died 2nd September, 1795.

V. Charles Skene, born 21st July, 1777, who carried on the line of this family.

VI. Mary Anne Skene, born 25th February, 1779, died 13th April, 1863.

VII. Elizabeth Skene, born 9th October, 1780, died 27th February, 1839.

VIII. Margaret Skene, born 23rd August, 1782, married Arthur Anderson of Deebank, and died 25th April, 1821.

IX. Andrew Skene, born 26th February, 1784, M.A., of Marischal College in 1802, passed advocate, distinguished himself at the bar, and became Solicitor-General for Scotland. He died at Edinburgh, 2nd April, 1835.

X. William Skene, born 26th February, 1784, was a Colonel in the East India Company's Service ; married Miss Campbell of Lochnell, and died without issue in 1854.

XI. Alison Skene, born 9th November, 1786, died in England in 1839.

Dr. George Skene died, after a short and acute illness, on 25th March, 1803, aged 61; and his wife on 16th January, 1802, aged 51.

VII.—DR. CHARLES SKENE,

M.A., 1795, M.D. (Edinb.), 1799, was a distinguished Physician in Aberdeen, and also 1823-1839, Professor of Medicine in Marischal College. He married, on 18th June, 1808, Margaret Ann Anderson, daughter of Anderson, Esquire of Linkwood, Elgin, by whom he had the following children :—

I. Mary Skene, born 25th May, 1809, died 22nd May, 1882.

II. George Skene, born 8th May, 1811, was an Ensign in the East India Company's Service ; died at Bechampore, India, 4th June, 1831.

III. Charles Skene, born 9th October, 1812, M.A. of Marischal College in 1830, captain in 79th Regiment Cameron Highlanders, and afterwards Superintendent of Indians, Canada.

IV. Andrew Skene, born 22nd April, 1814, assistant-surgeon in the 52nd Regiment ; died at Brecon, in Wales, 23rd January, 1846.

V. Margaret Skene, born 23rd June, 1815, died 9th November, 1818.

VI. Alexander Skene, born 10th February, 1816, was captain in the East India Company's Service, married, in India, Beatrice Marjory Herschel Cumberlege, daughter of Colonel Cumberlege of the Madras Cavalry ; both were killed in the Indian Mutiny, on 8th June, 1857, with their two children—

1. Mary Isabella Frances Skene, born 29th July, 1854.

2. Beatrice Harriet Annie Skene, born 11th December, 1855.

VII. Harriet Skene, born 26th August, 1818, died 16th October, 1866.

VIII. William Skene, born 14th November, 1819, died on 30th of same month.

Dr. Charles Skene died on 11th June, 1844, aged 66 ; and his wife on 19th November, 1819, aged 31.

VIII.—CAPTAIN CHARLES SKENE

now represents this family.

SKENE OF NEWTYLE.

╳ I.—ROBERT SKENE,

third son of Gilbert Skene of Tilliebirloch, by his wife Elspett Forbes, appears first at Milne of Commeris, one of the Tanistry lands adjoining Tilliebirloch, and afterwards at Slydie of Erdifork, in the neighbouring parish of Midmar. In 1589 he married Janet Forbes, and had two sons—

I. Robert Skene.

>29th June, 1589—Robert Skene and Jonat Forbes mariet.
>
>In 24th October, 1610, there is an obligation to Robert Skene, son to umquhile Gilbert Skene of Tilliebirloch, at Aberdeen, November, 1608.
>
>On 15th November, 1615, there is an obligation by George Williamson, burgess of Aberdeen, to Robert Skene at the Mylne of Commeris, in name and behalf of Robert Skene, his eldest son.

II. Alexander Skene, at Mylne of Commeris.

>On 16th June, 1616, there is an obligation to Alexander Skene, son to Robert Skene, at the Mylne of Commeris, for money lent at Kirkton of Echt.

Before 1620 Robert Skene had left Commeris, as on 16th June in that year, Alexander Skene, son of Robert Skene, "olim in Comeris," is procurator for Alexander Skene of Skene. He died in 1625.

⅄ II.—ROBERT SKENE.

On 21st September, 1615, Sir James Skene of Curriehill, Alexander Skene of that ilk, and Mr. Andrew Skene, senior, their cousin, of Chapelton, were admitted burgesses of Aberdeen, "gratis gratia concilii;" and, at the request of Sir James Skene of Curriehill, "Robert Skeyne, paynter and glasinwricht," was admitted freeman, and " Robertus Skeyne filius . . . " was admitted burgess of Aberdeen " gratis absque solutione ullius compositionis et hoc gratia ex rogatu honorabilis viri Domini Jacobi Skeyne de Curriehill." This last was the above Robert, as he is called younger, burgess of Aberdeen. Thus, on 25th March, 1630, there is a decreet Robert Skene, younger, burgess of Aberdeen, eldest son to the deceased Robert Skene in Slydie, of Erdifork, against W. Gordon of Abergeldie, on a bond to the deceased Robert Skene, dated 29th May, 1618, and again in a similar decreet, on 19th July, 1634, and again on 22nd July, 1642.

He married, in 1618, Marjorie Forbes ; and, on 1st April, 1629, there is a sasine in favour of Robert Skene, merchant burgess, and Marjoria Forbes, of a house " in vico lemurum ex occidentali parte."

He seems to have been a prosperous man, as on 17th September, 1628, he mortifies 100 merks for decayed gild brethren, and, in 1631, threescore six pounds thirteen shillings iiijd. for the maintenance of one of the ministers of the burgh, to serve the cure at the Kirk of Futtie ; and by his last will he left 1000 merks to the Box of the Gild Brethren of Aberdeen.

In 1633 he was treasurer of the burgh. He had by his wife, Marjorie Forbes, the following children :—

I. Christian Skene, born 20th September, 1619.
II. Alexander Skene, born 27th October, 1621.
III. William Skene, born 8th May, 1624.
IV. Marjory Skene, born 8th September, 1628.
V. James Skene, born 14th February, 1631.

He died in 1643, and a flat monument, in St. Nicholas Churchyard, bears the following inscription :—

HEIR LYES VNDER THE HOIP

OF A BLISSED RESVRECTION ROBERT SKENE MER

CHAND BVRGES OF ABD

WHO DEPAIRTED THIS LYFE THE 14 OF NO 1643

ALSO MARIORIE FORBES HIS SP

OVS WHO DEPAIRTED THE 10 OF

SEPT 1650

AS ALSO IAMES SKENE WHO DEPARTED

THE 8 DAY OF AUGUST 1694 AND QF

AGE 63 YEARS

with a shield, bearing the arms of Skene of Skene, differenced, and impaled with those of Forbes of Tolquhon, and the letters R. S. ; M. F.

III.—Mr. Alexander Skene of Newtyle.

On 15th January, 1625, Alexander Skene, eldest son of Robert Skene, burgess of Aberdeen, is admitted burgess "jure paternitatis et dispens. cum jure jurando quia pupillus est et infra ætatem"; and, on 20th June, 1648, he served heir to his father, Robert Skene, and is infeft in the tenement " in vico lemurum."

On 26th August, 1646, he was married at Kirkaldie to Lilias Gillespie, daughter of Mr. John Gillespie, minister of Kirkaldie who died soon after.

In 1656 we find him one of the magistrates of Aberdeen ; and in 1657 he acquired, from Sir Alexander Forbes of Foveran, the lands of Newtyle, in the Parish of Foveran.

In 1669 "Alexander Skene, a magistrate in Aberdeen, his wife Lilian became a quaker, also Alexander Skene himself. He narrates of himself that having once before his conversion to quakerism bitterly reviled the quäkers, he became seized with the complaint called Cynicus Spasmus, by which his mouth continually turned about, which lasted sometime" (MS.E). In 1677 he published a pamphlet with the title " The Way Cast up," and on the 5th of the fifth month, 1679, he wrote an address to the Presbyterians, entitled " A Plain and Peaceable Advice to those called Presbyterians in Scotland," by Alexr. Skene (London, 1681).

His other literary works, including MS.A., are noticed in the Introduction.

The arms of " Mr. Alexander Skene of Newtyle " are thus recorded in the Lyon Register : " Parted per chief azur and gules three skenes argent hefted and pomelled or, surmounted of as many woolf-heads couped of the third." Crest : " A dexter hand holding a corona triumphalis." Motto : " Sors mihi grata cadet."

By his wife, Lilias Gillespie, who died in 1697, he had the following children :—

I. Robert Skene, born 29th October, 1647 ; died young.

II. John Skene.

III. Lilias Skene, baptised 31st August, 1651.

IV. Alexander Skene, baptised 6th September, 1653; died young.

V. Cristen Skene, baptised 1st October, 1654; married, in 1673, Andrew Jaffray of Kingswells.

VI. Rachel Skene, baptised 11th December, 1656; died in 1661.

VII. Patrick Skene, baptised 27th June, 1659.

VIII. Anna Skene, baptised 1st June, 1661.

IX. Jean Skene, baptised 18th March, 1662.

X. Elizabeth Skene, baptised 30th May, 1669.

In 1680 he sold the estate of Newtyle, reserving certain liferents, and in 1681 there is a Ratification to William Gordon, under the reservations conceived in favour of Mr. Alexander Skene, late of Newtyle, and Lilias Gillespie, his spouse, and after their decease to Alexander Udnie of that ilk and his heirs, of the town and lands of Newtyle; also of a croft, lately occupied by John Skene, son to the said Mr. Alexander Skene; all conform to the rights and dispositions made to the said Alexander Forbes and Alexander Skene, by the deceased Sir John Turing of Foveran, reserving to Alexander Skene and his wife, liferent of part of the lands, and of the Manor House of Newtyle, conform to contract of alienation, dated 1680, between the said Mr. Alexander Skene and Lilias Gillespie, and the said John Skene and Helen Fullerton, his spouse, on the one part, and William Gordon and Agnes Blackburn, his wife, on the other.

✝ IV.—JOHN SKENE.

In 1659 John Skene, eldest lawful son to Mr. Alexander Skene, Baillie, is admitted a burgess of Aberdeen. "He was also a quaker, and became governor of New Jersey, in America, and died in 1687. He married Helen Fullerton, and a daughter of John Skene, son to Baillie Skene, in Aberdeen, laird of Newtyle, was married, anno 1699 or 1700, to Obadiah Haig, who died on his journey to Jersey" (MS.E).

V.—JAMES SKENE,

younger son of Robert Skene and Marjorie Forbes.

Like his brother, Alexander, he was admitted a burgess when under age, as on 18th September, 1635, when only four years old, "Jacobus

Skeyne, filius legitimus Roberti Skeyne mercatoris burgen. de Aberdeen recept. et admiss. in liberum burgensem et fratrem gildae jure paternitatis et dispens. cum jure jurando quia pupillus est et infra ætatem."

In the "Account of Learned Men and Writers in Aberdeen," after a short notice of Baillie Alexander Skene, there is the following notice of him—"His brother, James Skeen, was ane excellent Poet in the Scottish language. He wrote the Decalogue, the Lord's Prayer, and the Creed, in metre, printed by John Forbes, Aberdeen."

In the Diary of Alexander Jaffray of Kingswells, he mentions that there were two James Skenes, in Aberdeen, who were enemies of the quakers, and who were known as White James and Black James.

This James Skene was White James.

In 1666 we find him occupying the position of Lyon Depute.

He married Jean Hay, and had by her the following children :—

I. Robert Skene, baptised 23rd March, 1654. On 20th Sept., 1659, Robert Skene, eldest son of James Skene, burgess of Aberdeen, admitted in nonage and minoritie. He died on 19th October, 1660.

II. James Skene, baptised 2nd September, 1656; died 23rd May, 1669.

III. Lilias Skene, baptised 27th Sept., 1657 ; died 3rd November, 1660.

IV. John Skene, baptised 31st Oct., 1658. One of a series of silver archery medals preserved in the Grammar School, Aberdeen, bears on the obverse the arms (with a crescent for difference) crest, and motto of Skene of Newtyle ; and on the reverse the inscription " Ioannes Skeene octavo vicit, 1674. Virtvs vera svis marte vel arte favet." Another shows the arms of Skene of Skene with a fourth skene fessways in base and a crescent for difference ; the reverse being inscribed " Andreas Skeene quarto vicit 1667." This Andrew may have been one of the Ruthrieston Skenes.

V. Alexander Skene, baptised 12th February, 1660 ; died 20th March, 1661.

VI. Jeane Skene, baptised 10th April, 1661.

VII. William Skene, baptised 26th June, 1662.

VIII. Robert Skene, baptised 16th Nov., 1663.

IX. Andrew Skene, baptised 21st Feb., 1665.

X. George Skene, baptised 28th October, 1666.

XI. Anna Skene, baptised 28th June, 1668.

XII. Charles Skene, baptised 15th August, 1669.

XIII. Christian Skene, baptised 20th October, 1670.

His death is recorded on the tombstone—Also James, died 1694, aged 63.

VI.—WILLIAM SKENE,

his eldest surviving son. On 27th Sept., 1686, there is a sasine on a disposition by James Skene, merchant, in Aberdeen, in favour of William Skene, his eldest lawful son, of some woods, crofts, and parcels of burrow land at Newburgh, Sheriffdom of Aberdeen. Disposition dated at Newtyle, 6th August, 1686.

He was a writer in Edinburgh, and was made a macer of the Court of Session on 5th August, 1685. He married, in 1688, Christian Burd, daughter of Captain Edward Burd of Foord, by whom he had two sons :—

I. Edward Skene, who died in infancy in 1690.

II. Arthur Skene, who died in 1700.

On 29th December, 1730, Isobell Skene served heir in general to William Skene, her brother, macer in the Court of Session, son "quond. Jacobi Skene mercatoris in Aberden."

VII.—MR. ROBERT SKENE,

eighth child of James Skene, was minister of the Gospel. He had a son, John, who was Kintyre pursuivant, and predeceased him in the month of November, 1706. His will was confirmed on 22nd February, 1711, of the deceased John Skene, Kintyre pursuivant, and eldest lawful son to Mr. Robert Skene, minister of the Gospel, residing in Edinburgh, who is cautioner for his executor.

"On 23rd June, 1721, Mr. Robert Skene, minister of the Gospel, died 22nd and buried 23rd, foot of Halyeard's ground; and on 23rd Sept., in the same year, Anna Skene, daughter to umquhile Mr. Skeen, minister, died 22nd and buried 23rd, east Halyeard's ground" (Edin. Session Records).

Arms of Robert Skene and Marjory Forbes his Spouse, from a Stone in St. Nicholas Churchyard, Aberdeen.

CHAPTER IV.

SKENE OF DYCE.

I.—Mr. Patrick Skene,

fourth son to Alexander Skene XI. of Skene, commonly called the " little laird," by Elizabeth Forbes, his wife. Married on 30th May, 1591, Elspett Mercer, daughter of Laurence Mercer, burgess of Aberdeen ; and, on 10th September, 1592, is admitted a burgess of Aberdeen.

On 22nd May, 1594, there is a sasine by which " Providus.. vir Wilelmus Jak, burgen. de Aberdeen," grants "totam et integram terram suam anteriorem australem superius de presenti occupat. per magistrum Patricium Skene burgen. dicti burgi, vizt., aulam Cubiculum ly forgalrie cum solio et ly shop & jacen. in vico furcarum ad dandam sasinam prefato Magistro Patricio Skene et Elizabethe Merser ejus sponse."

He had by Elspett Merser the following children :—

I. Alexander Skene, who succeeded him.

II. Laurence Skene. 20th September, 1619, Laurentius Skene filius legitimus secundo genitus magistri Patricii Skene burgess of Aberdeen, admitted jure paternitatis. In August, 1629, we find Laurence Skene as servitor to Mr. Alexander Skene, writer, who was brother to Sir John Skene of Curriehill, receiving a gift of the Escheat, which pertenit of before to Thomas Smyth in Bandache ; and again, on 13th June, 1630, as servitor to Mr. Alexander Skene, writer, of the Escheat which pertenit to Patrick Leyth of Lickliehead.

III. Gilbert Skene, who carried on the line of this family.

IV. John Skene. He became servitor to the Earl Marischal; and, on 29th September, 1629, Joannes Skene, servus comitis Marescalli, is admitted a burgess of Aberdeen.

He is said by Mr. Alexander Skene to have "married, but had no children," but this is a mistake. He married Helen Durie, daughter of a burgess of Dunfermline; and, in 29th March, 1639, there is a decreet, John Skene, brother-german to Gilbert Skene of Dyce, and Helen Durie, his spouse, against George Durie, burgess of Dunfermline.

He appears, in 1666, as musician burgess of Dunfermline, and had a daughter, Anna Skene, married to Ninian Robertson, Baillie of Kyngarne.

V. Bessie Skene "married 1st, Thomas Forbes, called 'Dobrie,' a Polis word signifying good, to whom she bare a son and two daughters. Her son's name was Robert Forbes of Rubislaw, present provost of Aberdeen" (MS.A). "After Thomas Forbes's death, Bessie Skene, daughter to Mr. Patrick Skene, married George Johnstone of Cairnie, Baillie of Aberdeen, to whom she bare two sons and two daughters" (MS.A).

VI. Margaret Skene "married Mr. Black, burgess of Aberdeen, and thereafter to Alexander Burnett of Shedockslie" (MS.A). In the Burgh Propinquity Book it is declared, on 5th July, 1658, that "Margaret Skene, spouse of William Black, burgess of Aberdeen, was second lawful daughter of Mr. Patrick Skene, burgess of Aberdeen, who was fourth lawful son to Alexander Skene of that ilk, procreat betwixt the said Mr. Patrick and Elspet Merser, his spouse, who was lawful daughter to Laurence Mercer, burgess of Aberdeen. Gilbert Skene of Dyce, witness."

VII. Isobell Skene "married Andrew Knows of Pittside" (MS.A).

VIII. Agnes Skene "married James Innes of Tilleburies" (MS.A.)

Mr. Patrick Skene died in 1635, and, on 31st August, was "buried in the auld kirk."

II.—Mr. Alexander Skene.

On 15th May, 1638, Mr. Alexander Skene served heir to Mr. Patrick Skene, burgess of Aberdeen, his father, but lived only three years after, as on 2nd September, 1641, "Mr. Alexander Skene was buried."

Laurence Skene, the second son, appears to have predeceased him, and the line of the family was carried on by Gilbert, the third son.

III.—GILBERT SKENE OF DYCE

was a burgess of Aberdeen, and married, in 1628, Marjorie Buchan, daughter of William Buchan of Auchmacoy, who succeeded to one half of the lands of Dyce.

On 8th December, 1628, Gilbert Skene, burgess of Aberdeen, is infeft in the just and equal half of the barony of Dyce, and also in the Kirkton of Dyce, and on 6th January, 1629, in the half town and lands of Pitmedden.

By Marjorie Buchan he had the following children :—

I. Alexander Skene, born 1st April, 1630.

II. Gilbert Skene.

III. Mr. Patrick Skene, writer, in Edinburgh.

IV. Margaret Skene "married Mr. William Moir, Doctor of Physick" (MS.A). She appears to have married secondly to Gordon of Gordon's Mills, as in the Burgh Propinquity Book, on 24th July, 1695, "Proved by Alexander Skene of Dyce, &c., that Gilbert Gordon of Gordonsmill's mother was Margaret Skene, lawful daughter of the deceased Gilbert Skene of Dyce, procreat betwixt him and Margary Buchan, daughter of William Buchan of Auchmacoy."

He married secondly Barbara Forbes, daughter to William Forbes of Cotton, by whom he had—

V. Mr. William Skene, Schoolmaster at Haddington, afterwards one of the Masters of the High School of Edinburgh, who married Helen Pitcairn, and died in November, 1717.

The Testament testamentar and Inventory of the Goods, &c., of the deceased Mr. William Skene, Master of the High School of Edinburgh, who died in the month of November, 1717, was given up by himself upon the tenth of September same year, in so far as regards the nomination of his only Executor; and by Mr. Wm. Forbes, advocate, professor of law in the University of Glasgow, his cousin, whom he nominates his only Executor, in so far as concerns the Inventory. In his Will, dated at Edinburgh

20th Sept., 1717, he leaves a legacy to John Skene of Dyce, his nephew.

Gilbert Skene of Dyce died in March, 1665, and was succeeded by his son.

IV.—ALEXANDER SKENE OF DYCE—1665-1704.

He married, in November, 1652, Ann Johnston, daughter of Dr. William Johnston of Caskieben; and, on 24th April, 1655, there is a sasine Alexander Skene, younger, of Dyce, and Ann Johnston, his spouse, of the half of the lands of Beildeston.

He seems to have quarrelled with the Forbeses of Rubislaw, his relations, as in 1665 William Forbes of Cothellmill becomes surety for Alexander Skene of Dyce, Gilbert, and Mr. Patrick Skene, his brothers-german, that Robert Forbes of Rubislaw, Thomas, his son, and others, shall be harmless kept.

In 1672 Alexander Skene of Dyce, and Gilbert Skene, his brother, sell the feu-right of the lands of Pitmedden.

The arms of "Alexander Skene of Dyce, lineallie and lawfullie descended of the familie of Skene of that Ilk," are thus given in the Lyon Register: "Gules three Skenes argent pomelled and surmounted of alse many woolf's heads couped or, within a bordur ingrailed of the second." Crest: "A Garb proper." Motto: "Assiduitate."

There has been preserved an old Bible, printed in 1559, which belonged to the Dyce family, in which Ann Johnston, the wife of Alexander Skene of Dyce, records the family history, continued by her son, John. Her record is as follows :—

" 10th April, 1630, my husband, Dyce, was born.

2nd March, 1636, I was born.

11th month, 1652, we were married.

In 1664 we had 7 houses burnt, with their furniture.

3rd month, 1665, my husband's father died.

11th month, 1673, my mother died.

12th month, 1654, Barbara Skene was born.

7th month, 1660, John Skene was born.

10th month, 1662, Alexander Skene was born.

11th month, 1663, Andrew Skene was born.

5th month, 1665, Margaret Skene was born.

6th month, 1668, Ann Skene was born.

9th month, 1669, William Skene was born.

11th month, 1670, Gilbert Skene was born.

5th month, 1674, Patrick Skene was born.

7th month, 1677, Robert Skene was born."

His eldest son, John, thus continues the record—

" 15th of 11th month, 1688, my mother died.

Barbara Skene married to Forbes of Achortes in her 21st year of age.

Andrew was 15 years and one month old when he chose his own employment.

William was 17 years and two months when he went to Edinburgh. He died 1690.

Gilbert was seventeen years old when he went to Ireland.

4th of 1st month, 1704, my father died.

29th October, 1709, my sister, Barbara, died.

Robert was 15 years old when he went to his apprenticeship, 1693.

Andrew was married 1687.

Patrick Skene went to Dantzick last day of 1st month, 1689."

On 20th October, 1741, the Testament Dative and Inventory of the Goods, &c., of the deceased Robert Skene, late of Maryland, who died abroad upon the　　　　day of　　　　　　, 1736, is given up by Patrick Skene, sometime postmaster of Zamosky, kingdom of Poland, now residing in Aberdeen, brother-german to the said deceased Robert Skene, only Executor Dative decerned as nearest of kin to him by Decreet of the Commissaries of Edinburgh, 27th July, 1701. Among the debts given up is the balance of the fifth part, or share of the executry of the deceased John Skene of Dyce, his brother-german.

Alexander Skene of Dyce, who died on 4th January, 1704, was succeeded by his eldest son.

V.—JOHN SKENE OF DYCE—1704-1729

served heir to his father on 28th July, 1704 ; and, on 12th January, 1705, there is a charter of resignation Joannis Skene de Dyce ville et terrarum de Kirkton de Dyce, &c.

He thus continues the record in the old Bible :—

nt to Lisbon 15th July, 1680, entered prentice to Robert Farquhar, and burgess in that city, where I served him and his heirs ten 1 afterwards I served my cousin-german, Gilbert Moir. I was 20th January, 1709, with Margaret Farquhar, daughter to my naster, Robert Farquhar, and his spouse, Anna Marianna relict of Alexander Summer, merchant, and collector of the king's revenues in Wilker, with whom she had three children—two are alive. Alexander, the youngest, and Anna Catherine, the eldest, and Lord grant them grace that they may serve thee always. I lived in Radinegria.

Anno 1710 my wife was delivered of a son, John ; Godfathers, Gilbert Moir and John Farquhar; Godmothers, Anna Marianna Farquhar and Elizabeth Morison.

2nd May, 1711, had a daughter, Anna; Godfathers, Arthur Forbes and Wm. Caw ; Godmothers, Eliza Achum, S. Middleton.

Another daughter, Margaret, born 1712.

My son, John, died 1714. Margaret died 9th October, 1719. Alexander Summer, my stepson, of the king's footguards, died 1729."

John Skene himself died in the same year, and was succeeded by his brother.

VI.—ANDREW SKENE OF DYCE—1729-1732.

He was a merchant in Edinburgh, and in 1689 married Marion Russell, only daughter of John Russell, citizen of London, in which year there is a charter, by the provost and baillies of Edinburgh, to her as heir served and retoured to the late John Russell, her father, and to Andrew Skene, her husband, of portion of the land of Nethrogall, in Monimail. By her he had a son—

I. Alexander Skene (baptised 17th June, 1694; Mr. William Skene, master of the High School, is a witness), and a daughter—

II. Mary Skene, second wife of Robert Cumming of Birness, by whom she had two daughters—

1. Barbara married Dr. James Gordon of Straloch, or Birness, ancestor of General John Gordon Cumming of Pitlurg, and

2. Another daughter married James Gordon of Banchory, ancestor of James Gordon of Craig.

He acquired various lands in the parishes of Old and New Machar, Aberdeenshire.

On 26th July, 1712, there is charter of sale—Andree Skene mercatoris Edinburgensis de terris de Clubsgovill.

On 24th May, 1714, there is a sasine of Andrew Skene of Parkhill, in the lands of Clubsgovill Manor place thereof, Parkhill and fishings thereof, in Old and New Machar.

On 12th February, 1729, there is a charter of resignation and sale—Andree Skene de Lethinty et Alexandri Skene filius ejus unici legitimi natu Ville de Lethintye—and in the same year he serves heir to John Skene of Dyce, his brother, in the lands of Dyce, and is confirmed as his Executor Dative.

He died on 27th December, 1732, and was succeeded by his only son.

VII.—ALEXANDER SKENE OF DYCE—1732-1743.

On 28th February, 1733, Alexander Skene of Parkhill gave up an inventory of the goods, &c., of the deceased Andrew Skene of Lethintie, as his only son and sole Executor.

His last will was dated on 27th June, 1731, by which he left the estate of Lethintie to Andrew Skene, second son to the said Alexander.

In 1741, there is a discharge by Margaret Forbes, spouse of Alexander Skene, formerly of Parkhill, now of Dyce, of the sum, in a bond, to Andrew Skene of Lethintie, his father.

By his wife, Margaret Forbes, he had two sons—

I. John Skene, who succeeded him.

II. Andrew Skene, who succeeded his brother.

VIII.—JOHN SKENE OF DYCE—1743-1747

served heir in 1743 to Alexander Skene of Dyce, his father.

He had a natural daughter, Margaret Skene, who married William Smith, and had three sons—

I. Andrew Smith, afterwards Skene of Lethintie.

II. John Smith, a captain in the navy.

III. Adam Smith, advocate, in Aberdeen, and two daughters.

IX.—Andrew Skene of Dyce—1747-1815.

In terms of his grandfather's will, he succeeded, after his father's death, to the estate of Lethintie, and on 12th February, 1745, there is a charter of resignation —Andreæ Skene filii legitimi natu secundi demortui Alexandri Skene de Dyce vill. et terr. de Lethintie.

On 20th February, 1747, the inventory of the goods, &c., of the deceased John Skene of Dyce, is given up by Andrew Skene of Lethentie, now of Dyce, his only brother, with concurrence of Margaret Forbes, Lady Dyce, his mother.

He died in January, 1815, at the age of 82, and thus terminated the family of Skene of Dyce in the male line.

Andrew Skene, the last laird of Dyce, settled the succession to his estates by two deeds of entail, dated 19th Feb., 1794. By the first he settled the estates of Dyce, Parkhill, and others upon a series of heirs, the institute being John Gordon Cumming of Pitlurg, and among the substitutes, the Skenes of Skene, Dr. George Skene, physician in Aberdeen, and the Skenes of Rubislaw. By the second deed of entail he settled the barony of Lethentie and others upon a series of heirs, the institutes being Margaret Skene, relict of William Smith, and the heirs male of her body, and among the substitutes, Dr. George Skene, physician in Aberdeen, Captain James Skene, uncle to the laird of Skene, and James Skene of Rubislaw.

Under the first deed General Gordon Cumming of Pitlurg succeeded to the estates of Dyce and Parkhill, and assumed the name of Skene, quartering the differenced arms of Skene of Dyce.

Under the second Andrew Smith, eldest son of Margaret Skene or Smith, succeeded to the estate of Lethentie, and changed his name to Skene.

CHAPTER V.

SKENE OF WESTERCORSE AND RAMORE.

I.—JAMES SKENE IN BANDODLE,

second son of Alexander Skene IX., of Skene " by Lord Forbes' daughter."
He was a Notary Public, and the first of the sons of the family who
bore the designation of " in Bandodle," the Tanistry lands having been
acquired by his father.

In 1538 he appears as uncle and curator to Alexander Skene of that
ilk, his nephew, and in 1543 witnesses two charters as Notary Public.
In the same year James Skene in Bandodle is infeft in the Sunny third
of the lands of Blackball.

He married Janet Lumsden, daughter of Lumsden of Cushney; and,
on 20th May, 1546, there is crown charter of confirmation " Jacobo Skeyne
in Bandodill et Jonete Lumsdein eius coniuge super cartam illis
factam per Andream Fraser de Staneywood 13 Maij 1546 de toto et
integro annuali feodo seu feudifirma Triginta quinque Mercarum sex
solidarum et octo denariorum monete Scotie dicto Andreæ heredibus
suis et assignatis annuatim solvend. nomine feudifirme de totis et
integris terris de Westercorse et Norham in parochia de Coule per
honorabilem virum Willelmum Hurry de Pitfechie necnon superioritate
dict. terrarum."

The author of MS.B gives the following account of his family :—

" But to return to   Skene, he purchased the lands of
Ramore, and married   Burnett, daughter to Leyes. His name
was Mr. James, who begot six sons on her, whereof one was Sir John
Skene, first, Lord-Advocate, and thereafter, when he came from Den-

mark, on being secretarie to that embassy, with the Lord Marischall, he was made Lord-Register, and married al his children nobilie. He had 5 elder brothers, viz., the Guidman of Ramoir, and the Commissar of Aberdeen, and the Commissar of St. Andrews, and two Doctors of Phisick, viz., the one Professor of the College of St. Andrews, and the other the first Professor of Medicine at Aberdeen. Both of them were, upon their coming from France, falling short of money at London, had only a quardegue [quartecu] by them, and resolving to kill or cure where-ever they came, were heard to say one to another, Let us spend this, and then revenge Pinkie and Flowden, and being arraigned before the K., King James preferred the on to be his ordinar, the other his extrordin-arie Daughter [Doctor], and recommended them to St. Andrews and Aberdeen, for the love he bore to Sir John, their brother, who was the youngest of the sex, and went in and out first, and the eldest last. Their mother, finding her husband and Mr. James a bon compagnon, and haueing his friends with him, sat up at night drinking. She retired herselfe to a Buss of Birkis, in respect the Drink was almost done in the house, save only a tunned coug, and took herself to pray for her hus-band and familie, and thereafter she fell asleep, and being with chyld, it quickens, and she starts up and went to her husband, and told him that she would never grudge at his good fellowship any more, for God had revealed it to her that she was with a son, whose name was to be John who should be a father to the other fayve—and then brought forward the Tuning skell couge quhich was formerlie absconded from her hus-band, and began her own *hans in kelder*" (male child in the womb).

Like most family traditions, this account is not strictly correct, and James Skene, the father, seems to be confounded with Mr. James Skene, his eldest son.

His wife was, we have seen, not a Burnet but a Lumsden.

There is among the Curriehill papers a "genealogy of Sir John Skene, Clerk Register, Lord Curriehill," in which his descent is correctly stated. "The Laird of Skene was married to my Lord Forbes's daughter, and she had to him the Laird of Skene, the elder brother, and the Laird of Ramore, the second. The Laird of Ramore was married to the Laird of Cushnie, chief of the name of Lumsden, his daughter, in Aberdeen, who bore to him the Laird of Ramore and Sir John Skene, Clerk Register."

The story of the two doctors, also, rather falls through, for there was certainly only one of the sons who was a doctor and "mediciner to his Majestic," and there was at the time no Professor of Medicine in St. Andrews; but another of the sons, Duncan, was incorporated in St. Mary's College of St. Andrews in 1559. He was a Notary Public. He may, however, have been his brother's companion on this occasion, and made the remark, as he was noted for his witty sayings. He was Notary to the Edzeill and Crawfurd family, and in their correspondence there is frequent allusion to "Mr. Duncan Skene's daft diximes."

The following description of the "tunned coug" is given in "An Account of Scotland in 1679, by Thomas Kirke, a Yorkshire squire"— "Their drink is ale of bear malt, and tunned up in a small vessel called a cogue; after it has stood a few hours, they drink it out of the cogue, yest and all."

In MS.B the five elder brothers of Sir John Skene alone are given, but he had four younger brothers, as we shall see, making in all ten brothers, sons of James Skene of Westercorse.

Prior to the sixteenth century there was little outlet for the sons of such families, except to enter the church, or to have their names inscribed in the rental books as kindlie tenants of some outlying farm, which their descendants, if the laird was embarrassed, acquired in property, or else they descended to the condition of ordinary farmers; but in the beginning of the sixteenth century the increasing trade of the country, and the new life and new ideas infused into society by the Reformation, sent the younger sons to seek their subsistence in other fields. Those who would have entered the church became notaries public. Others either became burgesses of the county towns, or entered into the increasing trade between Scotland and Poland, in which Aberdeen took a large share, whence, if they were prosperous in trade, they again emerged and founded new county families, by purchasing land; while the foundation of the College of Justice, as well as of the College of St. Mary's at St. Andrew's in this century, afforded a new outlet for their energies in which they might acquire fame or fortune.

The history of these ten sons of Mr. James Skene, by his wife, Janet Lumsden, affords an apt illustration of the above remarks. They were—

I. Mr. James Skene, who succeeded his father.

II Mr. William Skene.

On 13th April, 1540, the Bishop of Aberdeen admitted, among others, as Notaries—

Magister Jacobus Skeyne,

Magister Wilhelmus Skeyne.

On 17th September, 1549, "Magister Willelmus Skene" entered King's College as a student in theology, and in the same year he is ordered. by the Bishop to be ready to take Priests Orders, at Easter, 1550, to take Minor Orders between this and the Feast of All Saints, the Subdiaconate at Christmas, and the Diaconate and Presbyterate, between that date and the said Easter.

In 1556 "Magister Gulielmus Skene in utroque jure licentiatus" is incorporated in St. Mary's College, St. Andrews.

In 1563 he became one of the Visitors of St. Salvator's College. In 1564 he was appointed Commissary of St. Andrews; and in 1565 "Magister Gulielmus Skene Juris licentiatus, Sti. Andree Commissarius et conservator privilegiorum" is elected Dean of the Faculty of Arts. In 1579 he was transferred to St. Salvator's College.

He married Margaret Martin, relict of Wm. Arthour, and died on 2nd September, 1582. On 17th February, 1586, the will of Mr. William Skene, Commissar of St. Andrews, is confirmed by Margaret Mertoune, his spouse, as executrix dative.

In his work, "De Verborum Significatione," Sir John Skene refers to a work "Mri. Wilielmi Skenei fratris mei Commissarii Sancti Andree;" and Sir James Melville says, in his Memoirs, "Commissare Wilyeam Skene was ane man of skill and guid conscience in his calling, learnit and diligent in his profession, and tuk delyt in nathing mair nor to repeat ower and ower again to anie schollar that wad ask him the things he had been teaching."

III. Mr. Alexander Skene. He appears to have been an alumnus of the University of Paris, as in an edition of Vaus' Grammar, published in Paris in 1553, there is an address "Alexandri Skeyne Juventuti Aberdonensi Grammatice studiosi," dated Lutetie, 16 Calend. Julii, MDLIII."

In 1563 he was an advocate before the Lords of Council, in

Edinburgh, and married Margaret Cockburn, relict of James
Lawson of Hieriggis, as on 13th April, in that year, there is a
contract between William Lesly of Balquhane on the one part,
and Mr. Alexander Skene, advocate, before the Lords of Council
and Session in Edinburgh, for himself and in name of Margaret
Cokburne, his spouse, on the other ; and, on 9th March, 1568,
there is a contract between John Lawson of Boghall, son and
heir of umquhile James Lawson of Hieriggis, Margaret Cokburne,
mother of the said John and Mr. Alexander Skene, her spouse,
on the one part, and James Wylie Skynnar, burgess of Edinburgh, and Margaret Leslie, his spouse, on the other.

In 1574 he became a burgess of Aberdeen, and acquired part
of the salmon fishings of Midchyngill, in the river of Dee; and in
a sasine in his favour, on 8th April, 1575, of a land on the north
side of Castle Street, Aberdeen, among the witnesses is Magistro Johanne Skeyne fratre germano dicti magistri Alexandri.

On 1st October, 1576, the Council Records of Aberdeen
contain the following :—" The said day the Provost, &c., grantit
and geiff license to Maister Alexander Skene, burgess of the
said Burgh, and Advocat, admitted to our Souerane Lords
Sessioun, before the Lords of Counsell, to duell and remain
absent of this Burgh, within the Burgh of Edinburgh, for the
space of three years, notwithstanding he be obleist. be the
Statutes, &c., to duell and remain within the same, in respect he
is presently ane heritable possessor of ane half nettis fishing of
the Mydchingill, &c., especiallie because the said Alexander
procuris for them before the Lords ; " and, on 9th October, 1579,
this permission is renewed for three years.

On 6th March, 1584, there is an obligation by Alexander
Quhitlaw of Ester Liffe, and others, to Mr. Alexander Skene
in Edinburgh, brother-german to Mr. John Skene, Advocat.

On 6th July, 1586, " Mr. Alexander Skeyne, Advocat, before
the Lords and Burgess of Edinburgh and Aberdeen, departit."

He left no issue, as on 12th July, 1586, there is a decreet at the
instance of Mr. John Skene, advocate, against Mr. James Skene
of Westercorse, his brother, in which Mr. John Skene, as heir of
provision, sues Mr. James Skene, as heir of conquest of their
brother, Mr. Alexander Skene, advocate.

Sir John Skene thus alludes to him in his work "De Verborum Significatione," under the word Bothua, "ut in lib. M. Alexandri Skenæi fratris mei germani quondam in supremo Senatu Advocati."

IV. Robert Skene. 1st October, 1571, Robertus Skeyne admitted Burgess of Aberdeen: Alexander Cullen, Cautioner.

In the deed by which Jacobus Nicolson resigns, on 19th Oct., 1574, the half fishings of Mydchingill to Mr. Alexander Skene, the witnesses are "Alexandro Cullen, Roberto Skeyne, burgen. de Aberdeen."

And on 24th July, 1575, Robert Skene is witness to a contract between Alexander Forbes of Auchintoull, and Mr. Alexander Skene, advocate, in which he is designed brother-german to the said Mr. Alexander. He was ancestor of the Skenes of Belhelvie and of Rubislaw.

V. Mr. Gilbert Skene applied himself to the study of medicine, in which he took a doctor's degree, and in 1536 was appointed mediciner or professor of medicine in King's College, Aberdeen. A memorandum in the records of King's College says, "he entered in Principal Anderson's time, and continued likely till after the Reformation, or the Assembly visitation in 1569."

It was while occupying this position of professor of medicine n: King's College, that he published the little tract on "The Peste," which was printed, as the title bears, at Edinburgh in the year 1568.*

In the same year he became one of the ordinary regents of the College; but, in 1571, there is a presentation, dated 6th November, by the rector, principal, regents, &c., of the College of Aberdeen, with collation of William, Bishop of Aberdeen, to Maister Gilbert Skene, doctor in medicine, of the Burse of medicine, otherwise called a prebendar of the said College, with the manse, hous, place, yardis, and croftis pertaining thereto; and on 20th August, 1587, he, with consent of the masters, disponed the mediciner's manse to Mr. Thomas Lumsden, rector, of Kinkell.

---

* This tract, with another, was reprinted for the Bannatyne Club, under the title of " Tracts by Dr. Gilbert Skeyne," with a prefatory notice of Dr. Gilbert by the editor of this work, and the above notice necessarily corresponds with it.

In 1569 he married Agnes Lawson, as appears from a contract, on 25th November, between Mr. John Spens of Condie, and Mr. Alexander Betoune, Erchdeine of Lawtheane, on the one part, and Mr. Gilbert Skene, Doctoure of Medicine, and Agnes Lausone, his future spouse, on the other. She was, as appears from another contract in 1583, relict of John Uddart, burgess of Edinburgh.

In 1571 Gilbert Skene, Doctor of Medicine, and Agnes Lawsone, his spouse, are infeft in the lands of Mekill Wardes, in the barony of Pitsligo.

In 1575 he appears to have finally settled in Edinburgh, as in that year he purchased from Mr. John Melrose a house in Niddry Street, Edinburgh. Here he practised as a doctor, and must have risen to some celebrity, as on 16th June, 1581, there is in the Privy Seal Record, "ane letter makand mentioun that our Soueraine Lord understanding that his wellbelovit Maister Gilbert Skene, doctour of medicine, has bestowed his haill aige bygane in ze studie of guid letters, and in speciale of medicine, and appointing him his own physician;" and, in the Act of Revocation of the Collectory-made by James VI. in 1581, there is specially excepted "the gift of pension to our wellbelovit Maister Gilbert Skene, our Mediciner, of the soume of Twa hundreth pundis money of our realme." He seems to have lived uncomfortably with his wife, and finally separated from her, as on 1582 there is an action of adherence at the instance of Agnes Lawson against Mr. Gilbert Skene, her spouse.

In 1593 Dr. Gilbert Skeyne sells his house in Niddry Street to his brother, Sir John Skene, for an annuity of 200 merks, from which we may infer that he had retired from practice. The house is described as lying on the south side of the Kings Hie Street, in the Vennel called Niddrie's Wynd, on the east side of the passage entrance of the same.

Dr. Gilbert Skene died in 1599, leaving no family, but survived by his widow, Agnes Lawson, who alleged that she had been named executrix, but was unable to procure a nomination; and, on 20th July, 1599, his nephew, Robert Skene, son of his eldest. brother, Mr. James Skene of Westercorse, was decerned

Executor Dative, and gave up an Inventory of his goods and gear; and, in 1602, another nephew, James Skene, brother's son to Mr. Gilbert Skene, is decerned Executor *ad omissa.*

VI. Mr. John Skene, afterwards Sir John Skene of Curriehill, ancestor of the Skenes of Curriehill and Halyards in Mid-Lothian.

VII. Mr. Duncan Skene. In 1559 Duncanus Skeyne is incorporated in St. Mary's College, St. Andrews. On 9th June, 1567, there is an obligation by William Richeson of Cranstoun, Riddell, Principale, and Thomas Hunter, burgess of the Canongait, suretie to Mr. Duncan Skene, brother to Mr. Alexander Skene, advocat.

In 1591 Mr. Duncan Skene, Notary Public, is infeft in an annual rent of £40 from the lands of Balnabriech in Forfarshire; and, on 11th March, 1594, there is decreet at the instance of Mr. Duncan Skene, brother-german to Mr. John Skene, Clerk of Register, against James Guthrie of Eister Balnabriech, and Christian Barroun, his spouse, and James Guthrie, their son and heir, for payment to him of two annual rents, one of £40, and the other of 40 merks, furth of the lands of Eister Balnabriech, due for the years 1592-93-94, to which annual rents he has right, by alienation and disposition, by the said James Guthrie, to him and his heirs lawful, to be gotten of his body; whom failing, to John Skein, lawful son to the said Mr. John Skein, his heirs and assigns, and concerning which there are two contracts between the said James Guthrie, his spouse and son on the one part, and Mr. Duncan Skene on the other part, both of the date at Balnabriech, 12th June, 1589, and registered in the Books of Council and Session, 11th February, 1594.

Mr. Duncan Skene appears, in several deeds, as a Notary Public, and seems to have acted in that capacity to the Edzell and Crawford families, and to have been resident at one time in the family of Lord Ogilvie, as appears from the papers of these families. In a letter from Lord Ogilvie to Sir David Lindesay, which is in Mr. Duncan's handwriting, and dated : Farnwell, 1st March, 1586, he adds a postscript for himself, to Sir David— " My Lord, my maister is sumquhat mair coleragious sen he cam haim furth of Ducheland, nor of befoir, swa I dar nor will nocht be hamlie witt his Lordschip with my daft diximes. I had

O

never ane busines heid. Albeit it be gryt, thair is mair wit about it nor within ye sam."

Mr. Duncan Skene died unmarried in 1602, and, on 11th June in that year, there are, in the Curriehill papers, the original minutes of Court, in the service of Mr. John Skene, younger, as air of tailzie and provision to the said umquhile Mr. Duncan Skene.   George Skene is Dempster of the court.

VIII. Mr. Thomas Skene was a writer.   He first appears in the Council Register of Aberdeen, and gives evidence of an apparently turbulent youth.   There is on 17th December, 1574, the Baillie's decern—Gilbert Henric to pay to Thomas Skene, ten shillings scots, and in May, 1574, the Baillies decern and ordain Wilyam Wishart to refund, content, and pay to Thomas Skene the soume of thirty-five shillings, probably connected with said business ; but, on 10th September, 1575, Thomas Skene confessit striking Harie   in ye arme with ane whinger, wherefore he was in unlaw, and William Foremen became suretie for the modification of his unlaw.

After Sir John Skene became Clerk Register, we find that Thomas had been made servitor to the Master of Elphinstone, and participated in the grants which, through Sir John's influence, were so freely bestowed upon different members of the family.   In the Privy Seal Record there is, on 5th February, 1594, ane letter maid . . . givand, grantand, and disponand, to his lovit Thomas Skene, servitor to Alexander, Master of Elphinstone, during all the days of his lifetime, all and baill the vicarage, pensionarie of Pittintagart, with the manse and glebe, &c., at his hieness disposal, by the decease of umquhile Mr. William Hay, parson of Turriff.   Thomas Skene married a Mowat of Balquhollie, and had three sons—

1. Mr. James Skene, writer, in Edinburgh.   In 1601 he became servitor to Mr. Robert Learmonth, advocate, son-in-law of Sir John Skene, and in 1600 he was present at the death-bed of James Skene of Westercorse (Acts and Decreets, 8th Feb., 1603).   In 1620 he married Anne Learmonth, his master's daughter, by whom he had a daughter, Helen ; and after her death he married a second time Elizabeth Mowtray.

In 1650 Mr. James Skene, served heir to Barbara Mowat, wife of Mr. Andrew Oswald, advocate, "filiæ avunculi."

On 13th Sept., 1655, James Skeyne, writer, and Elizabeth Mowtray, married; and on 30th May, 1656, James Skeyne, son to umquhile Thomas Skeyne, writer, and Elizabeth Mowtray had a son, James. His father died soon after, as on 17th Jan., 1658, umquhile James Skene, writer, and Elizabeth Mowtray, a son, John; but this family came to an end in the same year, as on 11th Nov., 1658, there is a sasine on precept by the provost and baillies of Edinburgh in favour of Jeane Skene, father's sister, and heir to the deceased John Skene, procreated betwixt the deceased James Skene, his father, and the deceased Elizabeth Mowtray, spouses, and Patrick Hamilton of Greine, her spouse, of a tenement in the village of Leith.

2. Robert Skene was admitted a Notary Public on 15th July, 1598, and settled at Turriff, probably owing to the connection of his mother's family with that part of the country, as there is an obligation by Walter Mowatt to Robert Skene in Turriff, dated at Turriff, 8th December, 1607.

In September of the same year he was admitted a burgess of Aberdeen, but his name occurs among the burgesses "rure manentes."

There is a sasine in 22nd May, 1616—Robertus Skene, in villa de Turriff, of a tenement in Aberdeen, formerly belonging to Thomas Skene, burgess of Aberdeen, in which Mr. James Skene, son of Robert, is a witness. This line cannot be traced further, but part of the protocol books of Mr. Robert and Mr. James Skene, both Notaries in Turriff, has been preserved.

3. Thomas Skene. He was admitted a burgess of Aberdeen on 16th July, 1602, and on 25th February, 1603, there is a sasine by Thomas Skene and Isobel Anderson, his spouse, referring to contract of marriage between them, with consent of Robert Skene, in villa de Turriff, his brother-german. He died, without issue, before 1616.

4. Jeane Skene married Patrick Hamilton of Greine.

IX. Andrew Skene. He appears as a burgess of Aberdeen as early
as the year 1564, and in 1571 he married Bessie Annand, of the
family of Annand of Ochterellon, and settled in Many, near the
northern boundary of Belhelvie, as on 1st March in that year,
" Andreas Skeyne, in villa de Many," resigns, in the hands of the
superior, for new infeftment to himself and Bessie Annand, his
spouse, " terra sua per Alexandrum Quhytcross nunc occupata
in vico inferiori ecclesie ex boreali parte inter terras Georgii
Wischart et Thome Merscone."

He appears sometimes in Aberdeen, and sometimes among
the " absentes," down to 1589, when, on 15th October, in that
year, " Andrew Skeyne, burgess of Aberdeen, departit."

He had a son—

I. George Skene. He appears, in 1602, as Dempster of court, in
the service of Mr. John Skene, son of Sir John Skene of
Curriehill, to his uncle, Mr. Duncan Skene, and in the same
year is executor, as brother's sone, to Patrick Skene, another
brother of Sir John Skene.

In 1611 we find him living at Knockhall, which then
belonged to Lord Sinclair, and in that year he is a juror in
the service of idiotcry of William Skene, son to Mr. James
Skene of Westercorse.

In 1613 we find him, in the Aberdeen Council Register,
called burgess, chamberlain to Lady Sinclair ; and, on 22nd
January, in that year, there is an action by George Skene,
brother's son to Sir John Skene of Curriehill, against Alexander Innes, in Garnwatter, for spuilzie, in August, 1612,
furth of the lands of Quoren, in the parish of Urquhart, of a
black horse and a mare.

In 1619 he becomes servitor to Turing of Foveran, and
in 1621 there is a precept by Turing of Foveran to George
Skene in Auchnacant, and we find him there in 1623, with
Barbara Anderson, his spouse.

In October, 1626, there is the redemption of ane tenement of land caleit the Stanehouse of Ellon, granted by
George Skene in Auchnacant, to Mr. Gilbert Annand, a
connection through his mother ; and the last notice we have
of him is in 1635.

X. Patrick Skene. On 17th May, 1580, "Mr. John Skene, Advocatus coram Dominis Concilii, Patricius Skene ejus frater germanus gratis gratia Concilii," admitted burgesses of Aberdeen.

Nothing is known of his history, except that he was twice married—first to Marjorie Hurrie, a daughter, probably of Hurrie of Pitfichie, who possessed Westercorse, under the Skenes as superiors, and whose death is thus recorded—

17th July, 1585, Marjorie Hurre, spouse of Patrick Skene, buried in the kirk; and, on 10th January, 1586, we have Patrick Skene and Marjorie Forbes mariet.

In 1589, Patrick Skene and his spouse are warned to remove from a house in the Gallowgate pertaining to David Fergusone.

He had no family, and died in 1601, as on 29th July, in that year, there is an edict, at the instance of Mr. Patrick Forest against the executors, the spouse, bairns, if there may be, intromitters with the goods and gear of umquhile Patrick Skene, burgess of Aberdeen. Compeirit Mr. Patrick Forest, procurator for George Skene, brother's sone to the defunct, desiring him to be decerned executor dative to him.

Mr. James Skene of Westercorse had two daughters—

XI. Bessie Skene, who married William Elzenor, burgess of Aberdeen, by whom she had two sons and one daughter—

1. Robert, burgess of Aberdeen.

2. John, "incola villae de Turriff," admitted burgess in 1607.

3. Bessie, married to Patrick Skene, in Bandodle.

24th November, 1579, sasine by William Elzinor in favour of "probe adolescentule Bessete Skene, sue future conjugi jam in sua virginitate existen." of a tenement in Upper Kirkgate.

17th March, 1585, Bessie Skene, spouse to William Alshenour, burgess of Aberdeen, departit.

XII. Mirabell Skene "married   Forbes, burgess of Aberdeen, and had a son, David, who lived with Earl Marischall; who had a daughter, Lucia Forbes" (Curriehill papers). Her daughter, Jean, is mentioned in 1613, as "sisters dochter to defunct" Dr. Gilbert Skene.

As previously mentioned in the account of the "little laird," James Skene, who was his uncle, and had been his curator, led his retainers to the battle of Pinkie, and was slain there in 1547.

II.—Mr. James Skene of Westercorse and Ramore,

the eldest son, succeeded his father, who, before he went to the battle of Pinkie, transferred his estate to his son, as appears from a crown charter of confirmation, " Magistro Jacobo Skeyne filio Jacobi Skeyne in Bandodil super cartam sibi factam per dictum Jacobum Skeyne in Bandodil de data 26 Februarij, 1547, de toto et integro annuali feodo triginta quinque Mercarum &c. de terris de Westercorss et Norham necnon superioritate dictarum terrarum."

He afterwards acquired the lands of Ramore, in Kincardineshire, and Mr. James Skene of Ramore is witness to a crown charter on 13th December, 1578.

On 18th January, 1587, there is an action at the instance of Mr. James Skene of Westercorse against Alexander Cuming of Culter, to find they have done wrong in demolishing the briggis callit Bowbrig, lying betwixt his lands of Carnyguhen, Ramoir, &c., on the north side, and his lands of Catterloche on the south. Mr. John Skene is his procurator.

He was twice married, 1st, to Janet Burnet, second daughter of Alexander Burnett of Leys, by whom he had the following children :—

I. Alexander Skene. On 27th April, 1582, " Mr. Alexander Skene, filius et heres apparen. Magistri Jacobi Skene de Westercorse gratis gratia Concilii," admitted a burgess of Aberdeen. He died in the same year, as on 4th November, in that year, " Mr. Alexander Skene de Prestoun Burgensis de Aberdeen ac Advocatus coram Dominos Concilii " resigns the fishings in Midchingill " in favorem her. masc. de corpore quondam Magistri Alexandri Skene junioris Burgen. de Aberdeen, filii et heredis apparentis Magistri Jacobi Skene de Westercorse ac patruelis ipsius Magistri Alexandri Skene senioris resignantis." Witness, Mr. James Skene of Westercorse.

II. Gilbert Skene, also a burgess of Aberdeen ; and, on 4th May, 1591, " Magister Gilbertus Skene Burgen. de Aberdeen frater germanus ac heres quondam Magistri Alexandri Skene junioris Burgen. de Aberdeen " is infeft in the fishings of Midchingill. He succeeded his father.

III. Robert Skene. 5th April, 1606, sasine to Robertus Skeyne filius legitimus quondam Jacobi Skeyne de Westercorse of the lands of Rannaloch, upon disposition to him by James Skene, son and heir of Sir John Skene of Curriehill.

He was twice married, 1st to Janet Skene one of the three daughters and co-heiresses of Arthur Skene of Auchtererne, by whom he had a son, Alexander, who served heir to his mother in 1621 ; and 2nd to Helén Robertson, relict of John Vaus, portioner, of Brochton, as appears from a notice of her in that year, and Robert Skene of Rannaloch, now her spouse. In her right he appears to have obtained property in Auchtermuchty; and, in 1620, he conveys Rannaloch and Brochholls, in the parishes of Kincardine and Cluny, to Alexander Skene of Skene, and after that date is usually designed as Robert Skene of Auchtermuchtie.

In the years, from 1597 to 1611, he appears as servitor to Sir John Skene of Curriehill. In 1599 he is designed son to James Skene of Raemoir, and in 1600 and 1601, brother's sone to Sir John.

IV. William Skene. On 13th November, 1611, "Gulielmus Skeyne filius Jacobi Skeyne de Westercorse," is cognosced as "non compos mentis fatuus et naturaliter idiota," and "Robertus Skeyne de Auchtermuchtie ejus fratri germanus primogenitus" is appointed tutor as "propinquior consanguineus ex parte patris dicto Gulielmo." Among the jurors is George Skene in Knockhall.

V. Janet Skene married, 1st, Patrick Innes of Tibbertie ; and 2nd, on 11th February, 1625, to John Forbes of Byth, Mr. John Skene, Clerk of Session, and Mr. James Skene of Ramore, being consenting parties.

Mr. James Skene of Westercorse and Ramore married a second time Elizabeth Strathauchin, as appears from a redemption by Alexander Cullen, provost of Aberdeen, of a tenement, over which 300 merks had been lent by Magister Jacobus Skene de Westercorse et Elizabeth Strathauchin ejus sponsa. He died in June, 1600, and his testament dative is confirmed in October, 1600, his son, Robert Skene, being appointed sole executor.

III.—MR. GILBERT SKENE OF WESTERCORSE AND RAMORE.

On 30th September, 1600, there is a retour—" Magister Gilbertus Skene heres masculus Magistri Jacobi Skene de Westercorse patris in annuo feodo &c. de terris de Westercorse et Norham necnon superioritate dictarum terrarum."

In 10th November, 1602, he is infeft in the lands of Kebety, in the parish of Midmar, and in 1612 we find him designed Mr. Gilbert Skene de Ramore.

He appears to have married a daughter of Forbes of Corsinday. He died in 1616, and was succeeded by his son,

IV.—MR. JAMES SKENE OF WESTERCORSE AND RAMORE,

who was then probably under age. He was admitted a burgess in 1618, but it was not till 20th July, 1620, that there is a retour Magister Jacobus Skene heres Magistri Gilberti Skene de Westercorse patris in dimedictate ville et terrarum de Corsinday, dimedietate terrarum de Muirton et Little Corsinday, dimedietate terrarum de Badenley, et terrarum molindinarum, terris de Kebetie cum pastura in foresta Coraenie in baronia de Cluny.

On 27th July, 1622, there is a similar retour in the lands of Westercorse and Norham.

Ramore was probably liferented by his mother, as it is not till 9th January, 1664, that " Jacobus Skene de Ramore heres Gilberti Skene de Ramore patris " is infeft in " terris de Caernquhin Ramore Catterloch et Tillibo."

He was succeeded by his son.

V.—ROBERT SKENE OF WESTERCORSE AND RAMORE.

On 18th November, 1661, there is a sasine in favor of " Robertus Skene nunc de Ramore nepos quondam Magistri Gilberti Skene de Westercorse filius quondam Jacobi Skene quondam de Ramore," in the lands of Carnquhine Ramore Catterloch et Tilnabo Molendini de Ramore.

"Robert Skene of Ramore descended of a second brother of the Laird of Skene" records arms in the Lyon Register: "Gules three daggers argent pomelled and surmounted on the poynts with alse many woolf's heads couped or, all within a bordur invecked of the second." Crest: "A birk-tree environed with certaine ears of oats all growing out of a mount proper." Motto: "Sub montibus altis."

He was three times married, 1st, to a daughter of Rait of Halgreen, 2nd, to Barbara, daughter of William Forbes of Cotton, and relict of Gilbert Skene of Dyce, and 3rd, to a daughter of Robert Irvine of Cults.

By his first wife he had an only daughter, Margaret Skene, who married James Hog of Blairiedryne, and brought the estate of Ramore into that family.

On 8th August, 1685, there is a sasine in favour of Margaret Skene, spouse of James Hog of Blairiedryne, and in 1691 there is a sasine in favour of James Hog of Blairiedryne, in the lands of Ramore, &c.

P

SKENE OF CURRIEHILL.

I.—Mr. John Skene,

sixth son of James Skene of Westercorse, and afterwards Sir John Skene of Curriehill.

The following account of his career is given by Sir John Scott of Scotstarvet in his "Staggering State of the Scots Statesmen for one hundred years, from 1550 to 1650," in his usual depreciatory style :—

"Sir John Skeen succeeded to be Clerk Register after Alexander Hay, and was preferred to the place by the moyen of my Lord Blantyre, his brother-in-law ; for their wives were two sisters.

"He was well skilled in the laws before he was advanced to that place, and got a sole gift for printing the Acts of Parliament and *Regiam Majestatem*, by which means he acquired a great deal of money from the country, for all heritors of land were obliged to buy them; but it did little good; for albeit he lived many years in the place, yet did he purchase but few lands, only he bought Curriehill and Ravelrig, of no great value ; all which was sold by his son, Sir James.

"He resigned his place to his said son in his old age; but Haddington, by his power, forced his son, Sir James, to resign the same in his favour, and got him made an Ordinary Lord of Session, which place Sir James brooked till his death, and was made president of the Session by King Charles. But being of a generous disposition, and having small means, he behoved to sell and dispone all, both in town and country, for defraying of his debts.

"Sir John's four daughters had little better success ; only Sir William Scott's wife [the author's mother], who got nothing by her father, had best success. But the other three—one of them married to Robert Learmont, advocate, the second to my Lord Fosterseat, and the third to Sir Robert Richardson of Pencaitland—their sons have disponed all their fathers' lands, and nothing is left thereof at this day."

The history of Sir John, as well as of his son, Sir James, can be traced from the infancy of the former, and it will be seen that the author of the " Staggering State " has rather distorted the facts in order to point the moral of his piece.

We have first, two notices, which may relate to Sir John in his early school days. On 13th July, 1541, the Town Council of Aberdeen "divide the Sang skuill between Sir John Futtie and John Black, singar, his depute ; the said John to have power to puneis and correct his awin twa brothers, Alexander Grayes twa sones, ane Skene and ane Lummisden, barnis of the said skuill, reserving the punysment of the remanent barnis thereof to the said Sir John himself, as superior thairof." 24th January, 1549, "Gilbert Kintor . . . conuikit . . . for ye inpading of daue andersoun Doctor in ye grammer skuhill of ye said bur^t in sanct nicklace kirk of ye said bur^t villand to haue strikin him And als ye said daue anderson and Jon robertsoun ar conuikit be ye said sorne be ye mov^t of ye said chancelar for ye out feching of ye barnis of ye said grammer skuhill and ye invading of ye said gilbert kintor and dauid kintor his broder throw ye qlk invading ye said dauid kintor was strikin and strublit be ane scolar callit skeyne w^t ane tre." Here we have him first in the Sang school, along with a Lumsden (and Sir John's mother was a Lumsden), and no doubt much benefited by the punishment and correction he received from Mr. John Black ; and then we find him leading the bairns of the Grammar School, and showing his prowess in defending their master. Mr. Grant, in his History of the Burgh Schools of Scotland, adds, "Tradition says that the scholar called Skeyne was the famous Sir John Skeyne, Clerk of Register, so well known to the students of Scots law and history" (p. 63), and the dates accord ; for, after passing through the course of studies at King's College, Aberdeen, he went to the University of St. Andrews ; and in 1556 Johannes Skene was incorporated in St. Mary's College. After taking his degree of Master of Arts, he was, in 1565, Regent of St. Mary's College, and one of the electors of the Rector.

Dempster, who was personally acquainted with him, says, in his Ecclesiastical History, "adolescentiam in Norwegia, Dania, Sarmatiaque magna parte consumpsit, ubi et linguas didicit exactissime boreales et mores polivit, et ingenium, ad magna surgens, ex virtutis et honesti praescripto formavit, vir candore animi et humanitate incomparabili, jurisprudentiæ ac rei antiquariæ peritissimus."

He alludes to this journey, himself, in his work, "De Verborum Significatione," "Ane pedder is called ane Marchand or Creamer quba bearis ane pack or Creame upon his back quba are cald bearares of the pudill be the Scottismen of the Realme of Polonia; quhairof I saw ane great multitude in the toune of Cracovia, Anno Domini 1569."

On 19th March, 1575, Mr. John Skene was admitted advocate; and, in 1577, he married Helen Somerville, eldest daughter of Sir John Somerville of Camnethan by his second wife, Catherine, daughter of John Murray of Falahill; her sister, Dame Nicolas Somerville, being wife of Walter, Lord Blantyre.

Mr. John Skene seems soon to have risen to great practice at the Bar, but according to the custom of the time, instead of being paid by fees as at present, he engaged "to procure" in all causes affecting a client, for a fixed annual payment. Thus we find a decreet, at the instance of Sir John Skene, advocate, against George Meldrum of Fyvie, for payment to him of 90 merks, as arrears of yearly pension of 20 merks, granted by the said George Meldrum to the said Mr. John "for service alreddie done, and to be done be ye said Mr. John to ye said George, in his office of procuratioune, in all his honest and lefull causses before the said Lords, and that for all his lifetime conform to the letter of pension subscribed by the said George Meldrum at Edinburgh, 20th May, 1580, and which arrears are for the years, 1588-89-90-91-92, &c."

In 10th June, 1577, he was granted an annual pension of ten chalders of meal out of the revenues of the Abbey of Aberbrothock for his labours in connection with a plan for forming a general digest of the Scottish laws; and in 1587 he was named a member of a commission to examine the statutes passed in the Scottish Parliament.

In 1589 Sir James Melville who, having been selected by the king to form an embassy to Denmark to conclude a marriage with one of the princesses, was directed "to chuse any man of law that ye please," for the purpose of discussing the question about the ylles of Orkney, says, as in his memoirs, "when I schew his Majestie that I wald tak with me for man of law Mester John Skein, his Majestie thocht then that there were many better lawyers. I said, that he was best acquanted with the conditions of the Germanes, and culd mak them lang harrangues in Latin, and was a gud, trew, stout man, lyk a Dutche man. Then his Majestie was content that he suld ga ther with me" (p. 566).

Mr. John Skene accordingly went to Denmark as one of the Ambassadors, and in the deed of agreement between the Scottish Ambassadors and the Danish Government regarding the Orkney Isles he is a party as "Joannes Skynaeus, juris consultus et supremi serenissimi Scotorum Regis Senatus Advocatus" (Privy Council Register, IV., p. 223).

In the following year he accompanied Colonel Stewart on an embassy to Germany. He was also ambassador to the States General in 1591.

In 1592 a commission was appointed by the Parliament to "survey the lawes and actis made in this present Parliament, and all utheris municipall lawes and actis of Parliament bygane," "and to consider qubat lawis or actis necessardlie wald be knawin to the subjectis," and to cause the same to be printed. Sir John Skene was one of the Commissioners, and the task was committed to him.

On 1st April, 1593, "ane letter was maid under the Privy Seal, appointing Mr. Johnne Skene one of his Majesties Advocates, because of the infirmity of Mr. David McGill"; and, on 19th September, 1594, there is a similar letter "makand and constitutand Maister Johnne Skene his hienes Clerk of his Register."

In 1598 the first part of the Acts of Parliament, from James I. downwards, compiled by Mr. John Skene, was published, and to this was appended his treatise "De Verborum Significatione," a most useful work, invaluable to the student of ancient Scottish history, and a monument of his learning and industry.

In 1604, by which time he had been knighted, Sir John Skene was named one of the Commissioners for the Union of Scotland and England, and in 1607 he completed his treatises of the "Regiam Majestatem" and "Quoniam Attachiamenta," and presented them to the Privy Council. In the letter recommending the work to James VI., he is termed "the Clerk of your hienes' Register in this estaitt, ane wyse, learned, and worthy clerk," and they add, that "the meanness of his estate and fortune not answerand to his witt, ingyne, and literature, may not furneische him moyane to publeis this wark, albeit compiled and digested be his travillis and studie."

In consequence of this appeal a sum of money was directed to be paid to him by the sheriffs, baillies, stewards, and other judges, as well as by the prelates, earls, lords, and barons of the Realm, and a Commission was appointed in order to fix this sum.

Among the Curriehill papers is the following receipt, " I, Sir John Skene of Curriehill, grantis me to have receivit fra Sir Patrick Home of Polwart, knight, the soume of ten pundis money, and that for his part of the taxation grantit be the Estaittis for imprenting of the auld lawes. Subscrivit with my hand at Edinburgh, the tent of March, 1609, S. John Skene, with my hand."

Sir John Skene held the office of Clerk Register till the year 1612, and we find him employing several of his relations as servitors or clerks. Among them were Mr. Andrew Skene, ancestor of the Skenes of Hal-yards in Fife, Mr. Robert Skene, son of his brother, Mr. James Skene of Westercorse, and throughout the whole time, James Skene, son of his brother, Robert Skene. The Record of the Privy Seal is full of grants to these servitors of escheats and nonentries, bringing with them considerable sums of money, in which it is probable Sir John himself benefited to no small degree, but his means, which must have been considerable, were not invested to any great extent in land.

In 1582 he had a crown charter " de loco vocat. lie Craig de Blantyre," in Lanarkshire.

In 1596 there is a crown charter to him and Helen Somerville, his wife, of the lands of Rannalloch, in Aberdeenshire.

In 1598 there is a charter to him and Helen Somerville, his wife, of the dominical lands of Reidhall, in Midlothian ; and in 1599 a charter to them of these lands, along with the east half of Gorgie. In 1604 he purchased the lands of Curriehill for 20,000 merks ; and there is a charter to them of the lands of Hill, commonly called Curriehill, in Midlothian, from which he took his title.

Sir John Skene's official life closes in 1612, when he resigned the lucrative and important office of Clerk Register, in favour of his eldest son, Sir James Skene, who was, however, persuaded to accept the office of an Ordinary Lord of Session instead, to the great annoyance of his father. Spottiswood, in his history, gives the following account :— " Sir John Skene of Curriehill, in 1611, on account of his age and infirmity, intending to resign his situation of Clerk Register in favour of his son, Sir James Skene, sent him to London with a letter of resignation, to be used only if the king should be willing to admit him. He was induced, however, to give in the resignation and accept a seat on the bench as an ordinary judge, when the more lucrative office was conferred on Sir Thomas Hamilton" (p. 517).

The resignation had proceeded upon a "Bond by Mr. James Skene, eldest lawful son to Sir John Skene of Curriehill, mentioning that his said father had resigned his office of Clerk of Register, to the effect the said Mr. James might be provided thereto, therefore the said Mr. James binds himself to pay to his said father all fees during his life, dated at Edinb., 16th March, 1606; Witnesses, Mr. Alexander Skene, son lawful to said Sir John; Robert Skene, son lawful to umquhile Mr. James Skene; and James Skene, servitor to said Sir John." This proceeding on the part of Sir James caused at once misunderstanding between them, which was eventually settled, and as part of the settlement, Sir John took out on 28th May, 1614, a crown charter to himself, Helen Somerville, his wife, and Sir James Skene, their son, of the lands of Curriehill. The letters relating to this disagreement will be found in the appendix.

Sir John Skene had by Helen Somerville, his wife, four sons and four daughters—

I. James Skene, afterwards Sir James Skene of Curriehill.

II. Mr. John Skene of Halyards, ancestor of the Skenes of Halyards, in Midlothian, who carried on the line of this family.

III. Mr. Alexander Skene. On 24th October, 1593, there is a contract between Mr. John Skene, one of our sovereign Lord's Advocates, and Helen Somerville, his spouse, on the one part, and Mungo Russell and Gideon Russell, his son, and apparent heir, on the other part, by which they were bound to infeft the said Mr. John Skene and his spouse in liferent, and Mr. Alexander Skene, their third son, and his heirs; whom failing, to John Skene, his brother, and his heirs; in an annual rent of 100 merks, &c.

Among the Curriehill papers is an obligation by Mr. Alexander Skene and his son, John, to John Skene of Halyards, for 600 merks, to obtain Mr. John being admitted an assistant and successor in the office of keeper of the register of Hornings, with his father in 1631; and a bond for a sum of money due by Mr. Alexander Skene, brother to Halyards, Joneta Syme, his wife and John Skene, his eldest son, keeper of the register of Hornings, to Jean Haliburton, relict of Samuel Somerville, in 1632.

The testament dative of umquhile Mr. Alexander Skene, writer, in Edinburgh, who died, 22nd March, 1638, given up by Janet Syme, his relict, spouse, and executrix dative, decerned to him by decreet of April, 1638, confirmed 3rd April, 1638.

IV. Mr. William Skene. On 3rd December, 1600, Mr. John Skene, Clerk of Register, and Helen Somerville, his spouse, " for the natural luif and affection, and natural kyndness which we beir to our weil belovit son, William Skene, being as yet unprovidit of ony living or moygane be us, and to ye effect he may have ane reasonabill beginning to preif to seek the knowledge of guid science, and be brocht up in vertew and leirning," infeft him in an annual rent of 60 bolls victual.

On 16th March, 1615, there is a decreet, at the instance of Mr. John Skene of Curriehill, one of the Privy Council, against Mr. Alexander Skene, sone lawful to the said Sir John, and brother and apparent heir to umquhile Mr. William Skene, youngest lawful son to the said Sir John, &c.

V. Jane Skene married Sir William Scott of Ardross, Director of Chancery, and their daughter, Eupheme, Countess of Dundonald (wife of the 1st Earl), was the lady referred to on page 6. Her sister, Helen Scott, married William, 2nd Lord Blantyre.

VI. Margaret Skene married Mr. Robert Learmonth, advocate, brother to the laird of Balcomie.

VII. Catharine Skene married Sir Alexander Hay, Lord Foresterseat. A daughter of this marriage was wife to Sir Archibald Johnston, who had by her Elizabeth Johnston, Lady Strathallan, wife of General Viscount Strathallan.

VIII. Euphemia Skene married to Sir Robert Richardson of Pencaitland. Sir John Skene died in year 1617.

17th June, 1717—Comperit Helen Somerville onllie executrix testamentar nominat be umquhile Sir John Skene of Curriehill, knight, her spouse, quba producit inventer of his guidis and geir, and maid faythe, &c.

Spottiswoode, in his Church History, speaking of his death, says, " he was much regretted by all honest men, for he had been a man much employed and honored with diverse legations, which he discharged with good credit, and now, in age, to be circumvented in this sort by the simplicity or folly of his son, it was held lamentable" (p. 517).

II.—MR. JAMES SKENE,

afterwards Sir James Skene of Curriehill, was admitted advocate on 6th July, 1603. On 31st August, 1605, he was infeft in the lands of Rannaloch, on a disposition by Mr. John Skene, one of the ordinary Clerks of Session.

On 2nd December, 1608, his father resigned in his favour the office of Clerk to the Bills, to which he was this day admitted. He was also conjoined with his father in the office of Clerk Register, but when his father resigned that office in favour of his son, in 1612, he accepted instead the position of an ordinary Lord of Session.

In 1619 a warrant was sent from the king " to warn Sir James Skene before the Lords of Secret Council to hear and see himself depressed for not communicating kneeling at Easter ; and, on 24th June, 1619, the Lords of the Privy Council, by command of the king, called Sir James Skene of Curriehill before them, and verle straitlie layed to his charge his disobedience to his Majestie's command and direction in not communicating with the rest of his Majesty's Council and Session in the kirk of Edinburgh, at Easter last, and for going to ane other kirk," &c. He pleaded that in that week he was Ordinar in the Utter house, and engaged on Saturday in examining witnesses, &c., which had prevented his attending the preparation sermon ; and he denied attending ane other kirk. The proceedings are printed in the appendix. It was generally understood that he was influenced by his wife, who was of a Puritan family.

On 14th February, 1626, he was promoted to the chair of President of the Court of Session ; and, on 2nd January, 1630, he was created a baronet by patent to himself and his heirs male whomsoever, which is recorded in the Register of Signatures on 26th January, 1630.

Sir James Skene married, on 7th December, 1603, Janet Johnston, daughter of Sir John Johnston of Hilton and Sheen, by whom he had eight sons, of whom two only survived, the rest having died young; and three daughters who were married. His sons were, as appears from the Session Registers—

Q

I. John Skene, baptised 24th April, 1608 ; died young.

II. John Skene, afterwards Sir John Skene of Curriehill, Baronet, baptised 21st October, 1610.

III. James Skene, baptised 20th April, 1615 ; died young.

IV. William Skene, baptised 10th October, 1616 ; died young.

V. Thomas Skene, afterwards Sir Thomas, baptised 25th June, 1618.

VI. William Skene, baptised 19th December, 1620 ; died young.

VII. James Skene, baptised 11th June, 1621 ; died young.

VIII. Samuel Skene, baptised 25th March, 1624 ; died young.

His daughters were—

I. Rachel Skene, baptised 16th February, 1612, married Sir Archibald Douglas of Cavers.

II. Euphame Skene, baptised 9th March, 1613, married Sir Archibald Inglis of Ingliston.

III. Helen Skene, baptised 24th October, 1619; married, first, Sir Robert Bruce of Broomhall, Lord of Session (and by him was mother of Sir Alexander Bruce, who succeeded as 4th Earl of Kincardine) ; secondly, the Honourable Sir Charles Erskine of Alva, fifth son of John, seventh Earl of Mar ; and thirdly, Sir James Dundas of Arniston, one of the Lords of Session.

Sir James Skene died on 25th October, 1633, when his death is thus recorded by Sir James Balfour, in his Annals :—20th October, 1633, dyed Sir James Skene of Curriehill, Knight and Baronet, President of the College of Justice, interred in the Greyfriars. He died, however, on 16th, and was buried on 20th October.

The testament testamentar of umquhile Sir James Skene of Curriehill, Knicht Barronet, President of our soverane Lordis College of Justice, who died on the 16th October, 1633, was given up by himself on 4th October, 1633, as concerns the nomination of his executors, legacies and debts, and by dame Jonet Johnstone, his relict, in name and behalf of Thomas and Helen Skenes bairnes lawful to the defunct, so far as concerns the inventory of his guids and geir, quhilk bairnes are onlie executor testamentaris nominat to their said umquhile father in this latter will. By his latter will he desires his body to be buried " in the kirk called the Grayfreir kirk, besyde the sepulcher of my umquhile father," and he nominates his said children, Thomas and Helen, his only executors. It is dated at Edinburgh, 4th October, 1633, and is witnessed by Sir Samuel Johnstone of Slains, advocate, and Mr. Archibald Johnstone. Confirmation dated 21st November, 1633.

His monument is on the outside of old Greyfriars Church, and bears the arms of Skene of Curriehill, and the following inscription :—

HIC CITVS EST HONORABILIS VIR DNS
JACOBVS SKENE DE CVRRIHILL MILES ET
BARONETA AC PRECES COLLEGII
IVSTITIÆ QVI OBIIT 15 DIE MENSIS
OCTOBRIS ANNO DNI 1633
ÆTATIS SWE 54

III.—Sir John Skene of Curriehill, Baronet.

On 16th December, 1636, he served heir to his father in the lands of Hill, commonly called Curriehill, in the Bailliry of Balernoke, in which he is styled "Dominus Joannes Skene de Curriehill hæres legitimus et propinquior hæres dicti quondam domini Jacobi Skene de Curriehill militis Baronetæ sui Patris"; and, in December of the same year, there is a disposition by Sir John Skene of Curriehill, Knight, Baronet, of the lands of Curriehill, in favour of Mr. Samuel Johnstone.

Sir John married Rachel Spiers, and after he sold the estate "he levied a regiment of men upon his own charges, and went to Germany and died there, leaving no children" (MS.B).

"Sir John Skene of Curriehill, who married Rachel Spiers, by whom he had only one son, who died in infancy. He afterwards raised a regiment of foot upon his own charges, with whom he went to Germany, where he died without surviving issue" (MS.D).

IV.—Sir Thomas Skene, Baronet.

"The President's second son died unmarried" (MS.B).

"Sir John of Curriehill had Sir James of Curriehill, who was President of the Session, and had Sir John and Sir Thomas, who dyed without issue" (MS.C); "and in him ended the whole male line of Sir

James Skene, eldest son of the Lord Register. The representation, therefore, devolved upon the descendants of his uncle, Mr. John of Halyards before mentioned " (MS.D).

Arms of Sir James Skene of Curriehill, from a Stone in Greyfriars Churchyard, Edinburgh.

Halgaards. Mitcham   date on the window 1630

SKENE OF HALYARDS IN MIDLOTHIAN.

I.—Mr. John Skene,

second son of Sir John Skene of Curriehill, Lord Register. " He being also a man of great knowledge in our laws, was appointed Clerk of the Bills, and one of the principal Clerks of Session."

On 5th March, 1614, Sir James Skene, on becoming a Lord of Session, resigned the Clerkship of the Bills to him.

" He afterwards acquired the lands and barony of Halyards, in Lothian, which became the chief title of his family " (MS.D).

There is a charter under the great seal, " Magistro Johanni Skeen de Halyards uni Clericorum Collegii Justitiae terrarum Baroniæ de Halyards, &c.," dated 24th March, 1650. " This was part of the ancient lordship of Liston, in the parish of Newliston, the original domain of the knights templars, afterwards of the lordship of St. John of Jerusalem " (MS.E).

He must have been a person of some accomplishment, as he is undoubtedly the author of the MS. collection of old Scottish airs, which has been printed by the Bannatyne Club, under the title of the Skene MS. It is supposed to have been written between 1615 and 1620, and at the end of the first part are the words, " Finis quod Skine," written in a hand which bears a strong resemblance to many specimens of his which have been preserved. The names " Magister Johannes Skeine," and " Magister Johannes Skeine, his book," appear on two of the fly-leaves. The editor adds, " the work bears internal evidence of its having been got up by a person of taste and judgment, exhibiting occasionally a simplicity, a beauty, and even a degree of elegance which, from anything we have seen of the productions of that age, we could scarcely have expected" (p. 15).

Mr. John Skene married, on 29th June, 1603, Alison Rigg, sister to William Rigg of Athernie, merchant burgess. Their contract of marriage, dated 4th June, 1603, is among the Curriehill papers.

By her he had three sons and six daughters—

I. John Skene, who succeeded him.

II. James Skene, born 17th April, 1622 ; and

III. Alexander Skene, born 20th May, 1625, who both appear to have died young.

IV. Helen Skene, born 9th May, 1605, married John Coupar of Gogar.

V. Margaret Skene married William Fairlie of Bruntsfield.

VI. Katharine Skene married Sir William Murray of Hermiston, second son of Patrick, first Lord Elibank.

VII. Jean Skeen married Sir Alexander Belches of Tofts, one of the Senators of the College of Justice.

VIII. Janet Skene, born 5th December, 1618, married, first, Major Home of Carlensyde ; and secondly, William Row.

IX. Alison Skene died unmarried.

Mr. John Skene of Halyards died in December, 1644. His will is here given, as a specimen of the language used in wills at that time :—

" I, Mr. John Skene of Halyards, one of the ordinar Clerks of Sessione, knawing nothing to be more certain nor death, the manner, time, and place to be most uncertain, mak my Testament and latter will as after followes. I thank my God and Jesus Christ for his manifold mercies towards me, but above all, for that great work of my redemptione, purchased to me in the blood of Jesus Christ, his onlie son, my Lord and Saviour, of whom onlie depends the salvatione of my soull. I mak, nominat, and constitute Mr. John Skene my onlie executor and universall legatour and intromitter, for his owne use, with my haill goods, geir, debts, soumes of money, and other moveabills perteining to me, the tyme of my deceis, quhan it sall be at the pleasure of God ; and I leave, assigne, and dispone my haill moveabill goods, soumes of money, to him with my blessing, perteining to me at the tyme of my deceis, and leaves the samyne in universall legacie to him, and maks him universall legator thereof, secluding all others, with power to him to intromitt therewith, use, and dispone thereupon at his pleasure, and to give up inventory, confirm this my testament. Item—I leave the soume of 300 merks to the poor of this burgh of Edinburgh. Item—I leave the soume of other 300 merks to the poor of the kirk and parish of Kirkliston, to help to be one stock for maintenance of the poor, to be employed at the sight of the gentlemen and minister, and kirk-session thereof. I leave to William Somerville, my servant, £100, and ordain my said executor to pay the said legacies within one half year after my decease. In witness whereof, I have written and subscribed these presents with my hand, at Edinburgh, the 26th day of April, 1641. Sic subscribitur Mr. John Skene, with my hand."

II.—MR. JOHN SKENE OF HALYARDS

succeeded his father in 1644.

"The said Mr. John's eldest son, Mr. John Skene of Halyards, married Mary Ker, daughter to   Ker of Mersingtone, who had two sons and two daughters" (MS.B).

Her marriage took place on 14th October, 1641, and she was daughter of James Ker of Mersington.

The sons were—

I. John Skene, who succeeded him.

II. Thomas Skene, who was an advocate, and married, on 6th April, 1677, Beatrix Hepburn, daughter of the Laird of Brunston, by whom he had three sons and two daughters—

1. Charles Skene, born 1st December, 1681, a sailor. Is mentioned, in 1714, as on board a third-rate man-of-war.

2. Francis Skene, born 5th September, 1684, an officer in the Royal Fusiliers, served in America, in 1737, where he died.

3. James Skene, mentioned in 1734.

4. Elizabeth Skene, born 25th May, 1678.

5. Catherine Skene, born 20th November, 1680.

Thomas Skene died in November, 1700, and, on 14th November, 1701, this testament dative and inventory is given up by Beatrix Hepburn, his relict, as only executrix dative, in virtue of the contract of marriage, dated 6th April, 1677, and in consideration of a decreet obtained by him on 16th August, 1701, against Charles, Francis, James, Elizabeth, and Katharine Skene, lawful children to the said deceased Mr. Thomas.

III. Alison Skene "married Mr. Alexander Swinton, Lord Mersington" (MS.B). One daughter of this marriage, Mary, married Brig.-Gen. Bruce of Kennet, and another daughter, Helen Swinton, married Colonel Charteris of Amisfield, and was mother of an only child, Janet, wife of James, 4th Earl of Wemyss.

IV. Helen Skene married Hugh Brown, apothecary chirurgeon of Edinburgh (MS.B).

On 31st July, 1666, there is a disposition by Mr. John Skene of Halyards, with consent of Mary Ker, his spouse, to John Skene, his eldest lawful son, of the lands of Halyards, with the principal messuage and manor place thereof, in the barony of Listoune and shire of Edinburgh.

He died before 1669, and was succeeded by his eldest son.

III.—JOHN SKENE OF HALYARDS.

There is, 22nd December, 1669, a renunciation by George Drummond of Carlowrie, in favour of John Skene, now of Halyards, of the lands and barony of Halyards, in the parish of Kirkliston, and shire of Edinburgh, held in reversion for the sum of 2500 merks, contained in bond of date 2nd December, 1664, granted by the deceased Mr. John Skene of Halyards, with consent of Marie Ker, his spouse, and the said John Skene, now of Halyards, designed in said bond their eldest lawful son and apparent heir.

John Skene originally studied law with Mr. David Wilson, writer, in Edinburgh, to whom he was bound apprentice in 1662, but afterwards entered the army, and is styled major in Sir William Douglas' regiment in 1688.

He married Janet Drummond, daughter to Drummond of Carlowrie, and had by her four sons and five daughters—

I. John Skene, born 16th February, 1675. He was an ensign in Lord Lindsay's regiment, and "was murdered by a Frenchman, by stabbing him in the heart, after the said ensign Skene's sword was broken, for which the said Frenchman was condemned, by a Council of War, to be shot to death in the Links of Leith, who thereafter got his pardon by the moyen of Sir Thomas Livingstoun, but was banished Scotland by the Privy Council, by the intent of his relations and friends. He (Ensign John) was not married" (MS.B). The duel took place at Kirkaldy in 1696.

II. George Skene, who succeeded his father.

III. Charles Skene, born 28th November, 1682, went to Virginia as a merchant, in 1704, and was never heard of again.

IV. Hugh Skene, born 3rd April, 1617, was ensign in General Lauder's regiment, and married in Holland Petronella van Sorgen. He died in garrison at Tournay, on 25th July, 1724, and had by her two sons—

    1. John Skene died at the age of 4, on 23rd February, 1726.

    2. Dromondus Skene died at the age of 5, on 6th December, 1727.

V. Eupham Skene married Mr. John Wilkie, minister of the gospel at Uphall.

VI. Janet Skene married Robert Kincaid of Over Gogar Mains.

VII. Helen Skene died unmarried.

VIII. Elizabeth Skene married the Rev. William Russell.

IX. Beatrice Skene died unmarried.

" John Skene having entered into some unsuccessful speculations with his brother-in-law, Drummond of Carlowrie, both became insolvent about the year 1680 " (MS.E). His estate was eventually evicted from him in the year 1694, and was purchased, at a judicial sale carried on before the Lords of Session by his creditors, by his brother, Thomas, who resold it in 1696 to Mr. Marjoribanks.

" It was sold to his brother for the sum of 36,446 merks, and resold to Mr. Edward Marjoribanks, merchant, in Edinburgh, for 44,000 merks." The decreet of sale is dated in 1696.

John Skene died in 1717.

" 27th February, 1717, John Skene of Halyards buried the 27th, 2 foot north Swintons, rough ston, aged ——."

IV.—George Skene,

eldest surviving son of John Skene of Halyards, was a lieutenant in the Fusiliers, which was Brigadier Row's regiment.

He married Elizabeth Currie, and had by her two children—

I. John Skene.

II. Elizabeth Skene.

He was wounded at the battle of Hochstedt, of which he died in 1733, and in 26th February, 1744, the testament dative of the deceased Lieutenant George Skene of the royal regiment of Scots Fusiliers, who died at Bath, 6th June, 1733, is given up by Elizabeth Skene, his daughter, with consent of Elizabeth Skene, *alias* Currie, his relict, as his curatrix.

R

V.—JOHN SKENE.

On 2nd February, 1756, the testament dative of the deceased
John Skene, only lawful son of Lieutenant George Skene of the royal
regiment of Scots Fusiliers, who died in the Canongate, 11th March,
1737, gyven up by Elizabeth Skene, only child, in life, of Lieutenant
George Skene, decerned executrix dative to the deceased John Skene,
her brother-german ; and with him died the last male descendant of Sir
John Skene of Curriehill.

On 22nd December, 1787, his sister, Elizabeth Skene, laid before the
Faculty of Advocates a petition praying for some help, as the great-
great-grand-daughter of Sir John Skene of Curriehill, who was the
Lord-Advocate in the year 1592, and received from them a pension of
£10. "She had likewise a pension of £20 a-year from Government.
After reaching an advanced age she died unmarried, and on 18th
January, 1796, the Faculty, on a representation by Mr. Russell, of
Selkirk, nearest relation of Mrs. Elizabeth Skene, lately deceased,
defrayed the expenses of her funeral.

*Arms of Skene of Halyards In Lothian, from the MS. of Sir David Lindsay the Younger
(styled in error, Skene of Skene).*

SKENE OF BELHELVIE.

I.—ROBERT SKENE,

son of James Skene, in Bandodle, afterwards of Westercorse, first appears in the Council Register of Aberdeen, on 23rd January, 1567, when he constitutes Mr. William Davidson his procurator, in all his actionis and caussis, and specialie agains Patrik Mamwir; and on 1st October, 1571, he is admitted a burgess of Aberdeen.

In 1572 he appears among the *absentes* in the burgess roll: his reason being that he had now settled in Belhelvie. This appears from an entry in the Council Register, on 9th March, 1572, when the magistrates give a decreet against Patrick Mamvir, for a debt due to Robert Skeyne in Bahelvie, payable either to him or to Andrew Skeyne in Aberdeen, who we have seen was his brother.

The parish of Belhelvie consists of—1st, the barony of Belhelvie, possessed at this time by the family of Glammes, and afterwards by that of Panmure. 2nd, a few separate properties, as Many, Colpnay, Pettens, and Westbourne belonging to the town, Blairtoun and Hophill, and the Kirktown of Belhelvie. The barony is the southern part of the parish, and extends to a small stream at Eggie. Through the centre of the barony a stream flows through a ravine past the present Belhelvie Lodge. It rises in the farm of Craigies, and passes through Whytecairns, Overhill, Old Overtown, Upper Potterton, Mylne of Potterton, and Mylneden, where it falls into the sea, and south of Mylneden, along the shore, were the farms of Fife and Blackdog. These farms, with the exception of Craigies, were the possessions of the Skenes in Belhelvie. The Mylne of Potterton, with Overhill and Old Overtown, was then known as the Over Mylne, and Mylneden as the Nether Mylne.

Robert Skene possessed the former. He was twice married, 1st, to a daughter of David Ædie, merchant, burgess of Aberdeen, by his wife Isobel Forbes, by whom he had—

I. Robert Skene, who went to Poland, and in 1593 was made a burgess of Posen. The following entry appears in that year in the records of the town of Posen—"Significamus tenore presentium quibus expedit, quod coram nobis, Proconsule, Advocato, Scabiciis totaque Communitate Civitatis nostræ suæ Regiæ Majestatis Posnaniensis personaliter comparens

Nobilis Robertus Skin, Scotice Skene, vocatus, annorum circiter 43 habens, supplicavit nos, ut eum ad communitatem nostrae civitatis Posnaniensis cum omnibus juribus, quibus alii concives et incolæ ejusdem civitatis gaudere agnosceremur. Nos petitioni ejusdem nobilis Skin (Skene) annuentes, ejusdem authoritate nostra ad communitatem aliorum Incolarum nostræ civitatis Posnaniensis associamus dando et concedendo eidem omnibus privilegiis juribusque civitati nostræ servientibus a die hodierna uti frui et pro semper gaudere."

(sequuntur subscriptiones.)

II. Gilbert Skene. There is a decreet against Gilbert Skene, in Over-hill, for a spulzie committed in 1584. He is again mentioned as in Overhill in 1597, with Robert Skene, his son, and likewise in 1602.

He appears to have married Marjory Rolland, and to have had two sons, Andrew Skene and Robert Skene, as we find the half lands of Overhill occupied, in 1602, by Andrew Skene and Marjory Rolland, his mother, and a fourth part by Robert Skene.

In 1603 we find Robert Skene in Overtown of Belhelvie, and Andrew Skene, another son, we find, 1609, in Overhill of Belhelvie.

III. David Skene appears to have gone as a young man to Poland, and was admitted burgess of Posen in 1586.

"Actum feria sexta post festam Sancti Bartholomæi Apostoli Anno 1586 David Skin Scotus jus civile suscepit die et anno quibus infra" (Extractum ex libro Albo civitatis Posnaniensis).

He returned, however, as early as 1593 to Belhelvie, as in 11th June, 1597, there is a horning against David Skene at the Mylne of Potterton, on a bond, dated at Aberdeen, 7th June, 1593, and served personalie upon him at his dwalland place of the Mylne of Potterton in the end of 1596.

In 1606 there is a bond by David Skene, at the Mylne of Potterton, as principal, and Robert Skene and Andrew Skene, in Townhill of Belhelvie, as cautioners.

David Skene was twice married : first to Udnye's sister, by whom he had—

1. Thomas Skene, mentioned in Potterton, in 1623, with a house. He was an elder of the Church of Belhelvie from 1623 to to 1632, and again from 1643 to 1645, when he was returned as ruling elder to the Presbytery.

   In 1629, on the failure of the sons of Gilbert Skene in Overhill, he succeeded to the possessions of Overhill and Overtown, and in 1638 we find him in Milnden. He married Sara Leask, a daughter of William Leask of Leask and Isabell Ogilvy, his wife, by whom he had—

   1. Robert Skene, born in Potterton, in 1621. He was ancestor of the Skenes of Rubislaw.

   2. John Skene, born there in 1628.

   3. Hew Skene, born in Overhill in 1631.

   4. A son, born in Old Overton in 1632.

   5. Alexander Skene, born in Old Overton in 1636.

   6. Anna Skene, married in 1639 to Alexander Forbes in Foveran, Thomas Skene, in Milnden, her father.

2. David Skene, second son of David Skene at Mylne of Potterton, went to Poland and became a merchant in Zamoski. He married Margaret Chalmers, daughter of Robert Chalmers, merchant, Dantzig, and had two sons and one daughter—

   1. George Skene, born in Zamoski 17th September, 1644.

   2. Alexander Skene, birth not recorded.

   3. Katharine Skene, born in Zamoski 3rd October, 1646, married David Adie of Newark.

David Skene at the Mylne of Potterton married a second time in 20th August, 1606, Claris Seaton, by whom he had one son and two daughters—

3. George Skene, afterwards Sir George Skene of Rubislaw.

4. Jeane Skene, married 8th May, 1637, to Alexander Clarke, son to William Clarke in Haltoun.

5. Marjory Skene married, 8th July, 1627, Alexander Hay in Foveran.

IV. John Skene, fourth son of Robert Skene in Belhelvie, appears, on 9th July, 1595, in Potterton, and on 12th March, 1598, in Whyte-cairns. He is last mentioned in 1599, and appears to have died without issue.

V. Thomas Skene is mentioned in the Privy Council Records as tenant, on 16th February, 1601, of Whytecairns, along with Gilbert Skene of Overhill, Robert Skene, his son, and David Skene, at the Mylne of Potterton. He is ancestor of the Skenes of Blackdog, &c.

VI. Violet Skene married, in 1602, John Forbes.

Robert Skene, in Belhelvie, married, secondly, on 6th July, 1574, at Forbes, Margrett Forbes, and had by her one son and one daughter—

VII. James Skene, who became servitor to Sir John Skene of Curriehill. He received numerous grants of escheat in the Privy Seal Records, and in one on 6th July, 1597, he is termed "James Skene, son to umquhile Robert Skene of Overmylne." In another, on 10th March, 1598, he is termed "James Skene, lawfull sone to umquhile Robert Skene, burgess of Aberdeen." On 20th June, 1599, he witnesses a deed by Mr. John Skene, Clerk Register, in which he is designed "brother sone to the said Sir John Skene;" on 27th January, 1604, he is decerned executor, as brother sone to Dr. Gilbert Skene, Sir John's brother; and again on 16th June, 1617, Robert and Janet Skenes are mentioned as "brether bairnes to the defunct" Dr. Gilbert Skene. He died in October, 1651, having married Jean Hamilton, and had by her—

1. Jean Skene, born 12th January, 1626.
2. James Skene, born 24th March, 1628.

1652. Testament dative of umquhile James Skene, writer in Edinburgh, who died in October, 1651, given up by James Skene, younger, sone lawful to the said umquhile defunct.

James Skene, younger, writer in Edinburgh, died before 1673, when we find, in the Curriehill papers, a bond, by John Skene of Halyards, to John Skene, sone to the deceased James Skene, younger, writer in Edinburgh; but with this notice we lose all farther trace of his descendants.

VIII. Janet Skene.

Robert Skene, in Belhelvie, died before the year 1597, and probably in the year 1593, as in that year we find a change taking place in the position of his family. Robert becomes a burgess of Posen in that year, and David returns from Poland, and becomes permanent occupier of the Overmylne, or Mylne of Potterton.

II.—THOMAS SKENE,

the youngest son by the first marriage, appears to have succeeded his brother John in the occupation of Whytecairns. The notices of this family are somewhat scanty, and are mainly derived from the parish records of Belhelvie. He seems to have been succeeded by

III.—GILBERT SKENE,

probably his son. In 1624 we find the marriage of Gilbert Skene and Margaret Smyth; and in 1626 we have mention of Gilbert Skene in Whytecairns. His successor was

IV.—PATRICK SKENE

in Whytecairns, who died in the year 1704, leaving three sons—

I. James Skene.

II. Andrew Skene in Whytecairns, married on 8th July, 1704, Elizabeth Perry (James Skene, cautioner for the man), and had a daughter, Margaret, and a son, John, born 12th April, 1710.

III. Patrick Skene settled in Old Aberdeen, and married in 17th June, 1701, Elspeth Rhind, heiress of Thomas Rhind, merchant, by whom he had—

   1. George Skene, born in 1706.

   2. Thomas Skene, born 13th January, 1713. In 1774 Thomas Skene, merchant, Old Aberdeen, only living son of Peter Skene, merchant there, and Elspeth Rhind, served heir to his mother. He was one of the magistrates of Old Aberdeen, and was well known as Baillie Skene of the Auldtown. He died without issue in 1797.

V.—JAMES SKENE

removed, in 1707, to the farm of Blackdog, leaving Whytecairns to his brother Andrew. He had the following children :—

   I. Patrick Skene, born in Whytecairns 9th July, 1699.

   II. Alexander Skene, born in Whytecairns 16th March, 1701, died in April, 1703.

   III. Isobell Skene, born in Whytecairns 8th April, 1703.

   IV. Thomas Skene, born in Blackdog 16th October, 1707.

   V. Jean Skene, born in Blackdog 22nd November, 1709.

   VI. Margaret Skene, born in Blackdog 25th May, 1712.

   VII. Elizabeth Skene, born in Blackdog 24th October, 1714.

VI.—PATRICK SKENE

in Blackdog, was succeeded by his son.

VII.—THOMAS SKENE

in Blackdog, had two sons—

I. Thomas Skene.

II. Alexander Skene, an officer in the army, who married Katharine Anderson, daughter of John Anderson, farmer, Slains, and had two sons and one daughter—

1. Thomas Skene, who died.

2. Alexander Skene, who settled in Australia.

3. Margaret Skene married George Auldjo Esson, accountant in bankruptcy, Edinburgh.

He married, 2ndly, Margaret Auldjo, daughter of George Auldjo of Portlethen ; and died 21st May, 1865.

VIII.—THOMAS SKENE

removed to the adjacent farm of Fyfe, and married Elspett Browne, by whom he had a large family.

I. Thomas Skene married Mary Gilderoy, and had by her—

1. Isabella Skene.

2. Thomas Alexander Skene, grain merchant.

II. David Skene in Langseat, married   Mill, and had by her—

1. Ann Skene.

2. Thomas Skene settled in Australia.

3. Elspett Skene.

4. Margaret Skene.

5. Eliza Skene.

III. Alexander Skene, farmer in Fife.

IV. William Skene went, in 1839, to Australia, and became a member of the firm of W. Robertson & Sons. In 1850 he dissolved partnership, and became the proprietor of an estate near Hamilton, which has since borne his name. In 1870 he was returned as a member of the Legislative Council, by the electors of the western province.

He married Jane Robertson, and died in March, 1877, leaving the following children :—

    1. Thomas Skene.

    2. Jane Catharine Skene.

    3. William Robertson Skene.

    4. Margaret Skene.

    5. David Skene.

  V. Jane Skene married John Crawford of Tarbathill.

 VI. Eliza Skene married John Jenkins.

VII. Laurence Skene, bank agent in Portree, married Jane Tolmie, and died, leaving four sons and two daughters.

Thomas Skene is now dead.

RUBIESLAW.

SKENE OF RUBISLAW.

I.—GEORGE SKENE,

son of David Skene, at the Mylne of Potterton, by Claris Seaton, his second wife, afterwards Sir George Skene of Wester Fintray and Rubislaw, was born in the year 1619.

" His father and mother dying poor, David Skene, merchant, in Poland, his elder brother, by the father's side, brought him over to Poland, and bound him apprentice to Mr. George Adie, then merchant in Dantzick, where he learnt his trade, by which he acquired a handsome fortune there, and returned with it to Scotland. Purchased the lands of Wester Fintray and Robeslaw, &c., and was made Provost of Aberdeen, which he kept for 9 years, before the Revolution. As Provost Skene never married himself, and his elder brother, David, and his wife dying poor in Poland, he sent for his two sons and the daughter, and brought them to Scotland, and put the eldest son, George, in fee of his estate of Wester Fintray under redemption, and married the daughter, Katharine, to David Adie, eldest son of Mr. George Adie, his old master. His nephews, George and Alexander, turned out quite profligate and debauched, and to supply their extravagances broke open Sir George's cabinet and robbed him, which, with their other conduct, so disobliged him at them that he redeemed the lands of Wester Fintray, and disinherited them, and they both went abroad and never returned, and he then settled the lands of Fintray upon David Adie's daughter, Giles, when she was married to the Laird of Skene, and the heirs male of that marriage. Sir George Skene was born An. 1619, and died in April, 1707, aged 88" (MS.D).

This account is substantially correct. His father died in 1631, when George was twelve years old. He was in Dantzig till about the year 1665, when he returned to Aberdeen.

In 1666 he purchased the lands of Wester Fintray, in which he was infeft 9th July, 1666. On 17th September, 1668, he granted a charter of these lands in favour of his nephew, George Skene, eldest son of the deceased David Skene, merchant, burgess of Zamoski, in the kingdom of Poland, and to the heirs male of his body ; whom failing, to Alexander Skene, younger son of the said David, and the heirs male of his body ; whom failing, to George Skene, eldest son of Robert Skene, sometime treasurer of Aberdeen, and the heirs male of his body ; whom all failing, to John Skene of that Ilk, and his heirs and assignees whomsoever, bearing the surname and arms of Skene. The contract of marriage, dated 8th February, 1690, by which Sir George narrates his having redeemed the lands of Wester Fintray, and settles them upon Giles Adie on her marriage with Alexander Skene of Skene, has already been quoted in the notice of that family.

On 9th April, 1669, he obtained a disposition from Andrew Skene of Ruthrieston and Robert Skene, Junior, his eldest son, of certain tenements of land in the Guestrow of Aberdeen.

In 1676 George Skene became Provost of Aberdeen, which office he held till the year 1685. In 1678, 1681 and 1685 he was sent by the town as commissioner to Parliament. In 1681, when James, Duke of York, came to Scotland, George Skene, with David Adie late Baillie, was sent by the Council to Edinburgh to wait upon His Royal Highness in name of the town, and to entreat his favour in what may concern the same ; on which occasion he received the honour of knighthood. In 1685, the Provost presented to the King an address on his accession to the throne, as James the Second.

In 1687 Sir George Skene acquired the lands of Rubislaw, by adjudication, from the Forbeses of Rubislaw. They were conveyed to "Sir George Skene of Fintray, knight, late Provost of Aberdeen, in liferent, during all the days of his lifetime, and to George Adie, lawful son to David Adie, of Newark, late Baillie of Aberdeen, procreat betwixt him and Catherine Skene his spouse, his heirs male, and assignees therein specified, in fee, heritably and irredeemably, but under reversion, redemption, or regress, conform to the letter of disposition, granted hereanent, of the date of the 29th October, 1687 years."

The lands were redeemed by an instrument of consignation and redemption, in 1706, by Sir George Skene, against George Adie, in virtue

Sir George Skene's House. Guestrow. Aberdeen.

of the power received in the disposition to alter the destination upon consignation of a certain sum; and by disposition, dated 13th December, 1706, Sir George Skene conveys the lands of Rubislaw to himself in liferent, and to Mr. George Skene, his grand-nephew, one of the Regents of King's College, in fee, and to the heirs male of his body; burdened with the sum of 14,000 merks, to be paid to Mr. David Adie, and an obligation upon all heirs or singular successors succeeding to or endowing the said lands, to bear the proper arms and cognisance of Sir George Skene, and to assume the surname of Skene.

The arms, recorded some thirty years earlier in the Lyon Register, are: "Gules a chevron argent betwixt three skens of the second hefted and pomelld or, surmounted of als many woolfs heads couped of the third tusked proper." Crest: "A dexter hand issuing out of ane cloud reaching a garland of Lawrell fructuated." Motto: "Gratis a Deo data."

On 24th March, 1707, Sir George Skene executed a will, nominating Mr. George Skene, Regent, his executor and universal legator, and died in the following April, and his death, with that of his nephew, Robert Skene, is thus inscribed in the burial place of the Rubislaw family in St. Nicholas Churchyard:

HIC IACENT CINERES DÑI
GEORGII SKENE A FINTRAY ET
ROBSLAW MILITIS NOVEM QUONDAM
ANNIS PRÆPOSITI AĒD QUI OBIIT 9
APRILIS 1707 ÆTATIS 88
AC ETIAM ROBERTI SKENE MERCATORIS
SUI NEPOTIS QUI OBIIT 30 OCTOBRIS
1693 ÆTATIS 72.

This Robert Skene was eldest son of Thomas Skene, who was eldest son of David Skene, at Mylne of Potterton, and half-brother of Sir George. On 1st April, 1662, Robertus Skene mercator filius legitimus quondam Thomæ Skene de Belhelvie is admitted a burgess of Aberdeen. He became treasurer of the town of Aberdeen, and married Janet Jaffray, daughter of John Jaffray of Delspro, Provost of Aberdeen, by whom he had—

I. Janet Skene, baptised 9th May, 1665; married, 27th January, 1694, George Gordon, son of Alexander Gordon, Provost of Aberdeen.

II. George Skene, baptised 24th June, 1666.

II.—Mr. George Skene of Rubislaw—1707-1708,

at the time he succeeded to the estate, in 1707, was Professor of Philosophy and Regent of King's College, Aberdeen, an office which he had held since 1686. "His stipend, as Professor of Philosophy, was £175 Scots, 15 bolls of bear, and 9 bolls of meal. The ancient mansion which he inhabited in Old Aberdeen, opposite the College, was taken down in 1816. He married his cousin, Catharine Adie, and had a numerous family. Tradition reports his having been visited, a year after his marriage, by three heavy misfortunes at the same time. A careless nurse overlaid his eldest son, by which the infant was smothered; the woman fled in the middle of the night and never more heard of. His house was consumed by fire, and the family obliged to take shelter with their neighbours. The third misfortune I do not recollect" (MS.E).

He had by Catherine Adie, daughter of David Adie of Newark, his wife, the following children:—

I. George Skene, who succeeded him.

II. Robert Skene died unmarried in March 1709.

III. Janet Skene married John Anderson, Professor in Marischal College.

IV. Katherine Skene married Alexander Thomson, advocate, in Aberdeen, and died 4th March, 1776, aged 73.

V. Margaret Skene married Thomas Finnie of Wellbrae.

He died at Rubislaw on 12th December, 1708, having possessed the estate only one year.

His death, and that of his wife, are thus recorded on the tombstone, after that of his father, Robert:—

NECNON Mʳⁱ
GEORGII SKENE DE ROBSLAW HUIUS
FILII QUI FATIS DECESSIT 12 DE
CEMBRIS 1708 ÆTATIS 41
ET CATHARINÆ ÆDIE SUÆ CONIU
GIS QUÆ OBIIT 7 SEPTEMBRIS 1738
ÆTATIS 59

III.—George Skene of Rubislaw—1709-1757,

served heir to his father, Mr. George Skene, Regent of King's College, and likewise to his great-grand-uncle, Sir George Skene, both on 12th February, 1709. The evidence taken in the latter service proves the descent from David Skene of Mylne of Potterton as well as the family of the latter.

"He married Helen Thomson, daughter to Portlethen, and step-daughter to his mother, Catharine Adie. They were ten years married without having any children, after which they had a daughter, Helen Skene, to whom, as the estate was a male fee, it could not have descended, so that her father executed a deed in her favour for 80,000 merks of provision. As a son was afterwards born, of the name of George, this precaution became unnecessary, and her provision was limited to 10,000 merks. She married, in 1753, James Duff, advocate, in Aberdeen, youngest son of Alexander Duff of Hatton, of which marriage was George Duff, captain in the navy, who was killed at the battle of Trafalgar, where he commanded the Mars line-of-battle ship" (MS.E).

The tombstone record continues:—

AC Georgii Skene de Robslaw eorum
Filii qui obiit 21 Julii 17 [57] Ætatis 58
Nec non Heleneæ Skene ejus Filiæ
Sponsæ Jacobi Duff Advocati
Abredonensi quae obiit 12 Mar
Anno MDCCLXIV Ætatis 30
cum Helena Thomson sponsa dicti
Georgii Skene Junioris de Robslaw quæ
obiit 29no Julii 1768 Ætatis anno 68vo

George Skene of Rubislaw was succeeded by his son,

IV.—George Skene of Rubislaw—1757-1776,

born in 1736, and married to Jane Moir, eldest daughter of James Moir of Stoneywood, whose history has been detailed in an interesting and graphic narrative by the late Dr. John Brown, in the third series of his "Horæ

Subsecivæ," p. 83, under the title of " A Jacobite Family :"—" Having three daughters before a son was born, he entered into a treaty with the magistrates of Aberdeen, superiors of the lands of Rubislaw, to have the holding altered from a male fee to heirs whatsoever, which was obtained upon payment of £250 sterling. It was intended by the late Mr. Skene that his son should follow the profession of the law, with which view, while a youth, he attended the office of his uncle, Thomson of Portlethen ; but unfortunately his disposition was of too lively a cast for so plodding a profession, and as none more congenial were suggested to him, his circumstances being independent, he yielded to the conviviality of his disposition, giving up his time to gaiety and amusement, and soon became the delight of the society he frequented in Aberdeen. He sang well, played on various instruments, composed humorous songs, caricatures, and lampoons, in which fun and good humour always predominated ; constantly inventing some amusing frolic, of which his uncle, Portlethen, a pompous, portly man, and his cousin, Miss Finnie, a starched, antiquated virgin, were frequent subjects. Indeed he not unfrequently subjected the whole inhabitants of the town to his frolics, by various successful and amusing hoaxes, which to this day continue to afford merriment in the narration, by those of his contemporaries still in life, who were witnesses of his inventive and good humoured disposition. With a view to wean him from those unprofitable pursuits, his friends prevailed upon him to go to Edinburgh, to study law, where he remained for some time, but without much improving his taste for that dry pursuit ; which, as happens not unfrequently with young men who have the misfortune to possess a moderate independence, ended in a resolution to abandon the attempt altogether, and rest satisfied with the fruits of his paternal fortune. The remainder of his life was passed at Rubislaw, in the fulness of convivial indulgence, which soon ushered in its train that surly monitor the gout, whose attacks became so frequent and habitual as to occasion his having recourse to the Bath waters, where the family passed a winter; but without success, as a severe attack in the stomach occurred in the year 1776, of which he died on the 24th January, at the age of 40" (MS.E).

His legal studies do not, however, seem to have been utterly fruitless, for, as all the male representatives of the Curriehill family who stood between that family and the Skenes of Rubislaw had become

extinct, he appears to have formed a plan to prove his own representation of the family, and take up the dormant baronetcy. With this view
we find him having his papers examined by an antiquary and genealogist
of some local celebrity, the late Mr. Rose of Banff; but an accident which
befel the charter chest destroyed many of the family papers, and
prevents us from knowing more than the result of the examination.
" Upon the death of George Skene of Rubislaw, on 24th January, 1776,
the charter chest was conveyed to Aberdeen, and deposited in the house
of the late Alexander Carnegie, Esq., Town Clerk. Being of iron, and
very weighty, it was left in a low, damp appartment, or rather cellar,
with an earthen floor, which, in the period of one-and-twenty years that
it was suffered to be exposed to damp, so completely rotted the bottom
of the chest, that upon its removal, the bottom remained on the ground,
reduced to an ochry clay, and with it a layer of about three inches thick
of the old family parchments and papers, in a state of destruction utterly
irredeemable, in fact resembling a mass of rotten tobacco, which fell to
pieces on being touched " (MS.E).

Mr. Rose, however, had noted some of its contents in his note
books, in which are the following entries :—

" Sir James Skene of Curriehill, created knight baronet, which I have
seen at Robslaw."

" Skene, Sir James, of Curriehill, knight and baronet, President of the
College of Justices, died at Edinburgh, interred in Greyfriars, 20th
October, 1633. Represented by Robslaw."

His early death probably prevented the claim from being prosecuted,
and the patent which seems to have come into his possession perished
with the rest of the destroyed papers.

George Skene of Rubislaw left the following children, by his wife,
Jane Moir, who died in Edinburgh on 29th March, 1820, aged 79,
having been 44 years a widow.

I. Margaret Skene, born 4th September, 1767; married Colonel
Ramsay of the 2nd or Queen's Regiment of Foot, and had issue.

II. Helen Skene, born 13th August, 1768; remained unmarried, and
died at Florence in 1841.

III. Catherine Skene, born 20th Oct., 1769; married Sir Henry
Jardine, King's Remembrancer of Exchequer, and had issue.
She died in 1838.

IV. George Skene, born 14th December, 1770.

V. Jean Skene, born 5th December, 1771; died in infancy at Rubislaw.

VI. Maria Skene, born 22nd December, 1773; died in infancy at Aberdeen.

VII. James Skene, born 7th March, 1775.

V.—George Skene of Rubislaw—1776-1791.

"George Skene, a minor, succeeded his father in 1776, chose the profession of the army, and was sent to Douay, in France, to promote his studies at the military academy there, and upon his return got a commission in the 46th Regiment of Foot, then in Ireland, where he remained three years; and, having attained the rank of lieutenant, returned to Scotland near the close of his minority, in order to be served heir to his father, an event which, though then in the vigour of health and youth, it was not his fate to accomplish. He had gone to Aberdeenshire for that purpose, in summer, 1791, from whence he proceeded, for his amusement, to visit the Highlands, travelling on horseback, in the course of which he stopped at Nairn, on a very stormy night of rain, when a family with ladies arrived late, whom, as the house was full, it was impossible to accommodate; and they, being averse to proceed further, during bad weather, unfortunately applied to Mr. Skene to give up his room. With this request he generously complied, though unwell at the time, ordered his horse, and set off to ride to Inverness in a cold and stormy night, where he arrived, drenched with rain. An access of fever was the natural consequence, which he incautiously disregarded, and proceeded next day to visit Beauly, where it became so violent that it was necessary to send back to Inverness for a carriage to reconvey him there to Ettles' inn, where, in two days afterwards, he expired in presence of Mr. Ettles, the landlord, who narrated the circumstances afterwards to me. His body was conveyed to Aberdeen, and interred in the family burying-ground in St. Nicholas Churchyard, but a week after he had left that town, in the bloom of health and youth, on the 30th September, 1791, in his 21st year" (MS.E).

VI.—James Skene of Rubislaw—1791-1864.

The following notice of Mr. Skene occurs in the opening address delivered to the Royal Society of Edinburgh on Monday, the 4th December, 1865, by Sir David Brewster, who had been through life his personal friend :—

" James Skene of Rubislaw was born on the 7th March, 1775. His father died in the following year, leaving a widow and a family of seven children. In 1783, Mrs. Skene removed to Edinburgh for their education, and James, who was then the second son and youngest child, was placed at the High School ; and was the last survivor of a host of distinguished men who were his class-fellows.

" In 1791, after he had left the High School, he succeeded to the family-estate of Rubislaw, by the death of his elder brother ; and at the age of twenty-one, he was sent to Germany to complete his studies. After acquiring a knowledge of the French and German languages he returned to Edinburgh, and was admitted to the Scotch bar in 1797. Here he formed an acquaintance with Sir Walter Scott, which ripened into a close and life-long friendship. Mr. Skene had early shown a love of art, and a singular talent for drawing, to which Sir Walter alludes in the introduction to the 4th canto of Marmion, which is dedicated to Mr. Skene—

'As thou with pencil, I with pen,
The features traced of hill and glen.'

" In 1797 Mr. Skene was appointed cornet of the Edinburgh Light Horse, one of the earliest regiments of volunteers, which was organised mainly by the efforts of Sir Walter Scott. After walking the Parliament House for a few years, Mr. Skene revisited the continent in 1802, and travelled over the greater part of Europe during the next few years. In this journey he became acquainted with Mr. Greenough, President of the Geological Society of London, and travelled for some time with that distinguished geologist. He thus acquired a taste for geology, and was afterwards elected a member of the Geological Society.

" In 1806 Mr. Skene married Jane, daughter of Sir William Forbes of Pitsligo, Bart., and settled on a small property he possessed in Kincardineshire, where he spent the next eight years of his life.

"In 1816 Mr. Skene returned to Edinburgh, for the education of his children, when he joined the different literary and scientific societies, which at that time were not in a very flourishing state. He became a member of the Royal Society in 1817, and as Curator of their Library and Museum, an office which he held for many years, he did eminent service to that important department of the Society. He was also a member of the Antiquarian Society, and took an active part in its reform and restoration.

"During his residence in Edinburgh, Mr. Skene explored and sketched the various buildings in the Old Town that were remarkable for their antiquity or historical interest, and he has left a valuable collection of these sketches, which we trust may be given to the public.   .

"Mr. Skene held for many years the office of Secretary to the Board of Trustees and Manufactures, and in this capacity he did much for the promotion of the fine arts in Scotland.

"In 1838, when the health of some of his family required a warmer climate, he went to Greece, and settled in the vicinity of Athens. In an elegant villa, built by himself, he spent eight years ; and he has left behind him a series of beautiful water-colour drawings, upwards of 500 in number, of the scenery and antiquities of that interesting country.

"On his return to England in 1844, he took up his residence in Leamington. He afterwards went to Oxford, and resided in a curious old mansion, called Frewen Hall, where he enjoyed the best literary society in that seat of learning. After a residence there of nearly fifteen years, he died on the 27th of November, 1864, in the 90th year of his age.

"Mr. Skene was a man of very elegant tastes and numerous accomplishments. He had a great general knowledge of science as well as of literature, and spoke with fluency French, German, and Italian. He was, as Sir Walter Scott said, 'the first amateur draughtsman in Scotland,' and was the author of two volumes of Illustrations of the Waverley Novels. But though he used his pencil more than his pen, yet he made several contributions to the Transactions of the Societies to which he belonged, and was the author of the excellent article on painting in the Edinburgh Encyclopædia."

The preceding notice, though long, is valuable, as proceeding from the pen of so eminent a man as Sir David Brewster, and has therefore been inserted in place of an original notice of Mr. Skene, which would not come so appropriately from his son. It may be added that the full page illustrations to this volume are from his drawings.

His body was removed to Edinburgh, and interred beside the remains of his wife, who died in November, 1862, in his burying-ground at St. John's Episcopal Church there. He was survived by the following children :—

I. George Skene, born at Edinburgh, 23rd October, 1807.

II. William Forbes Skene, born at Inverie, 7th June, 1809.

III. Eliza Skene, born at Inverie, 21st October, 1810, married at Athens in 1840, the Baron Charles de Heidenstam, Swedish Minister at Athens, and died 21st February, 1886, leaving issue.

IV. James Henry Skene, born at Inverie, 3rd March, 1812. He entered the army, and after serving some years in the 73rd Regiment, sold his commission, and settled in Greece, and in 1832 married Rhalou, daughter of Jakovaki Rizo Rangabé, the head of an old and influential Fanariot family, by his wife, Zoe, daughter of Eustache Lapati, Secretary of State for Moldavia. He eventually became attached to the service of Lord Stratford de Redcliffe, English Ambassador at Constantinople, and for his services during the Crimean war was appointed Vice Consul at Constantinople, and afterwards Consul-General at Aleppo, from which office he retired in 1880, and died at Geneva on 3rd October, 1886. He was author of the " Frontier Lands of the Christian and the Turk;" " Anadol, the Last Home of the Faithful;" "Rambles in the Syrian Deserts;" and " With Lord Stratford in the Crimean War." He left the following children:—

1. Felix James Henry Skene, Clerk in the House of Lords, married, 15th December, 1871, Jane Elizabeth Huddleston Hossack, second daughter of Angus Hossack, Esq., and has issue, besides a son and two daughters died in childhood—

William Forbes, born 5th August, 1873.

James Henry, born 3rd December, 1877.

George Alexander, born 6th July, 1880.

Ethel Mary. Zoe. Olive Maud.

2. Reverend George William Charles Skene, Rector of Barthomley, Crewe, married, in 1885, Mary Maud, daughter of the late Honourable Edward Morris Erskine, Minister Plenipotentiary

at Athens and at Stockholm, and widow of William John Percy Lawton, Esq. of Lawton Hall.

3. Zoe Skene married, in 1855, the Reverend William Thomson, D.D., Provost of Queen's College, Oxford, preacher of Lincoln's Inn, and chaplain to the Queen ; in 1861 appointed Bishop of Gloucester and Bristol, and in 1862 Archbishop of York, and has issue—

Wilfrid Forbes Home, born 29th March, 1858, banker in York.

Jocelyn Home, born 31st August, 1859, Captain Royal Artillery, married, in 1886, Mabel Sophia, daughter of the Rev. Canon Paget.

Basil Home, born 21st April, 1861, Commissioner of Colo, Fiji.

Bernard Henry Home, born 9th January, 1874.

Ethel Zoe, married, in 1887, the Rev. F. W. Goodwyn.

Zoe Jane.

Beatrice Mary, married, in 1886, Henry Edward, only son of T. H. Preston, Esq. of Moreby Hall.

Alexandra.   Madiline Ita Mary.

4. Jane Skene married, in 1863, the Reverend Lloyd Stewart Bruce, Canon of York, and fourth son of Sir James Bruce of Downhill, Bart. She died in September, 1880, leaving issue—

Robert Douglas, B.A., born 30th March, 1867.

Lloyd Hervey, born 21st April, 1868.

Francis Rosslyn Courteney, born 14th August, 1871.

Wilfrid Montagu, born 26th October, 1874.

Ellen Mary.

Zoe Mary, married, in 1885, Rev. Charles Spencer, Newham.

Irene Mary.   Grace Guendolen.   Rosamond Hilda.

Helen Jane Theodora.   Edith Agnes Kathleen.

V. Catherine Skene, born at Inverie, 9th May, 1815, married in 1841 John Foster Grierson, Esq., Queen's Printer for Ireland, and has one surviving son.

VI. Caroline Christian Skene, born at Edinburgh, 23rd November, 1818, married, in 1840, Alexandre Rizo Rangabé, her sister-in-

law's brother, who has filled the office of Greek Minister at Paris and at Berlin. She died in 5th December, 1878, leaving issue.
VII. Felicia Mary Frances Skene, born at Aix en Provence on 23rd May, 1821, is unmarried, and resident at Oxford. She is authoress of "Wayfaring Sketches among the Greeks and the Turks;" "Use and Abuse;" "Hidden Depths;" "The Divine Master;" "The Lesters, a family record;" and other Novels and Tales.

VII.—GEORGE SKENE OF RUBISLAW—1864-1875.

George Skene, the eldest son, was educated at the High School of Edinburgh, and on finishing his course there, having adopted the sea as a profession, entered the sloop of war the Gannet, in which he served, as a midshipman, for eighteen months. Having then, at the request of his mother, given up the sea, he was sent with his brother, William, in 1824, to Hanau, near Frankfort, for the prosecution of their education. In 1826 he was entered a student at Trinity College, Cambridge, and, in 1829, he passed advocate, and commenced practice at the Bar. In 1832 he married, on 26th April, Georgiana Monro, daughter of Dr. Alexander Monro of Craiglockhart, Professor of Anatomy in the College of Edinburgh. In 1837 he was elected by the Faculty to the Chair of Universal History, in the University of Edinburgh, which he held till 1841, when he was offered one of the Sheriffships of Glasgow, which he accepted. In 1855 he was appointed Professor of Law in the University of Glasgow, which chair he occupied till 1866, when he retired and took up his permanent residence in Edinburgh.

By his wife, Georgiana Monro, he had the following children :—
I. James Francis Skene, born in 1833, and passed advocate in 1854. He died on 22nd September, 1861, at the age of 29, on a voyage home from Ceylon, which he had visited not long before.
II. Maria Isabella Skene remains unmarried.
III. Jane Georgina Skene married, 16th June, 1864, George Michael Fraser Tytler, secretary to the Bank of Scotland, younger son of James Tytler of Woodhouselee, and died 14th June, 1871, having had issue, besides two sons and a daughter who died in childhood—

    1. Maurice William, born 18th June, 1869.

    2. Georgina Mabel Kate.

  IV. Katherine Elizabeth Skene married, on 20th June, 1861, George Chancellor, W.S., second son of Alexander Chancellor of Shieldhill, who died in 3rd April, 1875.

His wife, Georgiana Monro, died in 4th June, 1868, and after her death he married secondly, in 1870, Catherine Elizabeth Tytler, daughter of James Tytler of Woodhouselee.

After his retirement from the Professorship of Law, and his return to Edinburgh, Mr. Skene devoted himself entirely to works of charity and benevolence among the poor of the old town of Edinburgh, where he was looked up to by all classes as a judicious and sympathetic friend and helper. In the winter of 1870 he met with a severe accident, which lamed him and impaired his health, and, in 1874, became aware that a fatal disease was undermining his life, and that he could not survive many months, a fate which he met with unusual calmness and fortitude, and on 2nd January, 1875, he passed quietly away in the sixty-ninth year of his age.

Mr. Skene was a man of much subtlety of intellect and of unusual acquirements, which he united with an ardent temperament that led him to the cultivation of strong religious principle, and to the exercise of an untiring and self-denying devotion to works of charity and benevolence.

VIII.—WILLIAM FORBES SKENE

was educated at the High School of Edinburgh, and after a session at Edinburgh College, was sent to Germany to prosecute his studies with his brother, George. On his return he spent a session at St. Andrews, and then, after serving an apprenticeship in the firm of Jardine and Wilson, of which his uncle, Sir Henry Jardine, was senior partner, he passed Writer to the Signet in 1832. In 1865 he received the degree of LL.D. from the University of Edinburgh, and in 1879 that of D.C.L. from the University of Oxford. In 1881 he was appointed Her Majesty's Historiographer for Scotland, an office which, with that of Her Majesty's Limner for Scotland, held by Sir S. Noel Paton, is the sole remains of the ancient Royal Household of Scotland. He has written "The High-

landers of Scotland," 1837 ; "The Four Ancient Books of Wales," 1869 ;
"The Coronation Stone," 1869; "Celtic Scotland," 1880; "The Gospel
History for the Young," 1883 ; besides editing " The Dean of Lismore's
Book," " The Chronicle of the Picts and Scots," and three volumes of
" The Historians of Scotland." He is also editor of this volume.

He is now the male representative of the families descended from
James Skene, who was second son of Alexander Skene of Skene, by his
wife, a daughter of Lord Forbes.

*Arms of Sir George Skene of Wester Fintray, from a Stone formerly in the
House of Rubislaw, now in the possession of the Editor.*

U

APPENDIX Nº. I.*

SKENE OF RUTHRIESTON.

I.—ROBERT SKENE,

paynter and glassenwright, Aberdeen, on 21st September, 1615, was admitted Freeman, and that gratis, but payment of any composition at the request of Sir James Skene of Curriehill.

He married Catharine Donaldson, and had by her—

I. Andrew Skene.

II. James Skene.

> 30th March, 1655—James Skeyne, lawful son to the deceased Robert Skeyne, glazier, was admitted a burgess of gild, James Skene, burgess of Aberdeen, cautioner. This was the brother of Newtyle, commonly called white James, and the James Skeyne admitted was known as black James. He married in 10th February, 1657, Janet Lumsden, by whom he had three sons, who died young, and three daughters.

> 20th June, 1685—Christian, Elizabeth, and Margaret Skene, lawful daughters to the deceased James Skene, elder, merchant in Aberden, sell their right to the lands of Rudrieston to the town.

III. William Skene died young.

IV. John Skene, a posthumous son.

> 9th December, 1635—Robert Skene, painter, buriet.

* The connection of the following families with that of Skene of Skene has not been ascertained, and they are therefore inserted in an Appendix.

II.—ANDREW SKENE.

In 1637 Andrew Skene served heir to Robert Skene, vitrearius burgen. de Aberdeen.

In 1642 Andrew Skene, eldest lawful son to umquhile Robert Skene, glasenwright, burgess of Aberdeen, being past 14 years, chooses John Forbes and Gilbert Skene, merchants, burgesses, for his curators.

There were at this time a considerable colony of Scotch merchants in Holland, and for their protection a functionary, called the conservator of Scotch privileges, was stationed at Campvere. It was an office similar to that of the more modern Consul. We find Andrew Skene filling this office from 1653 to 1665, and in 1664 Andreas Skene, mercator de Campvere, is admitted burgess. James Skene, burgess, cautioner. In 1667 he was Dean of Guild of the town of Aberdeen, and acquired the property of Rudrieston, and in 1667 Andrew Skene of Ruthrieston, and Andrew, his son, acquired the lands of Pitmuxton, with the office of mair of fee of the Sheriffdom of Aberdeen.

He married Christian Skene, daughter of Mr. Andrew Skene of Overdyce, and widow of David Drummond, factor in Campvere, by whom he had—

I. Robert Skene.

II. Andrew Skene.

    In 12th October, 1667, is the admission of Robert Skene, eldest son to Andrew Skene, Dean of Guild, as a burgess ; and on 3rd June, 1672, of Andrew Skene, second son of Andrew Skene of Ruthriestone, as a burgess.

    In 29th July, 1673, there is a disposition by Andrew Skene of Rudrieston, and Christian Skene, his spouse, and Robert and Andrew Skene, his lawful sons, to John Moir, of the lands of Rudrieston.

    Robert Skene, the eldest son, appears to have predeceased his father. On 25th June, 1667, he had married Margaret Farquhar, daughter of Alexander Farquhar, burgess of Aberdeen, and had two daughters and one son—

1. Christian Skene, born 6th April, 1668.
2. Margaret Skene, born 23rd September, 1669.
3. Andrew Skene, born 24th December, 1670, who died young.

And in 1680 there is a discharge by Andrew Skene, younger of Pitmuxton, to Margaret Farquhar, relict of deceased Robert Skene, his brother.

Andrew Skene was succeeded in the estate of Pitmuxton by his second son, to whom it had been conveyed in 1668.

III.—ANDREW SKENE OF PITMUXTON.

There is, on 23rd September, 1676, a discharge by Andrew Skene of Pitmuxtone and Isobell Donaldson, his spouse, in favour of John Donaldson, merchant burgess in Aberdeen, recorded 1st May, 1680 ; and in the same year Andrew Skene, younger of Pitmuxton, discharges Margaret Farquhar, relict of the deceased Robert Skene, his brother, of the effects and cabinet of papers he left with her three years ago, when he went to Holland.

He had by her—

I. Andrew Skene.

II. Mary Skene,

and must have died before 1700, as on 3rd December, in that year, is a marriage between John Clark, merchant, and Mary Skene, daughter of the deceased Andrew Skene of Pitmuxton.

He was succeeded by—

IV.—ANDREW SKENE,

who was an apothecary in Aberdeen. He married Margaret Kirkton, by whom he had—

I. Andrew Skene.

II. Alexander Skene.

In 1717 there is a charter to Andrew Skene, apothecary in Aberdeen, and Andrew, his son, of the lands of Pitmuxtone.

He died in 1737, when his will is recorded. He was succeeded by his eldest son.

V.—Dr. Andrew Skene,

physician in Aberdeen ; and, in 1738, Andrew Skene, chirurgeon in Aberdeen, eldest son of the late Andrew Skene, chirurgeon, and of Margaret Kirkton, his wife, serves heir to his brothers.

He married Margaret Lumsden, a daughter of Lumsden of Cushnie, and had by her the following children, mentioned in the Burgh Propinquity Book, 3rd April, 1765 :—

I. Mr. Andrew Skene, minister at Banff, died 2nd December, 1792.

II. Margaret Skene of Aberdeen, unmarried.

III. Dr. David Skene, physician, Aberdeen.

IV. Marjory Skene, married to Gilbert Jaffray in Kingswells.

V. Mary Skene of Aberdeen.

VI. Katharine Skene of Aberdeen.

VII. George Skene of Aberdeen.

On 24th August, 1767, died Dr. Andrew Skene, physician in Aberdeen, in the 65th year of his age.

In 1769, Mary Skene married Andrew Thomson of Banchory.

VI.—Dr. David Skene

died 27th December, 1770. A biographical sketch of David Skene, M.D., of Aberdeen, was read before the Royal Society of Edinburgh, in 1859, by Mr. Thomson of Banchory. He says, "From MSS. still existing [in Aberdeen University Library] in every branch of natural history, which are probably but a part of what he wrote, it appears that Skene pursued the study of nature to an extent and with an accuracy previously unknown in Scotland ; and from letters addressed to him by some of the most eminent men of the time, it is evident that his merits were thoroughly recognised by his contemporaries. His early death prevented his giving any part of the fruit of his labours to the public."

SKENE OF AUCHTERERNE.

The property of Auchtererne, afterwards called Waterearn, is in the parish of Logie Coldstone, and the Skenes seem from an early period to have had a hereditary right to the vicarage of Logie, in connection with which they had a possession called Tullinturk, in the neighbouring parish of Kincardine O'Neill. It is extremely difficult to trace a connected pedigree of this family.

In 1443 we find Robertus Skene, vicarius de Logymar; and, again, a hundred years later, we have in 1551 Mr. Robert Skene, vicar of Logy; and, in 1555, he appears as Mr. Robert Skene in Tullinturk. In the register of the Privy Seal we find—" Preceptum legitimationis Jacobi Skeyne, Arthuri Skeyne, Johannis Skeyne, Roberti Skeyne et Gilberti Skeyne bastardorum filiorum Magistri Roberti Skeyne, vicarii de Logymar in communi forma apud Edinr. penult. die mensis Februarii, 1553." The first Skene of Auchtererne we find on record is—

I.—JOHN SKENE,

who married one of the two co-heirs of Auchtererne of that ilk. On 18th February, 1506, there was a charter to John Skene and Margery Auchtererne, his spouse, one of the daughters and heirs of John Auchtererne, and the heirs of the marriage; whom failing, the nearest and lawful heirs of the said Margery, of the half of the lands of Auchtererne, with the half of the Blackmill.

II.—JAMES SKENE IN TULLINTURK, AFTERWARDS OF AUCHTERERNE.

In 1536 James Skene in Tullinturk has the reversion of the half of Garlogy, and, 3rd June, 1540, there is a charter to James Skene in

Tullinturk and his heirs, of the west half of Auchtererne and half Mill, on the resignation of John Skene and Margery Auchtererne, his wife. Then on 7th December, 1543, there is ane brieve maid to Maister Robert Skene, vicar of Logie, his airis and assignees, ane er ma, of the gift of the ward of the west half of the lands of Auchtererne, with the pertinents quhilk is pertainet to umquhile James Skene, portioner of Auchtererne, while the said half lands shall happen to be in the hands of the Queen, by reason of ward, thro' decease of Marjoria Auchtererne, liferenter of the same, or of the said umquhile James, till the lawful entry of the heir, being of lawful age; and also of the marriage of William Skene, sone and heir of the said umquhile James, and failing him, the marriage of any other heirs of the said James.

III.—WILLIAM SKENE OF AUCHTERERNE

married a sister of Patrick Forbes of Pittalochie, and had by her a son and two daughters—
  I. John Skene.
  II. Janet Skene.
  III. Eupheme Skene.
  He died before 1571, as on 21st November, 1571, then in the record of the Privy Seal "ane letter maid to Maister Robert Skene, his airis and assignees, ane er ma, of the gift of the ward of the west half of the Mylne, Mylne lands, and Tullerbe of the same land, whilk pertainet to umquhile William Skene, portioner of Auchtererne, and now thro' his decease being, as when it shall happen to be, in our sovereign lord's hands, by reason of ward, and also of the gift of the marriage of John Skene, sone and heir of said umquhile William Skene."

IV.—WILLIAM SKENE IN TULLOCH, AFTERWARDS OF AUCHTERERNE,

was second son to Mr. Robert Skene, vicar of Logie, and married Janet Skene, one of the daughters and co-heirs (through decease of her brother John) of William Skene of Auchtererne, and afterwards his widow, Margaret Forbes, her stepmother.

In 1571 he acquires one half of one half of Auchtererne from Eupheme Skene, the other co-heir.

On 1st March, 1588, Alexander Skene, eldest lawful son of Arthur Skene in Tullocht, has, in 1584, a 19 years' tack of the vicarage teinds of Migvie.

In 1600 Arthur Skene appears as portioner of Auchtererne.

On 23rd March, 1593, there is on the register of the Privy Seal a precept of a charter confirming a feu charter by Eupheme Skene, one of the two heirs of William Skene, portioner of Auchtererne, proprietor of the lands aftermentioned, with assent of George Forbes, her husband, to Arthur Skene in Tulloch, and the heirs male procreated between him and Margaret Forbes, his spouse, whom failing as their heirs whomsoever of the half of the shadow half of the town and lands of Auchtererne, with the half of the lands of Tulloch and Drumino.

In 1604 Arthur Skene, portioner of Auchtererne, conveys to Alexander Gordon of Lesmoir, one half of the shadow half of Auchtererne, Tulloch, and Druminie.

Arthur seems to have had three daughters, one of whom, Janet, married Robert Skene of Rannaloch, younger son of James Skene of Westercorse, and had by him a son, Alexander.

V.—ALEXANDER SKENE OF AUCHTERERNE.

In 1621 Alexander Skene served heir to Janet Skene, his mother, in the third part of the shadow half of Auchtererne, third part of shadow half of Tulloch, and third part of the shadow half of Drummond.

Alexander Skene died in 1645.

There is the following tradition of him:—

" A younger brother of Skene of Skene got the lands of Auchtererne, of whom is come Mr. Alexander Skene, who was a learned physician, and dyed in Peterso, in Poland, who by solid argument caused a priest burne his Byble. This man was the true heir of Auchtererne, sometyme called Wattererne, quhilk holdes in Barronie of the king, but now is become vassal of the Earl of Marr and Aboyne, and the titles theirof belonges to the house of Pitsligo, and titular and patron of Colston" (MS.C). His daughter, Margaret Skene, served heir to her father, Alexander Skene, who died twelve years before, in the same lands in 1658.

In 1697 there is a disposition by Alexander Skene of that ilk, heir served to John Skene, his father, narrating a disposition by Margaret Skene, only lawful daughter of the deceased Alexander Skene, portioner of Auchtererne, her father, dated 18th April, 1656, disponing to said John Skene the third part of the lands of Auchtererne, Tullo, and Drumon, and conveying the same to his brother, George Skene.

This was George Skene of Auchtererne, who, in 1720, purchased the lands of Carraldstone.

APPENDIX Nᴼ· II.

FOREIGN LETTERS, ADDRESSED TO SIR JOHN SKENE BETWEEN
1586 AND 1598.*

1.

S. D.   Nobilis et Doctissime vir amice observande.

Veniam dabis ut spero huic importunitati literarum mearum, quas ad
te, licet gravioribus negociis satis occupatum, dare non dubitavi, partim
amicitiæ nostræ initæ erga, partim quoque ut tibi significarem me pictur-
arum illarum, nihil adhuc accepisse.

Nescio an pictoris culpa, an vero illius cui has ad me deferendas
dedisti acciderit, solum hoc sato me neque auditione quidem quidquam
hactenus de illis intelligere potuisse.   Quidquid sit responsum tuum
omnino mihi crit expectandum antequam hinc discedam, quod ut ad me
quamprimum expedias te pro mea erga te observantia vehementer oro.

Ad iter meum quod attinet nolo te ignorare me id ex animo confecisse,
neque mihi in eo quidquam adversi accidit, præterquam quod et Aēræ et
Dublini paulo diutius hærere coactus fui adversante vento.   Redii tamen
in hanc urbem Deo beneficio salvus et incolumis.

Ea quæ in perlustranda Scotia vestra mihi in mentem venerunt.
Aēram cum primum venissem tuo isti clienti meoque conductori ad te
perferenda dedi : Sed ille nescio an sponte an vero oblivione literas
meas discedens in diversorio reliquit atque ad te vacuus rediit, quod ideo
addendum esse putavi, ne forte mea negligentia illud fuisse factum
existimes.

Cæterum abs te vir nobilissime peto me tui amantissimum ut redames,
et de me unice id tibi persuadeas, me non solum veram et sinceram
amicitiam tecum perpetuo colere velle, verum etiam per literas memoriam

---

* From the originals preserved in Her Majesty's General Register House, Edinburgh.

tui ad te testaturum esse quotiescunque occasio mihi se obtulerit. Oro Deum ut te patriæ et nobis amicis tuis diu incolumem servet, et te tuoque omnes ab omni malo semper protegat.

Salutat te plurimum et officiosissime Lavinus noster. Vale. Londini 16 Cl. Octobris Anno salutis LXXXVI.

tui studiosissimus.

CAROLUS BARO ZEROTINUS.

Nobilissimo et doctissimo viro domino Joanni Skenæo amico suo plurimum observando louinge Frende Sr. Johne Skene at Edenbourge.   Edimburg.

2.

S. D. An mea tibi postrema epistola reddita sit, nescio . sed cum serenissimo Rege tuo in Dania te hyemasse non dubito fortasse occupationes obstiterunt, ne responderes . volui tamen ego ad te iterum paucis scribere, offerente se occasione per D. Renecherum veterem amicum nostrum istuc proficiscentem, quem etsi ubi carum esse per se non dubito, vt mea causa tamen cum cuncta amplectione et ore docebit is te de rerum nostrarum statu et rebus communibus eritque vice epistolæ. Ubi audiveris eum et cognoveris eius consilium ac rationes, bene feceris si et ad Regis tui colloquium aditum ci aperueris . plura non potui per occupationes. Bene et Feliciter vale: ac serenissimo Regi tuo me subiectissime commenda 18 Junii Kal. Anno 90

CAS. PEUCERUS.

D.

Brevitatem epistolii excusabit
D. Renecherus.

Nobilitate doctrina, prudentia et virtute excellenti D. Johanni Scheneio consiliario præcipuo serenissimi Regis Scotiæ etc. amico veteri et carissimo.

3.

Monsieur,

l'esperoye de vous aller veoir et me resiouir auec vous du bon estat de votre maison et accroissement d'honneurs dont Dieu et votre

Roy honorent voz vertuz, mais comme je pensoye monter à cheual, on m'a coupè les estriers, comme vous dira Monsr le Docteur Moresin. Au reste apres avoir fait plusieurs voyages en Italie et en France assez hereusement, auec des S^{rs} de plus grande marque que ceulx que vous avez cogneu a Wittemberg, finalment m'estant retiré á ma maison en Sauoye auec ma femme, par la rage de la guerre i'ay esté mangè et pillé de tous costez comme par trop voysin de Geneue, qui estoit le but et siege de la guerre en ce paye là, et me defaillant l'industrie de pouuoir plus gouuerner ma barque parmy taut de tempestes, voyant que je ne me pouuoye maintenir dauantage en ma maison sans naufrage de ma religion, j'ay tout laissé par force. Et apres auoir sciournè plus de deux ans en la maison du viceroy de Boheme en enseignant son filz le Baron de Neu-hauss, desirant de reueoir les uniuersitez d'Allemaignè ennuyè de leurs quereles et combats en faict de la religion parmy leur gar aus, je suis venu en Angleterre là ou j'ay esté trompè de plus de la moiete. Et ne scay encores quelle fin prendront mes affaires. Vous asseurant que si ce n'eust esté la singuliere bonté et courtoisie de M^r. Antoine Bacon (qui m'a retirè en sa maison me fauorisant plus que ie n'ay iamais merité en son endroict, sinon en tant que l'aymant et honorant de tout mon coeur, il a pensé de m'estre obligé par ses propres faueurs) ie n'auroye plus de boys poure faire feu ou flesche. Et me semble que la fortune (si je doits ainsi parler) deuroit estre lasse du jeu et laisser reposer ceste pauure pelotte, qui ne scauroit plus rejaillir ny bondir. Mais ce sera quand il plaira a ce bon Dieu, lequel je prie de vouloir continuer ses faueurs en toute votre maison et vous donner un entier accomplisse-ment des saincts et vertueux desirs que j'ay tousiours honore en vous. Je vous prie aussi de vous vouloir resouuenir de l'amitie que vous m'auez porté a Wittemberg et m'aymer comme ie vous honoreray toute ma vie. De Londres ce 22 de Nouembre 1594.

Votre tres affectioné a vous obeir et seruir,

Le Doulx,

CATHARINUS DULCIS.

Beatus me, si rescripseris cum amica significatione tuæ erga me bene-uolentiæ sis fœlix cum dulcissimis tuis liberis.

Clarissimo viro domino Joanni Skynæo, Magno Magnatorum in senatu summo Scotiæ, domino et amico summa fide obseruando.

Edimburgum.

4.

S. P. Quamvis Clarissime Et Doctissime Domine Skynæ, amice amantissime, ab eo usque tempore, ex quo primum noticia inter nos et amicitia orta atque inita est, continuis itineribus et variis occupationibus impeditus fuerim, quo minus aliquid ad te perscribere, minusque aliquid non tam de tua ipsius valetudine, quàm de tuo tuorumque reliquo statu, quem secundissimum semper optavi, comperire potuerim; Animo tamen hoc maxime tempore, quo præsentium lator, minister meus, aliorum expediundorum negociorum gratia in Scotiam ablegandus fuit, inprimis incidit, ut quæ tui status præsens ratio ac conditio esset, intelligere satagerèm, tecumque, si omnia tibi ad nutum et voluntatem fluerent, plurimum lætarer: Ncc tamen intermitterem, quin à te amanter rogarem, ut huic ministro meo, si forte tuo vel consilio vel auxilio in sibi commissi negocii expeditione indigeret, benevole succurrere promteque adesse non gravarere, Tibique persuaderes, quicquid ei meo nomine præstares, mihi fore acceptissimum, et me ad omnia amicissimi et tibi addictissimi animi studia et officia semper paratissimum pollicereris. Quibus te divinæ Clientelæ commendatum volo. Dabantur Hafniæ Quarto Junli Anno 1595.

Mag^{tiæ.} et Amplitudinis

tuæ observantissimus

HENRICUS RAMELIUS.

Clarissimo Et Doctissimo Viro Domino Johanni Skynæo Juris Utriusque Doctori, Et Parlamenti Edinburgensis Advocato, Amico suo singulari.

5.

Salue quam plurimum mi nobilissime et charissime D. Skenæe.

Dici non potest quanta non modo iucunditate amicissimæ tuæ literæ me affecerint: sed etiam quam grata fuerit mihi presentia nobilissimi et generosissimi uiri D. Vilhelmi Stuardi, qui easdem exhibuit. Cui sanè præsertim in tanta eius festinatione et meo quoque inopinato Praga discessu, pro summis meis viribus conabar mea officia offerre, quod id ipsum ipsemet uti spero fatebitur. Deduxi eum quoque ad supremum Regni Bohemici præfectum D. de Noua Domo, cujus amicitia illi spero profuturam. Omnes sanè hujus uestri hominis integritatem prudentiam et dexteritatem amamus . quæ ex ipso uultu et sermone apparet . ideo ut sæpe nostratibus dixerim Deum in locis illis Septentrionalibus et occidentalibus hoc nostro seculo excitare et semare sibi homines, qui aliquando, orientales et meridionales nationes ex Babilonica captiuitate, sint liberaturi: et ueris Israelitis contra blasphemiam et Tyrranidem Gog et Magog et Dei istius Mauseos opem laturi in modo ista monstra et feces Sathanæ de quibus et tu quoque in literis tuis conquereris turbarent, hac omnia. Sed turbabit et hos aliquando Dominus ille Jehoua Elohim Spiritu uertiginis, ut in propriam perniciem suam turbata aqua ipsimet in ea merguntur.

Hoc nunc dico Deum aliquid singulare meditari in hoc bello turcico, ad quod tam remotæ gentes singulari zelo Dei pulsi ultro sua auxilia offerunt, ueluti serenissimus Rex tuus et Moscouitarum Princeps . cujus amplissimam legationem cum donis maximis que aliquot tunnus auri superant. Dominus Stuardus vester hic Pragæ uidit, et a me hesterna die ad eos deductus fuit, de capta a Cæsereano milite Arce Strigoniensi in Hungaria, et de occupatis aliis tribus munitionibus etiam a milite nostro in Croatia, et cæsis plus quam decem millibus turcarum . adeo ut hoc anno 95, turcarum tam a nostro quam a Transyluani milite ultra quinquaginta millia saltem in acie periâre paucis nostris Dei singulari protectione desideratis. Nos itaque hic omnes jam a triennio in procinctu esse cogimus, et plus arma quam literas et musas meditari; sed hæc hactenus.

De felicissimo rerum tuarum statu, summa cum animi uoluptate cognoui. Veré ergo beatitudo illa a Regio Propheta Psal : 128 decantata, tibi diuinitus contigit . in qua ut tibi dominus Deus ad ultimum uitæ tuæ curriculum benedicat eum ex animo precor.

De mearum rerum statu scito, me post longas illas quindecim annorum peregrinationes peragratis pene præcipuis Europiacis Regnis excepta uestra Scotia et Hispania, etiam in Asiam excurrisso, ubi et nos per literas ut scis salutauimus. Quo sanè in loco cum per quinquennium ab oratore Cæsareo et ab ipsa maiestate Cæsarea detinerer, et diutius etiam detineri debebam, oblata insuper mihi spe obeundi muneris oratoris seu legati Cæsarei, malui potius Domi meæ Arator, quam i bidem Orator fieri, et bobus paternis ut Horatius canit paterna excolere rura, proculque remotus talium ab aulis. reverso ergo mihi in Bohemiam, sua M^{tus.} Cæsarea obtulit et injunxit Sessionem in Senatu appelationum Regni Bohemici, in quo adhuc hæreo.

Vxorem quoque singulari sorte diuina mihi datam duxi ex anti-quissima et illustri familia Baronum a Wartumberg, ex qua aliquot liberos suscepi, sed tantum filius et filia in uiuis sunt. Princius ad quem per D. Stuardum literas quoque dedisti meus collega est . verum qui hanc religionem Catolicam in qua tecum mecumque æducatus fuit summo-pere et deridet, et blasphemat, ita ut cautè tibi imposterum ad ipsum scribendum sit. Quod sanè peccatum si per ignorantiam committeret excusabilior forsan esset, uerum terrestria curat nostrum autem muni-cipium mi D. Skenæe in cœlis est unde et illustrem illum aduentum magni illius Dei Saluatoris nostri expectamus, qui suas promissiones tanquam DEUS ille mentiri nescius, suis temporibus suis adimplebit cultoribus. uiderint ergo isti hypocritæ et derisores Deumue an potius se ipsos fallant.

Nos interea licet corpore remoti, Spiritu tamen Christi æterno et indissolubili vinculo coniuncti, sanctorum illam communionem etiam in hac mortalitate, insitando alii alios per literas seruabimus: recordaturi aliquando etiam horam in illa æterna societate, ubi non opus crit Epistolis, sed nos omnes erimus Epistola in Christo.

Ceterum id quod initio discendum erat . unicè et Summopere tibi commendo Magnif. et illustrem Baronem, Dominum Johannem Dionisium a Zierotin, que tibi hasc emeas literas tradit. Est in hæc familia ualde illustris et in Bohemia et in Morauia . et uitricus huius D. Fredericus a Zerotin Vice Rex Morauiæ. Fratris etiam nomen et fama huius D. Johannis non dubito quin tibi in Scotia sit nota, utpote qui hæc loca peragrauit. Et licet uterque non magnæ staturæ est; tamen in istis parvis doliis non tam quantitas quam qualitas materiæ spectanda est. In summa adeo cum tibi commendo, ut neminem magis commendare quam quid quid huic Baroni a te et a serenissimo Rege tuo gratiæ et fauoris et promotionis ad aliquid apud uos uidendum demonstrabitur . id nobis universis factum puta . est etiam hæc familia carum opum ut quosuis illustrissimos Principes at uiros tante et pro dignitate in Domo sua excipere posset ut interea taceam de pietate in Deum, et summa constantia in ea retinenda, et promouenda. Bene et felicissime uale uiueque æternum mi D. Skenæo. Datæ 13 Septembris anno 95.

Tui obseruantissimus frater

VUENCESL. BUDOWEIZ
a Budoria.

Nobilissim et Magnifico uiro Domino Johanni Skenæo, Supremi Senatus Regni Scotiæ assessori, et Archiuorum Regni Præfecto, Domino et fratri suo antiqua fide et constantia charissimo et obseruandissimo Edinburgum.

6.

S. Etsi pudet me quod tam longo tempore nihil ad te scripsi, confido tamen te pro humanitate et benevolentia erga me tua hanc inter-missionem officii mei in scribendo minus grauiter laturum esse mihique veniam daturum, præsertim cum neminem habuerim hactenus cui meas tuto ad te darem.

Audio antem te in patria tua maxima authoritate, apud tuos popu-lares ualere, et te in gratia serenissimi Regis uestri esse, ut et tibi gratulor et mihi gaudeam. Amicorum commodis non minus ac meis propriis libenter lætari soleo.

De me hoc tantum tibi dicere possum, me Dei beneficio in re me-diocri uel ultra etiam mediocritatem Prage uiuere et artem medicam exercere. Senex ferè vxorem duxi ; et quidem diuinitus mihi con-ciliatus has nuptias non possum dubitare, cum a Deo petiuerim bonum coniugium, et huius donum esse hoc sciam referente etiam sapiente rogo. Cæterum oro æternum Deum ut te Reipub. conseruet, que tui similes que paucos habeat audeo dicere, et tamen cuilibet nullo unquam tempore magis fuit opus, quam in hac uicissitudine rerum omnium dum ruinam omnia minantur et interitum.

Noua si que hic sunt ex illustri et generoso D. Barone Joh. Dionysio fratre domini Caroli Zerotinij nostri cognosces. Commendare tibi cum nihil attinet. Genus et heroica ipsius indoles dubio procul eum tibi satis commendabunt. Bene et feliciter uale nobilissime domine Schinae amice vetus ac obseruande. Dominus Deus te et omnes tuas actiones perpetuo gubernet et incolumem diu conseruet. Datæ Pragæ 14 Septem-bris 1595.

Tui obseruantiss.

Venceslaus Lauinius

AD. ROSEMBERGICUS.

Nobilitate virtute et eruditione præstantiss. domino Joh. Schinæo Serenissimi regis Scotiæ consiliario digniss. domino et amico veteri ac plurimum observando. Eidinburgi.

W

7.

Nobilissimo et doctissimo Domino Skeneæ S. P.

Quam gratæ imo quam gratissimæ mihi fuerint literæ tuæ, quas ad me per nobilissimum virum D. Guilhelmum Stuardum dederas, puto te iam ex responso meo cognovisse Respondi enim per Generosum Baronem D. Johannem Dionisium a Zerotin, quem tibi euntem in Scotiam commendaueram, et adhuc unice commendo, non dubitans quin si ad vos uenerit, hæc commendatio aliquod ponderis sit habitura.

Scripsi ad te quoque de rerum mearum statu, tum etiam de bello nostro contra Turcas. Ac quia nobilissimus et strenuus Eques D. Guilhelmus Stuarduas nunc ad uos reuertitur intermittere nolui, quin candem aliquod literarum ad te darem.

Quantum uero ego in promovendo hoc tanto et tanti uiri negotio laborauerim, uelim ut ex illo hæc potius quam ex me cognosces. Quam primum huc uenit, data ipsi fuit a sua majestate Cæs : (ut aulico stylo loquimur) audientia, et deinde excurrit ad uidenda nostrorum militum prope Strigonium Castra, his peractis iterum Pragam uenit, quem ad nonnullos præcipuos Regni nostri uiros ad contrahendam cum illis noticiam et amicitiam deduxi . qui sanè ob eximias heroicas dotes et peritiam rei militaris, omnibus quam gratissimus erat, ut interea taceam de illa in tam forti et strenuo milite et duce, morum suauitate, et in primis uero pietate. O utinam non negligeremus hoc bonum, et utinam plures eiusmodi essent . qui non modo hominibus sed potius Christo contra blasphemas illas et crudeles gentes turicas militare uellent. Imo quid nonnullæ nationes christianæ bellum contra Turcas gerendo efficiant, imo quam potius turpiter perfidè et sceleratè ad hostes filii Dei deficiant et nos prodant, id proh dolor experimus . modo oculos ad mare mediterraneum conuertito. Si ergo bellum contra turcas gerendum uti oportet est occidentalis et septrionalis miles ad hæc quam idoneus esset. Nam huic militi nulla cum turca affinitas, et miles hic plus ferre et pati potest. accedit ad hæc quod ex ipsis fundamentis uerbi Diuini et non consuetudine aliqua politica Christum et spem in eo repositam discunt et hac scientia ueluti armis intrinsecis omnium fortissimis sese contra tantum hostem muniunt, unde et illa externa arma uerum suum robur et uim sumunt . nam sine his omnia arma humana sunt instar machinæ magnæ, ex qua quis solo tantum globo absque puluere iaculari cupit, et qui quæso fieri potest ut terrestre illud et tam graue pelletur absque intrinseca in aliqua spirituali. Hæc ideo huc addo ut demonstrem quantum momenti sit christianum militem contra Turcas habere posse . alias certè ob licentiam carnis facilis est ad hostes spontaneus lapsus. Ac certè si Turca mutationem patietur sicuti aliquando id euenturum est idque extrimissimis promissionibus Dei, necessum erit ut maior pietas si non in plebeio milite et saltem in ducibus appareat, utque remotis superstitionibus in nomine sacro sanctæ et incomprehensibilis Trinitatis arma sumamus et alii aliorum tolleremus infirmitates, conuerso omni zelo nostro contra communem nominis Christiani hostem . alia ab ipsis turcis nobis malum et ruinam imminuerit. Sed hæc hactenus, et quidem properante calamo necnon propter uarias occupationes aliter scribere licuit. De rebus Vngareis et aulæ nostræ statu a domino Stuardo cognosces. Plura scribere nox uelat. Bene et felicissime uale mi charissime D. Skenæ. Iterum uale, donec in æterna uita æterno nostro Seruatori Christo uero Deo et uero homini coniungemus. Datæ Pragæ 21 Octobris an : 95.

Tui obseruandiss.

VUENCESLAUS BUDOWEIZ

Non perlegi.   à Budoria Consil : Cæs.

Nob ss : et præstantissimo uiro D. Johanni Skenæo, sereniss : Regis Scotiæ consiliario, et eiusdem Regni archiuorum præfecto. D. et fratri suo ueteri fide æterna charis. et col.

Edinburgum.

8.

S. P. Et præter uotum et contra expectationem meam accedit, Vir Clarissime, quod ego non iuerim in Scotiam, ut ueteris ac antiqua fide amici dulcissima consuetudine fruerer, lectissimam tuam uxorem uiderem ac communes utriusque uestram liberos pro mutuo amoris nostri affectu amantissimé amplecterer. Sed quæ est rerum mearum constantissima inconstantia, dum necessitate cogor obsequi illorum placitis qui non tam mei quàm sui commodi causa meam operam conducunt, factum est ut post multos cogitationum uelut æstus marini fluxus et refluxus, cum jam cogitarem de discessu adscitus fuerim in familiam Illustris ac Inclyti D. Domini Joannis Dyonisii Baronis e Zerotin qui et ipse cum non satis fauentes Calydonios deos dicam an Nymphas? experiretur, ab itinere retractus vi morbi, consilio medicorum et amicorum iter isthuc suum in aliud tempus differet, ac ubi ex febri tertiana convaluerit propter metû motuum qui etium hîc timentur in Galliam profecturus est. Interea tamen quo est heroico animo fratris Caroli quem nosci, æmulus in amandis tui similibus hoc est viris cordatis synceris et grauibus, iussit ut ego te ipsius nomine peramanter salutarem simulque omnia studia et amica officia offerem, Nobilis Henricus ab Eberbach ejus præfectus, vir singulari fide et prudentia plurimam salutem quoque tibi adscribi iussit, ac ad te transmittit literas communium nostrorum amicorum Dominorum Budouitii et Lauinii cum aliquibus aliis ad Inclytum Stuardum quas oro ut diligenter reddi cures. De rebus meis nihil lætum omnia redacta in fiscum saubaudi ; noster Lodouicus Robineus in Pictonibus seu de la Chauuiniere mortuus est, Musancherius viuit et valet. Si Deus volet nos saluos esse Parisiis, illhinc diligenter de omnibus scribam quæ putabo ad nostram amicitiam pertinere. Cæterum oro Deum Optimum Maximum ut tibi et totæ familiæ benè faciat, Vale et ama. Londino, die festo Sancti Georgii 1596.

T. A. studiosissimus et obseruantissimus.

CATHARINUS DULCIS.

Clarissimo viro Domino Joanni Skinæo J. Cto. apud Scotos magno Rotulorum Magistro, Domino et amico suo singulari fide et obseruantia colendo.

Edimburgum.

9.

Serenissime Potentissimeque REX ac Domine Domine clementissime.

Gratissimis animis amplexi sumus Serenissimæ Majestatis Vestræ iusique justiciæ et in nostrates favoris et clementiæ studium quod miris modis nobis prædicarunt cives nostri ejus navis exercitores et mercatores, qvam subditi Illustris Domini Comitis Orcauen, præteritis annis ad Insulam Unstam Ditionis Majestatis Vestræ vi et manu cæperunt ac spoliarunt. Nam quod eorum mandatarius Ornatissimus Joannes Ehlerus, post peractam juris omnem feruie solennitatem nihilominus sententia definitiva in causa rerum direptarum principali destitutus est.

Id potentiam adversarium potuisse, assensum suum nunquam accommodante Majestate Vestra sumus persuassissimi. Ipsa enim uti accipimus . factum non solum serio adversata, et ad transigendum de damnis illatis Dominum Comitem Orcanensem sedulo adhortata est ; sed et arbitrium causæ dirimendæ benignissimè ipsa suscepit, et detrectante hoc Domino Comite prædicto Ehlero civi . . . via aggrediendam gratiam authorit . . . et . . . tis tantum studio proprio non aliquo ipsius mer . . . licita est. Nobis qvidem nihil accidere gratius potuit gravi in tantâ civium nostrorum adversitate, habere eos propiciam Serenissimam Majestatem Vestram. Proinde ne verbis ægrare posse immensum beneficium videamur, quas debere nos gratias agnoscamus nihil hîc dicimus, sed ut prioribus in nostrates benignitatis studiis unum etiam hoc adjicere dignetur etiam atque etiam verbis diligentissimis humilimè rogamus. Nimirum ut authoritatem suam Regiam apud augustissimum Sessionis Consilium, quo remissam eam controversiam accepimus pro regiâ pietate interponat ne novum adoriendi Processum et rem actam denuo agendi necessitas civibus nostris imponatur, sed revisis prioris judicii actitatis, qvod bonitas qvod æquitas qvod immota justiciæ Regula, qvod Gentis utriusque consvetudo, qvod denique publicæ tranquilitatis utilitatisque ratio svaserit et dictitaverit citrà personarum respectum aliquem statuatur atque definiatur ac tandem aliquando cives nostri benevolentiæ potius et humanitatis officia meriti æstimationem navis et rerum injuriâ ablatarum haud difficulter consequantur ac tam Justicia et Clementia Majestatis Vestræ gravi propria innocentiâ et meritis adjuti facultatibus suis redintegrentur. Ita DEUS Optimus Maximus Serenissimam Majestatem Vestram diutissimè salvam et incolumem, Regiâ fortunâ florentissimam et Regnandi prosperitate gloriosissimam misericordissimè tueatur. Nos vero quantum justiciæ commendatio potuerit ad clementiam, tantum collati in cives nostros beneficii memoriâ ad humilimum ut obsequium afferat, sedulo sumus effecturi. Ejusdem Majestatis Vestræ Gratiæ et favori nos quoque humilimè commendamus. Datæ Gedanidie xxiiiiª mensis Anno Domini Mo Do xcvio.

D . . . 'tis Vr . . .

Obsequentissimi
Præconsules et Consules
Civitatis Gedanensis.

10.

Literæ tuæ, Vir Clarissime atque amplissime, mirum in modum me oblectarunt, quod per eas intelligam mei apud Dominam tuam non tantum conseruari memoriam verumetiam amicitiam obseruari ac coli integram: qua in re faris quod humanitate tua atque candore insigni dignam est: ego equidem quantum in me est lubentissime enitor ut amicitia tua dignus reperiar, hoc enim me monent ac jubent amplissimæ beneuolentiæ tuæ mihi præstitæ testimonia, quæ tenacissime memoriæ meæ inherent, semperque dum viuam inherebunt atque d. T^{e.} obiunctissimum tenebunt. Quod legum regni editionem te moliri ais, Jubente rege; Majestati suæ, regno, omnibusque quorum interest, gratulor quod te virum amplissimum eique rei omnibus modis quam maxime idoneum, tam doctrina quam facultaté ac studio præstantem habeant, qui id exequatur; tibi in hoc mugitanti, ut ex animo succedat exopto, ac dolorem sane opus tam necessarium inopia chartæ infectum iri. Vellem sane, quantum possem, isti defectui opem ferre; attamen cum nec in hac regione aut chartæ conficiatur, aut ea, qua opus est, quantitate, aut qualitate, venalis extet, profiteri cogor me id officii non posse præstare quemadmodum typographus tuus testabitur. Si alia quapiam in re d. T. gratificari, potero, habebis me quam obsequentissimum. Cæterum ingentes ago gratias quod de statu regni isthuc quædam mihi perscribere volueris: Deum precor ut tam vobis quam nobis incolumem seruet religionem et patriam. Nobis hic capto Caleto atque itidem Ardeatensibus, bellum grauius incumbit, Cardinalis archidux exercitum victoria elatum ipse animosus in Flandriam eduxit, Ostendæ obsidionem cogitarat, sed cum summa diligentia isti oppido et munitionibus et armoria, et omnibus aliis rebus necessariis quantum fieri potest prouiderimus videtur alio tendere, Hulstam scilicet aut Axeliam Flandriæ, nobis Zelandis admodum vicinis, ita quod maximi belli laboribus detinemur, atque involvimur, non tam viribus nostris confisi, quæ sane Jam sint exiguæ (Gallia enim adhuc dum partem copiarum nostrarum habet, tum etiam per classem Anglicanam alia pars non contemnenda abducta est) quam Dei armipotentis auxilio; Eum nobis precamur propitium, atque etiam rogo ut te conseruet. Vale vir clarissime atque amplissime meque ut facis amare perge. Middelburgo, 23ª die Junij 1596.

T. D. addictissimus

Jacobus Valche.

Clarissimo Amplissimoque Domino Johanni Scheneo Regiæ Majestatis Scotiæ sacri præfecto Consiliario dignissimo atque amico imprimis obseruando.

II.

Dum in Scotiam iter affectat affinis meus Joannes Ehlerus quondam Spect: Domini Joachimi Ehleri ordinis senatorii Filius, rediit mihi in mentem de nostra consuetudine in Germania quondam nobis intercedente tum cum opera et benevolentia tua nunquam mihi obliteranda uterer. Huncce igitur Ehlerum cum ob redintegratam mihi memoriam tui, tum ipsius etiam causa sine meis ad te literis pervenire nolui. Illam tibi quoque non ingratam fore confido si novi veræ humanitatis Genium qui olim mihi jucundissimus accidit. Hic vero Ehlerus quem dixi litem habet in Judicio Consilii sessionis quod in Scotia vestra est, habet autem jam diu eamque occasione navis cujusdam ad insulam Unstam direptæ. Quo nomine cum jam antea Illustrem Orcanensem Comitem apud consilium secretum convenisset cum a spolii Actione absolutum esse mihi retulit, remissa de cætero causæ cognitione ad illud quod dixi Consilium sessionis vestræ. Hic quod maximopere vereatur ne lis in immensum crescat, et ille moræ pertesus et sumptuum Justissimam causam deserere cogatur in tua benevolentia maximum sibi patrocinium collocavit. Atque isthoc omine se tibi per mei commendari voluit. Peto igitur a te per veterem illam consuetudinem nostram quando eo loco positus es ut possis, Velis huncce affinem meum authoritate tua et gratia adjuvare, quô sentiat potuisse aliquid apud te sibi autem plurimum profuisse commendationem meam. Nec tenebo te pluribus ne plus literis meis quæ tuæ humanitati tribuisse videar. Vale itaque namque consuetudinis memoriam perpetuo serva. Gedano 6 Julij Anno 1596.

Tui . . . observantissimus

GERHARDUS BRANDES

Nobilissimo juxtaque clarissimo Viro Domino Joanni Scænæo etc. Amico plurimum honorando.

I2.

S. Generos i Nobilissimi magnifici et doctissimi viri, facit summa humanitas et erga me benevolentia vestra, iam pridem mihi satis semperque perspectu comprobataque vt nihil esse, quod non pro jure seu lege amicitiæ me et vobis debere existimem, et vicissim a vobis auserim expectare Proinde vobis presentes ministros meos Petrum Forbus et Laurentium Velichero, si qua illis consilio et auxilio vestro opus fuerit peramanter commendo. Ac, quemadmodum hoc oneris fidei vestræ permittere non vereor Ita vicissim omnem operam studium officiumque meum, ut vobis in quibuscunque vestralibus vestro nomine si quidem eius aliquando hic à me prestari ut poterit et debebit, unice defero. Porro, cum per presentes occupationes plura non liceat, vos nunc hisce brevibus, summos factores et amicos meos, Dei omnipotenti protectioni commendo. Haffniæ V Augusti Anno 1596.

Vestrarum dignitatum

Studiosissimus

HENRICUS RAMELIUS.

Nobilibus generosis et magnificis viris, D. D. Johanni Schinæo et Petro Junio: et amplissimis Schotiæ regni senatoribus et consiliariis regiis et amicis summa observantia perpetuo colendis etc. Vtrius coniunctim vel seorsim singulis dentur.

13.

Gratissima mihi fuit significatio pristinæ erga me benevolentiæ tuæ dum quo loco literas meas habueris verbis haud vulgaris affectus plenissimis ostendisti. Mirum porrò in modum, me tenuit memoria et commemoratio tua jucundissimæ conversationis nostræ ; quæ res tantò mihi majus desiderium excitat tui quantò tutius illam nobis perpetuam fore, quamvis longissimo terrarum tractu dissitis mihi, jubes, omnino persuadeam : illud vero de pari voluntate et constantia mea judicium tuum, et si id quoque jucundissimum mihi accidit, tamen conscientiâ animi mei fretus jure quodam meo illud mihi deheri tua fac quæso cum pace dixerim. Proinde dum mutuo hoc foedere fructum amicitia legere, hoc est omnia humanitatis et propensi animi studia me vis expectare et dignum veteri tuo instituto facis ipse et ego in eodem officio, si vincere non datur saltem ut haud multum concessisse videar sedulam operam dabo. Ehlero nostro quid ante hàc præstiteris jam ex aliis cognovi, et hinc est, quod te idem imposterum etiam facturum facile mihi polliceor. Equidem agnosco quicquid hujus præstiteris ab amicitia nostra proficisci, siquid tamen causæ ipsius bonitati dare volueris proprium hoc virtutis æquabilitatis tuæ esse nolim dissimules, Ideoque ne plus verbis consequi velle quam voluntatis tuæ fiducia suspicionem moueam hactenus satis. Rerum nostrarum statum cognoscere desideras : is quidem hoc tempore talis est, ut scriptionem definitam non recipiat ita omnia nutu et metu Pontificis complentur. De cladibus Christiani exercitus et capta Agria tibi jam non potest esse novum atque hinc quod Turcicus Imperator jam propius finibus Poloniæ imminet, Rex noster diu multumque sollicitatus pro foedere cum Germanorum Imperatore concludendo comitia regni generalia ad medium Februarii habenda edixit, utique de nostro Germania fœdere nulla mihi spes, sed quicquid tandem erit quod tempus tulerit reddam te certiorem me quoque Deus Optimus Maximus laboriosa admodum in statione locavit sed patriæ intuitu cui prodesse contigit, omnia facilè perfero. De amicis olim communibus quid fiat haud probe constat. Jacobus vero Fabricius et tui amans superat, teque ut plurimum sibi carum resalutat : quem ego quoque bene ac diutissime valere nostri non immemorem ex animo opto. Calendis Februarii. Anno 1597.

Cui observantissimus et ad omnia paratus

GERHARDUS BRANDES.

Respondi 27 Martii 1597 per Patricium Someruell.

Clarissimo viro nobilitatis generis virtute et eruditione præstanti, domino Johanni Sceneo etc. Domino amico observando.

14.

S. P. Clarissime et Ornatissime Skinæe, amice singularis, Quamvis hoc tempore, quod scriptione, satis dignum esset, non habeam; committere tamen non volui, quin oblata commoda scribendi occasione hisce te salutarem, et officium, studium, ac benevolentiam in te meam attestarer; Simul quoque abs te amanter contenderem, ut hunc juvenem, qui hasce reddit, tibi commendatum habeas, eique tua opera, et benevola in literatos promptitudine, sicubi eam imploraverit, adesse haud gravate velis. Est namque ab illustrissimo Principe, Domino Johanne, Duce Slesvici Holsatiæ etc: cujus fiiliorum institutioni aliquandiu præfuit, huc in regnum commendatus. Ubi cum hactènus nonnihil hæserit, Scotiam, ac exinde Angliam perlustrare animum induxit. In quo suo proposito se tuo favore non parum adjutum iri confidit. Quicquid ergo benevolentiæ, et studii in illum mei causa contuleris, bene positum esse intelliges, Et me vicissim ad similia vel majora, ubi par usus id tulerit, tibi devinctum reddes. Quibus te Deo Optimo Maximo commendatissimum volo. Vale Dat. Hafniæ 12 Aprilis, Anno 1597.

T. Studiosissimus

HENRICUS RAMELIUS.

Post Scripta.

Amicissime Skinæe, Cum has obsignassem, venit in mentem, me superiori æstate ministrum, qui lanam rudem et pelles ovinas, ad meos domesticos usus ibidem coëmeret, in Scotiam ablegasse; ac eundem post reditum suum, nescio de quibus difficultatibus, quibus ejusmodi lanam et pelles ex regno vestro asportari inhibitum esset, a nonnullis prætenderetur, conquestum esse. Officiosè itaque te hisce rogare volui, ut prima quaque occasione significare mihi non molesteris, quænam ejus rei sit ratio, Utrum videlicet cuivis, ejusmodi pelles et lanam coëmendi et asportandi facultas pateat et concedatur, An vero a Ser: Reg: Ma.tis de singulari gratia, cum ad privatos solummodo usus eas coëmi curem, obtineri et impetrari possit vel debeat. Feceris in hoc rem mihi gratissimam, et me tibi ad quæcunque officia obligabis. Vale feliciter. Datum ut in literis

Dignitatis tuæ

Studiosissimus

HENRICUS RAMELIUS.

15.

S. Cum nuper apud vos essem Vir Clarissime, impetravi a Serenissimo Rege donationem redituum quorundam in Annandalia ad usum visitationis, qua instituta est ad plantationem Ecclesiarum in desolata illa regione. Eam manu Regia subscriptam memini me tibi tunc exhibuisse, ut tua opera Thesaurarii et Collegarum Suffragiis pro more confirmaretur. Sed Thesaurarium gravis morbus destinebat, teque ac Collegas tuos publica negotia ita distrahebant per id tempus, ut Concilii convocandi prærepta sit omnis occasio. Seorsim tamen ferè singulos

super hac re conveni, qui consensum suum haud gravate promittebant.
Quare fretus imprimis benevolentia Thesaurarii affinis tui, et amicitiâ tuâ,
mitto ad te eam ipsam donationem Regiâ manu munitam, ut in concilio
vestro vestris suffragiis et subscriptionibus corroboretur. Clementissimus
Rex istud propositum visitationis et plantationis iis in locis adeò
adprobavit, cum de hac re ageremus: ut affirmâvit de suo insuper se velle
elargiri ad eum tam necessarium usum. De vestra propensione et
voluntate prorsus confido, præsertim si intercedat authoritas et studium
tuum in hoc negotio conficiendo. Quod a te exspecto et vehementer
expeto. Quod si non conficiatur cessabit opus præclarum magno cum
detrimento illarum Regionum. Quis enim suo sumtu poterit sustinere
tantum onus? Et proxima Synodus Deidonensis prorogavit nobis
visitandi munus ea lege, ut impensæ nobis subministrarentur. Hoc
quidquid est, Vir Clarissime, fidei et benevolentiæ tuæ commendo. Porro
factu est mentio a Regia Majestate in illa Synodo de visitatione Acade-
miarum per viros idoneos. Et nos quoque idoneos viros valde optaremus
rei literariæ scientes et faventes: Te verò imprimis scientissimum et
scholarum exterarum et nostrarum ac una tecum Thesaurarium propter
æquitatem et authoritatem cum Domino Johanne Prestono. Non dubito
quin opera vestra magnum commodum allatura esset Academiis, si vestri
similes viri Ecclesiastici deligerentur Rob. pontanus, Nicol. Dagleisius,
Jacobus Nicolsonus, et tales viri probi et docti. Jam ignosce importunitati meæ: Satis te impeditum nimis detinui. Vale vir præstantissime.
Andreapolis ad d. xxiv. Maij 1597. Tibi addictissimus Johan. Jonstonus.

Clarissimo viro domino Johanni Skenæo assessori et consiliario
serenissimi Regis in Suprema curia. Edinburgi.

[*On the outer folds of the Letter are written these notes*]:—

1266 betuix Magnus 4 Alex^r. 3.

The annuell of Norroway is dischargit be Christianus 1. 12 May
1469.

Annuell of Norroway dischargit in the contract of marriage,
8th September 1468 and thairefter dischargit 12 May 1469.

m. c. constituit 12 de procuratoribus marchi sterlingorum and
m. c. 3 de arbitrament. is maid of quinque solidi sterlingorum.

16.

Quanquam neminem prætermiss. quemquidem ad vos peruenturum putarem cui literas non dederim, in hanc tamen partem peccare me malim, quam diuturno silentio, supinæ negligentiæ et ingrati animi suspicionem incurrere. Cum autem, ad tempus hîc in obscuro lateam, isque orbis terrarum angulus me teneat, in quo aut nihil rerum nouarum, aut si quid sit, incertis id authoribus ad nos perlatum subticere quam literis mandare tutius fore existimem, nihil prius mihi in presentiâ occurrebat, quam ut meam de vestra vestrorumque salute solicitudinem imprimis declararem vestrasque literas cum hoc nomine mihi desideratissimas esse tum si quid sit in meis rebus firmius de eo me libenter fieri uelle certiorem: Meâ quippe interesse putabam, me ad vos quàm sepissimè scribere, quare velim mihi hoc ipsum condones, si meæ necessitudini obtemperans, nostraque sanguinis conjunctione fretus minus videbor meminisse constantiæ tuæ confidere videor te mea causa quæ honeste possis libènter nec grauatè esse facturum, magnum tamen speraui apud te (pro mole negotiorum quæ te quotodie obruit) tum propter incerta viarum si quæ fortè interciderent, crebriores meas literas ponderis habituras, quibus (licet tuo in me adfectui nihil · addi posset, et non solum naturalis hominis ad hominem adiunctio sed ciuilis cognomenti necessitudo, Imo arctior familiæ ejusdem conjungatio, eaque tandem quam mihi tecum esse, voluisti conjunctio et familiaritas, longiori orationis ambitu mihi interdicant) te tamen grauioribus ut dixi negotiis districtum et intentum, de meis rebus sæpius compellandum esse existimaui. Peto igitur à te non conquisitis verborum lenociniis sed eâ orationis simplicitate quâ intelligis debere me me petere ab homine tam mihi necessario tamque familiari ut mea negotia quorum procurationem (quæ tua fuit humanitas) in te suscepisti explices et expedias, cum jure et potestate quam habes, tum quod commodo tuo fieri possit authoritate et consilio, et si forte difficiliores crunt ut rem etiamnum sine controversia confici nolint, haud alienum tua dignitate putabis esse quam charum me habeas ut intelligant mihique vel absenti et longè dissito ad eorum contumaciam reprimendam et animos frangendos præsidii in te satis esse experiantur: quò, si quod speramus impetrauerimus, tuo beneficio nos id consecutos esse indicemus; sic tuorum erga te observantiam excitabis, aliosque, hoc tuo patrocinio, ad tuum nomen suspiciendum et colendum accendes;

quod beneficium mihi non erit tam charum, quam pietas erit in referendâ gratiâ jucunda. Ego in te videre scirem, cum hæc ad te scriberem, quantopere si alius esses in hac petitione (ut res meæ fluunt) mihi foret elaborandum, plura scriberem. Nunc tibi (ut superioribus meis vnis atque alteris feci) omnem rem et causam meque totum trado et commendo uxorem tuam selectissimam illam matronam et cui ego secundum parentes plurimum debeo propriè et in primis deinde fratres liberosque tuos quam possum amanter et officiose saluto: vestramque in me benevolentiam raram hactenus et singularem virtute et observantia meâ indies justiorem facere studebo. Vale Helmstadij Cal: Junij 1598 Hæc raptim

Vestræ dignitatis studiosissimus

GULIELMUS SKENÆUS.

Clarissimo et doctissimo Sexto Scotorum regi a tablino reconditiore senatu M. Johanni Skenæo patruo ac Mecænati suo: sal:

Edinburgum quæ est in Scotia vel Aberdoniam.

17.

Benigne Mecænas et Reverende Patrue, Salue etc.

Si valetis, bene est, nos quidem valemus. Secundum jam mensem Helmestadij subsistimus, unde nos antè literas ad vos dederamus, is dies erat 12 Maij, sed Hamburgi seniente peste, quando isthinc ad vos perferendas curaverimus, aut intercidisse aut ad vos perlatas nondum esse, suspicor: Itineris mei jam Dei gratia confecti; quis sit futurus fructus, aut ubi manendum adhuc non satis video, adeò in incerto posita sunt omnia. Magnam experior in doctore Liddelio humanitatem, ut non satis mirari possim, illius in studiis meis promovendis studium singulare et industriam indefessam. Est eâ naturâ ut populares summo amore prosequi, et modis omnibus quibus potest, erigere soleat, hanc eius piam et in omnes bonos propensam voluntatem si non auxerunt, saltem excitarunt tuæ literæ, amoris et benevolentiæ plenissimæ, quibus tantum illi injecisti studium, ut nihil quod mea causa suscipi possit, illi arduum aut difficile videatur ; vir est bonus, pius, et eruditus, qui cum non posset mihi ex animi sententia gratificari, hanc mihi rationem saltem prescripsit meas

res componendi: Scito (quod antea non provideram) in hac inclyta
Academiâ in studiosorum gratiam, quorum facultates angustæ sunt,
quatuordecim mensas communes, a principe extructas esse, quibus qui
accumbunt, gratis omnino non vivunt, sedecim taleros pro victu exsol-
vunt, quod reliquum est, princeps, (qua est in literarum studiosos munifi-
centiâ) æconomo, a thesaurario suo, quotannis representat, et lautè sane
et genialiter victitant. Quare cum tanta hîc sit annonæ caritas, si in
mensam communem primo quoque tempore cooptarer bene consultum
rationibus meis existimat, Liddelius, quoad uberiorem facultatem maiora
præstandi, ars et natura indulserint. Cum hic obscurus sim et edicto ex
aula, non ita pridem sit cautum, ne cives peregrinos post ponantur, tanto
competitorum numero, èo res redacta est, ut istud beneficii consequendi
spes omnis præcisa sit, nisi tuam authoritatem apud Reginam, de illius
literis commendatitiis ad sororem, auferendis interponas, iisque quoad
fidei possit, in hunc sensum conscriptis.

Factum est ut Republica vestra literaria penitus perspecta, eiusque
celebritatis amore accensus, Gulielmus Skenæus Scotus, pius et modestus
adolescens, et de cuius indole meliora speramus, uberioris ingenii culturæ
Lauriendæ erga, apud vos in inclyta Julia Academia aliquandiu subsistere
exoptet, cumque illius facultates exiliores sint, quam ut eum sustentare
valeant, et nonnullum in literis nostris tenuitati suæ præsidium, arbitrare-
tur, eas, amicis illius quibus deesse non poteramus, depræcatoribus,
non ægrè impetravit, quem velis ita commendamus, ut maiorem in
modum commendare non possimus, et quandoquidem bonarum literarum
studiosis, a vestra magnificentiâ bene consultum esse, ex illius ad nos
literis non obscure, colligimus: Rogamus ut etiam illi hac in re com-
modetis, et in aliis omnibus, quæ sine vestra molestia facere possitis,
eumque in vestram fidem suscipiatis ut intelligat nos scripsisse de se,
nostramque commendationem non vulgarem fuisse. Erit id nobis
vehementer gratum.

Hoc (mi patrue ac Mecænas optime) non rarum est, non ita pridem
nostras quidam M. Georgeus Strang, Edinburgenus qui ad vos rediit,
eodem beneficio, iisdem literis fruebatur, noli itaque putare, me arduum et
difficile quiddam a te contendere; sed quod nostratium plerisque antè
indultum est, et licet, ut dixi magnus sit petitorum numerus, Hæ Literæ
tanto erunt nobis subsidio ad aditum tum apud Principem tum apud viros
doctos patefaciendum ut eos omnes, qui idem nobiscum ambiunt, non

videatur Liddelio ἀδυνατον, vel facile obducere: omnium utique studiorum plus minus octinginta, quid si mille dixerim? omnium inquam qui hic vivunt, gloria et æstimatio ab aula pendet: et a Principis commendatione: Hisce serenissimæ nostræ Reginæ literis, et tuas adiunges ad D. Adamum Crusium veterem tuum amicum, et summæ hic authoritatis, quibus rogabis ut aditum mihi apud principem faciat, mihique suam prestet in omnibus operam, ut cui tu honestissimè cupias, idque tibi gratum fore: Quid si etiam Dominum Doctorem Liddelium medicinæ doctorem et in inclyta Julia Academiâ Helmestadiensi, superiorum mathematum professorem salutaveris, cuius nomine summam tibi dico salute mquique mihi tua causa, in omnibus quoad fieri possit, indies gratificari non desunt: sed ista tuæ erunt prudentiæ et sapientiæ, quem non fugit in omnibus, quid deceat et quid minus; ista pluribus non persequor ne proverbium illud in me competat. Sus Minervam: Ego primum ignotus ab amicis et æstimatione inops, in ignota regione dolere, et ingemere ut frontem ferirem (ut ait Cicero) sed iam paulo facilius fero desiderium patriæ et amicorum, modo tu bene valeas, a quo nostra salus pendet Hedelberg aut cogitabam, si fuisset integrum, sed quia tua videbatur voluntas ut nisi adducto indicio et explorate id fieri posset, nihil properarem, et quia longum est iter et infestum, et pro annonæ laxitate quam sperabamus, eiusdem difficultatem mirum in modum experiamur, Basileæ aiunt et Hedelbergæ admodum compressam esse ex literis multorum quotidie ad nos perferatur, nondum mutamus sententiam nec constituemus quicquam, donec literas vestras acceperimus, et enim mihi nullo loco deesse vis, negocia nostra domestica tuæ pristinæ erga nos humanitati etiam atque etiam commendo, ad tua innumerabilia beneficia quæso, si me amas, hoc adde vt cum nostræ profectionis author fueris et caput (virtus inquam tua quæ currenti stimulos addebat) meæque tenuitati solus et unicus adjutor fueris, nihilo etiam minus extra patriam viventis rationem habere velis, quo in annos ad studia mea excolenda, ex iis quæ ad nos jure spectant, aliqua subsidii spe tenemur ut magis secure liceat in legum amœnissimus viretis exspatiari, unde rerum mearum præsidia putem expectanda, hic siquidem tantus est literatorum concursus ut tyronibus et neophytis non sit locus. Ranustis ex edicto principis silentium et modus impositus, est, aliarum facultatum professores hic sunt supra viginti: qui diligenter vident ne quid detrimenti patiantur a lectoribus privatis, quamobrem si aliqua mihi spes ex meo affulgeret, quoad eos progressus nostra fecisset industria vt sua virtute nostram tenuitatem sustentare posset et libere profiteri audierem: tum alió me conferrem vt res tempusque postularent hoc si fiat ita te videam, vt mihi gratius nihil posset accidere, Tuamque amplitudinem (mihi crede) illustrabit vt cum ab omnibus absentium iuxta præsentium amicorum curam gerere prædicaberis, in quos præclarè stabit Isocrates, ὃι φαυλοι παροντας φιλους μονον τιμῶσιν, ἀπουδαις δέ καὶ μαχραν ἀποντας ἀγαπῶσι. Hæc hactenus non quod diffidens tuo in me adfectui, vt cui nihil in omni vita propositum erit magis, quam vt quotidie vehementius, te de me optimè meritum esse lætere, sed rei magnitudo me monet, et sera parsimonia in fundo est. Novi quidam scribam regiam angliæ (quod absit) fatis cessisse, id si verum, quin hactenus audiveritis non dubito, at Philippum Hispanorum regem supremum obiisset diem sunt qui apud nos pro certo adfirment, sub cuius mortem, classem ingentem in Anglos provectam, justo Dei judicio exorta pestilentia et tabe mirè disjectam et afflictam esse persuadere nobis conantur, quorum suggestu et imprimis Liddelii ista scribo: Bene igitur vale, ne forte gravioribus (vt par est) districto molestus sim, et illas commendatitias quam primum mittas velim, ubi si te mihi commodum dederis, a te omnia habebo et divitiis superabo crassim. Iterum vale et uxori, selectissimæ illi feminæ de nobis imperpetuum benè meritæ, et liberis tuis ex me officiosam salutem dicito cui te diu salvum præstet et incolumem divinum innuen:

Hæc raptim et subito offerente se tabellario qui Rostochium tenderet 16 Julij.

Tuæ prudentiæ
observantissimus cliens
Gulielmus Skenæus.

18.

Gratia Dei et Patris Christi sit cum tua dignitate in omnem æternitatem.

Amplissime ac nobilisime Domine si una cum tua familia valetudine quam optima eo præditus, et felici rerum successu exanimi sententia frueris id mihi usque adeó est acceptum, tamque auditu jucundum, ut eo mihi nihil acceptius nihilque auditu jucundius accidere queat: Ad me vero quod attinet, tua amplissima dignitas sciat quod animo et corpore divino beneficio quám optimé sim affectus et constitutus, meaque professio quæ in linguæ hebrææ explicatione in hac inclita Academia mihi est demandata et concredita, non infeliciter procedat. Nam pro ratione hujus Academiæ et horum temporum auditores satis multos habeo qui meis laboribus non solum quam optimé sunt contenti sed etiam Deo pro illis agunt gratias quam maximas. Præterea magnifice Domine universus totius Germaniæ status præcipiti metu suspectus, et tenui filo humanitus loquendo suspensus est Nam veræ et orthodoxæ filii Dei Ecclesiæ unde quaque damna et pericula imminet.

Nam præter Turcas et Hispanos de quibus ad nobilissimum et honestissimum Adolescentem Jacobum Balendinium scripsi, domestici hostes eam undique infestant, et opprimere conantur, Flaccianaca enim turba et pontificii quam durum et dirum inauditæ, diabolicæ acerbitatis virus in eam evomant, quantisque convitiis et maledictis illam agitent et conspuant vix prout verbis exprimi. Clamitant pleno gutture, et impudente ore omnia probra in innoxias profundunt, addunt etiam quod effrenis debacchandi licentia sit summa religio et viva veræ fidei ἐνέργεια atque luculentum Spiritus Sancti testimonium Mullerus etiam Wittenbergae ex suggestu publicè Sanctam Mariam filii Dei matrem Calvinistam appellavit, ob id quod ex Angelo Dei, quæsiverit, quomodo filium paritura sit cum virum non agnoverit, omnibus modis dolendum esse dixit, quod sanctissimi quique calvinistico veneno sint infecti; hæc in publica concione cum magna populi applausu per sarcasticum risum ebuccinavit, eaque res typis est excusa et in lucem emissa, sic omnes appellant Calvinistas qui hujus aut illius rei vel dogmatis rationem quærunt.

Volunt sibi simpliciter credi sive verum dixerint nec ne, volunt etiam Sancti Dei verba secundum literam ubique accipi, blatirant etiam Deum tam potentem esse ut ea facilè efficere queat, quæ verbis concepta et enunciata sunt de vero et genuino corum sensu non sunt admodum solliciti, Deum omnipotentem esse pleno gutture clamitant, quasi Deus omnia sine discrimine et voluntatis demonstratione factus sit, certè Dei potentia est solum voluntatis ejus ministra. Nam quæ Deus vult et decernit voluntate, ea efficit et producit sua infinita potestate. Itaque à voluntate ad potentiam est conclusio vera, sed à potentia ad voluntatem concludendi ratio et admodum periculosa et blasphema: Nobis enim non alia Dei omnipotentia cogitanda est, quám quæ cum illius voluntati et sapientiâ congruit, quæ autem omnipotentiam cum ejus voluntati sine

Y

ejus demonstratione committunt, impii et temerarii sunt, et Deum quodam
modo in ordinem cogunt, cum Deus nequaquam ob id omnipotens sit,
quasi ille ea facere velit quæcunque temeraria hominum et vana cogitatio
conceperit et fieri voluerit; Sed ideo dicitur omnipotens, quod omnia ea
facere possit, quæcunque verbo se facturum indicavit, Mirum sane
omnibus modis est, quod illud hominum genus de Dei omnipotentia tam
liberé apud imperitam multitudinem deblateret, et non aliter garriat,
quam si omnipotentiam Dei ad sua frigida commenta et vanissima
somnia comprobanda jure quodam conductam et quasi obstrictam
haberet. Certé omnipotentia illis non solum est speciosum effugium
apud promiscuam turbam, sed etiam est favorabilis prætextus. Væ a
illis, quod omnipotentiam Dei omnium errorum quasi operculum et
integumentum faciant. Cogor his addere unum quod Marpurgi et Martii
factum est a superintendente Doct. Leuchlero, qui in publica concione
audacter et confidenter hac proferre non erubuit sicuti dixit . si Deus me
ad hominem creandum in consilium vocasset, consuluissem ipsi imò
jussissem ut sinistram aurem non creasset sed ejus loco nasum posuisset,
ac loco nasi unum magnum oculum pro utroque oculo fecisset, tam
absurda et blasphema proferre illis summa est religio. Ante quadri-
ennium Cassellis simile quoddam contigit a Domino Johanne Winkel-
manno qui eo tempore fuit ibi aulicus concionator, is in quadam concione
in orthodoxos immodicé invectus est, ita ut Wilhelmus Làndgravius
piissimæ memoriæ ipsum repræhenderit, dicens moderatius et parcius
de illis dicendum et loquendum esse, cui Winkelmannus indixit satis
impudenter, diecns : Will dein E. dem H. Geist das maul stopfen, h.e.
Vult tua clementia Sp. S. os obturare. Talia semper proferunt, et addunt
se Calvinistas jam vicisse. Certé vicerunt eos non argumentis sed
conviliis et mendaciis, argumenta ex divinis literis petita nulla admittunt,
sed scommata, calumnias, et omnis generis probra in orthodoxos evomunt
et expuunt, et qui hoc non faciunt eos suspectos habent et Calvinistas
esse clamitant. Sic ipsis calumniand. protervia est [*torn*] vera suæ
Ecclesiæ nota. Profectò magnifice domine cum controversia nullis
argumentis componi et finiri queant, omnibus modis metuendum est,
illas Deum hastis Turcarum dirimere velle, de quibus ad Jacobum
Balendinium copiosé scripsi, Ea cujus literis Turcarum copias et conatus
tua magnificentia cognoscere poterit. Postremo clarissime Domine
ante mensem Casparus Peuccrus constantissimus et ipsissimus filii Dei

Martyr hîc Heidelbergæ fuit, qui tuam dignitatem plurimum salutare jussit, haec erant ejus verba. Johannem Schinneum meum veterem et carissimum amicum meis verbis officiosé saluta. Mi Domine Vix est credibile quam sit adhuc vegetus, cum jam agat feré annum 70. Virium nulla est facta debilitatio, solummodo oculi illi aliquantum caligant.

Vale magnifice Domine, in filio Dei quam beatissimé et me Rennecherum tuum veterem et carissimum amicum amare perge. Jacobum Balendinium communem nostrum amicum officiosissimé salutaris quæso. Emdæ magna seditio exorta est inter comitem et cives propter religionem de qua alias. Datum Heidelbergæ. 9 Aprilis.

Tuæ ampliss. dignitati addictissimus,

HERM: RENNECHERUS.

[*In different hand*] HERMANNUS RENNECHERUS.

Magnifico ac nobilissimo viro Domino Johanni Schinneo Serenissimi Regis Scotorum Consiliario dignissimo veteri fautori ac Domino suo summa observantia colendo.

Edenburgum in Scotia.

APPENDIX Nº· III.

Ad
Joannem Skenævm Collegam
Suum in Senatu et Archiotam.

Tandem hoc palimpsestum in manus vulgi exijt,
    Tersum, elaboratum, elegans.
Sed forte nescis quid tulerit hic Hercules
    Bovile purgans sordidum :
Crede mihi multa devoravit tædia,
    Multos trymixos ebibit.
Ite, ite, vappæ desides, Germaniam
    Lustrastis, et qui Gallias,
Nec quid reportastis domum præter novas
    Amystides, ceu syntheses.
Loquuntur ista qualiter se gesserit
    SKENÆVS in puertia,
Vbi vix per ætatem attigit Rempublicam,
    Rebusque sese immiscuit,
Ad Teutones, Anglos, Danos, et Battavos
    Legatus ilico mittitur.
Jd qua fidelitate, munificentia
    Testatur ista Principis.
Qui hunc legit ex tot millibus reducem, cui
    Archiva Regni crederet.

Tanti est benigno, et liberali Principi
 Servire, qui nullum suæ
Benignitatis qualitercunque meritum,
 Dimittere exsortem solet.

P. ROLLOCVS.

Ad
Joannem Skenævm Archivorvm
publicorum Regni Scotiæ custodem dignissimum,
Carmen Epicon.

Recte (ita Dij faveant cœptis, cursusque secundent)
Dum cessant alij, prope solus publica curas
Commoda ; securus rerum, SKENÆE, tuarum,
Si prosis aliis : hoc vere est non sibi nasci,
Sed patriæ : nam quam patriæ, doctissime, partem
Debueras ortus, magno cum fœnore reddis.
At postquam virtus meriti non immemor vnquam
Digna laboratis despondit præmia curis,
Et licuit, tandem chartis te reddere nunquam
Ante tuis, primum blattis epulanda relicta,
Magnorum consulta patrum, Regumque priorum
Jussa, sacro veneranda metu, temerandaque nulli,
Impune, in puras educis luminis auras.
Nec solum sole, et cœlo te auctore fruuntur,
Verumetiam (meriti tanta est fiducia) rerum
Jam sibi tractandas, audent promittere habenas,
Vis, furor, et fraudes, terras formidine solvent.
Et quæ despectæ, sub tristi carcere leges
Obductæque situ, et multa caligine tectæ
Aruerant ; nivea per te nunc veste refulgent :
Et manibus Domini, et patrum, populique feruntur.
Quin etiam fontes legum, et cunabula pandis,
Quoque cadant juris deducta vocabula ab ortu,
Quidque ferant, docto hoc tradis dictata libello.
Macte animi, nulli deerunt virtutis honores,
Nec meritis pretium : tenet, æternumque tenebit,

Imperium STEUARTA domus, nec contigit vnquam
Gratior, aut cui plus debent hæc tempora PRINCEPS,
Qui quanquam laudes longe transgressus avitas
Quamque inter Reges assurgat celsior omnes,
Solus amat doctosque colit, doctissimus ipse,
Solus amat verum, et veterum vestigia recti,
Jllius mandata ferens melioribus annis.
Majorem Europæ partem legatus obisti,
Js tibi, sed facilis, merito, sed plura merenti
Praesentis virtutum ergo, despondit honores,
Pluribus aucturus ; sed nos quod possumus vnum
Te memores meriti, æterno sacrabimus ævo.
Et quanvis primæ peragentur secula vitæ,
Nobilis omne tamen vives, doctissime, in ævum,
Dum Sol sidereo ponet discrimina mundo,
Et memores repetent seri tua scripta nepotes,
Phœnicemque suo cineri superesse videbunt.

Aliud

Dum lucem tenebræ, tenebras lux alma sequetur,
  Dum STEUARTA domus Regia sceptra feret :
Non merite SKENEÆ tui morientur honores,
  Phœnicem cineri scis superesse suo.

THOMAS CRAGIVS.

Archiotæ D. Skenæo, &c.

Nec tu nullus eris, cui tot prius abdita Princeps
  Credidit Archivis jura ruenda suis.
Primus ab his, tantum patriis cum legibus addas
  Lumen, erit calami gloria prima tui.

PATRICIVS SANDISVS.

Ad virvm clarissimvm
D. Joan. Skenævm.

Qva SKENÆE domo, quibus es majoribus ortus,
Quaque tuum longa ducas ab origine nomen,

Ignorem licet (extremo quod dissitus orbe,
Vix hausi latitans tantæ primordia famæ)
Viva tamen summo de pectore flumina vidi
Ire indefesso per secla sequentia cursu.
Dum veterum ponis leges ex ordine Regum,
Quæ terra procul, et cæca caligine mersæ,
Delituere prius, picto ludibria muro.
Tu tamen ausus eras, regale notus in aula,
Vndique melifluos legum diffundere rivos,
Pandere et obscura primas ab origine voces ;
Vt Regum summis, atque imis jussa paterent :
Vt cædes, vt furta, doli, scelerataque fraudum
Impietas (horrendum odium mortalibus ægris)
Lurida præpetibus fugerent sub tartara pennis.
Tu, SKENÆE, doces quanto conamine Reges,
Nobilitate pares, et avito sanguinis ortu,
Dissimiles animis, similes pietate, potentes
Imperio, cuncti justo moderamine legum
Incubuere suæ multum decus addere genti.
Insignes STEUARTA dedit domus vnica leges,
Qua duce, non metuit sævos gens ista tumultus.
Quis nobis impune hostis prior intulit arma,
Ausus et insano Martis contendere bello?
Legibus haud vnquam gens est melioribus vsa,
Nec plus consilio, virtute, potentibus armis,
Angustis poterant mortales sedibus vlli.
☞ Quis te Justitiæ, quis pacis amantior alter?
Infido quis te, PRINCEPS, clementior hosti?
Quis vera pietate Prior? tua fama per orbem
Spargitur, ignotas inter celeberrima gentes.
Magnanimis figis leges et sceptra BRITANNIS:
Et quondam duo regna, tuo, REX, subjicis vni
Imperio, superas omnes virtute, Priores,
Et meritis nomen longe transcendis avitum:
Astra velut nitido vincit splendore Selene.
Te celebres SKENÆE manent per secula laudes,
Nominis et major post mortem surget imago,

Quod sacras Regum tantorum scribere leges
Non metuis, cernent seri tua facta nepotes,
Ingenium, viresque tuas super aethera tollent
Laudibus, æterna moriens celebrabere fama.
Omne tuum merito nomen florebit in ævum.
Celsior et Princeps, cui tota BRITANNIA paret,
(Qualem Justitia, qualem pietate videbunt
Nulla senescentis, sic fama est, secula mundi)
Praemia digna tuis meritis feret: ille disertis,
Facundisque favet longe facundior vllo.

Aliud ejvsdem ad evndem
Skenævm.

Littora dum tumidis resonantia fluctibus æquor
Verberat, et tellus ictibus icta gemit:
Donec Sol roseo properet festinus ab ortu,
Occiduas cursu dum parat ire domos:
Magna tuæ in terras famæ volitabit imago,
Et çelebris toto lex erit orbe tua.
Et tua scripta palam multorum ante ora ferentur,
Mæonidæ nec erit laus tua laude minor.

WILHEL. SIMONIDES,
Britannoduni gregis Pastor.

Ad. Cl. V. Dn. Joannem Skenæum Archivis praefectum, pro infinitis
suis laboribus in libros Regiae Majestatis et in amicitiæ
tesseram ἐγκωμιαςικὸν.

Magna tibi SKENÆE, tuo nunc gloria facto
Exsurgit: priscas dum promis in ordine leges;
Et Regum reseras jussa, ac monumenta priorum;
Semisepulta quidem, multisque incognita seclis:
Sic generi antiquo nos reddis: et inclyta per te,
Omnibus in lucem, pia virgo ASTRÆA refulget:
Nuper, ab indignis, nobis rediviva lacunis:
SCOTUM ergo eximium, nunc felix SCOTIA, jactes
Ipsa tuum: felix tantis natalibus vna.

Quid tibi pro merito, poterit promittere virtus?
Quis te, virtutesque tuas, ignorat ineptus?
Justitiæ, jurisque comes, Themidosque Sacerdos,
Qui nobis, patriæque decus, qui pectore toto,
Virtuti invigilas, meritoque exsurgis in altum.
Macte equidem virtute tua, (vir maxime) felix
Pone metum, æternum spondent tibi sydera honorem.
Et vivet nunquam perituræ gloria famæ :

Nil duraturum mundus creat, ignis et aer,
Cunctaque corruptis, obeunt clementa figuris.
Quin et purpureus stellarum exercitus, alto
Cardine cœlorum, occasus patiuntur et ortus :
Quicquid habens ortum, finem timet : omnia poscit
Terra, vorace sinu : nihil immortale sub astris :

Ast opus exactum est, quod non Jovis ira, nec ignis,
Nec poterit ferrum, nec edax abolere vetustas,
Regia dum vasti, resonabit machina mundi.

Ergo vale SKENÆE, tibi laus maxima : sic tu
Progredere, O felix, fatoque accede vocanti,
Invidiaque omni major, super astra triumpha.

JOANNES RVSSELLVS, J. C. et in
supremo Senatu, Advocatus.

APPENDIX Nᵒ· IV.

LETTERS CONNECTED WITH TRANSACTIONS BETWEEN SIR JOHN SKENE AND HIS SONS.*

..

LETTER FROM THE ARCHBISHOP OF GLASGOW TO KING JAMES.

Most Sacred and Graciouse Soveraigne—

I resavit your Maiesties letter the first of November, commanding me to declare ànent Sir Jhon Sken and his childrenis effairis, on qhose syd the agrement fayled, and particularly if the twentie day of Julj last wes precislie appointed for agrement of al materis controvertit amongst tham, and conditioun maid, that if the Father fulfilled not suche thingis as wer on his part desyrit, Sir James suld be fre of al conditionis maid to his brother, Mr. Jhon. Pleise your Maiestie, the truthe is, that hafing resavit your Maiesties letter to deal with tham for thair agrement in May last, I travellit to haif it done according to these groundis qhiche wer layit be your Maiesties servant, Jhon Murray, to tham bothe, at thair being at Courte, qhiche war thir: That Sir James suld gif his father surtie for sex and threttie hundreth merkis Scots, to be payit to him yeirly during his lyftym, and that without ony conditioun to be done be the father; and for Mr. Jhon, his brother, that how soon he suld obtein Sir James to be infeft in the landis of Curreyhil, and ane sex thousand merkis lying vpon Saltoun, and mak payment to him of the sowm of twelf thowsand merkis, that sa soone he suld haif the office of Clerkschip provydit him. Qhen I preasit Sir James to gif his father surtie, he excusit himself that he culd not do it, unlesse he wer infeft in Curyhil and that sex thowsand

---

* These letters and those under the next head are taken from "Original Letters relating to the Ecclesiastical Affairs of Scotland" printed by the Bannatyne Club.

merkis. As I laboret the Father to infeft him, he refusit, except his brether wer satisffeit ; so I wes forcit to leave that point, and se if I culd agre the brether. In treating with tham, a questioun fel in, qho suld pay the father his last yeiris dewtie. Sir James alledgit that he suld haif twelf thowsand merkis clear, and if he wer compellit to gif his father sex and threttie hundreth, it wald diminische so muche, and conditionis suld not be kept to him. Mr. Jhon his brother answerit, that it wes reason his father suld be payit furthe of the profit of the office be tham that had brukit it, and for him self, he wald pay the twelf thowsand merkis appointet be Jhon Murray. Finding this stay, I desyrit tham to referre the mater to the said Jhon, his declaratioun and a wryting to be sent to Jhon be eche of tham, qharin thai suld referre tham selfis in that point to his determinatioun; qhiche thai wer content to do; And because the father was-impatient of al delay, I travellit earnestly with him to grant me the twentie day of Julj, till I mycht resaif answer in the point questioned between the brether from Jhon Murray, and at that tym I promisit to mak end of the busines ; After earnest entreatie, I obtenit his gud wil for that continewatioun, and this wes the cause of appointing the twentie of Julj, at qhiche day I assurit the Father, according to the hopis I had, that materis suld be endit to his contentment ; but to Sir James or his brether, I maid no conditioun, nor had not occasioun to mak ony.

In the mean tym, I travellit with Sir James, that he suld pay the yeiris dewtie to his father ; and if Jhon Murray determined the questioun on his syd, this money suld be repayit be his brother to him ; quhairvnto he yieldit. About the 20 of Julj, Jhon Murrayis answer returnit, declaring that Sir James suld pay the yeiris dewtie to his father. Sir James, thocht not wel contentit with the answer, sayit he wold acquiesce ; then I presit Mr. Jhon to obtein his brother infeft in the landis of Curryhil, and the sex thousand merkis of Saltoun. He answeret, that his father wold infeft him in Curryhil, but not in the sex thousand merkis, qhiche wes disponit to another brother. I requyrit him to se that recompensit otherwyse, because this wes a part of Jhon Murrayis decreit. He answerit, that he wes in hope, be Jhon Murrayis friendschip, to ben repossessit to his place of horningis be the Clerk of Register, and if that wer done, he wold fulfil conditiounes, otherwyse he culd not, without vndoing him self. We spendit in this sum sex or seven dayis.

Persaving great difficulties to compone matteris between the brether, I dealt with Sir James that he wold satisffie his father in gifing him securitie for his yeirly dewty, and for al other thingis tak his hasart of his father's gud wil; quhairunto at last he yeildit, and namit sum seven or eight cationeris with him in the band, qhiche I gaif his father, and he wes thairwith content. Qhen the band wes in forming, the President, be occasioune of a complaint maid to him anent the delyvering of a bil, meanit to the Lordis, that thair culd be no order, sa lang as one of the number of Sessioun had the command of that office, and vrgit muche the repayring of this; qhairvpon Sir James him self, and other freindis, desyrit me to speak to his brother, and craif his answer, qhither or not he wold accept the place vpon the conditionis. The Sessioun rose a day after or two, and being to go towardis St. Androise for sum effairis, I kept a meting between tham in Sir James' garden at Edinburgh; William Creichtoun of Ryhill wes with me, and ane Forbes, a freind of thairis. Mr. Jhon wes lothe to vndertak for the sex thowsand merkis of Saltoun. I presit him earnestly to do it, and that tryst left materis to his advysement vntil the fyve and twentie of August, at qhiche tym, meting at Edinburgh, Mr. Jhon declarit he wold fulfil al conditionis, and for the sex thowsand merkis of Saltoun, qhiche his father could not be inducit to gif Sir James, he suld pay him other sex thousandis, on this maner, that is, relief the landis of Curryhil of four thowsand merkis, with hiche burthen Sir James suld ever acceptit the sam, and mak him suretie for other two thowsand at the decease of his father and mother. Sir James stood a qhyl that he wold haif no other sex thowsand than that of Saltoun; but qhen I had declarit him how this wold be thocht very vnreasonable dealing, he left it, and schew himself content with that point. Then we talkit of the twelf thowsand merkis, and how it suld be payit. Sir James presit instant payment. Mr. Jhon offerit surtie to the term. At last, because Sir James wold not resigne the office without the money wes numerit, Mr. Jhon maid offer of the sam presently: then I thocht al had been endit. I inqyyrit Sir James if thair wes ony more to be done or spoken of: he said, nothing but sum particularis that he and his brother wold talk of amongst tham selfis, qhiche suld tak no money from him. We suld haif met the morn after and concludit, but Sir James excuisit himself that he wes diseasit, and sent his gudfather and sum other freinds to mein his cace, and request me to be freindly. I told tham, my travelis wer only be your Maiesties command, that I had procedit after suche maner, and brocht tham to agre in al thingis, nothing restit but to perform. They told me, Sir James 'culd not quyt the office without great losse, and wold had me to propone other conditionis, qhiche I eschewit.   So persaving the schift, I prayit tham to muif him to gif his father securitie, else I wold mak my report to your Maiestie, as I wes commandit, and for the brether, I wold leif that busines to another tym.   They said he suld. Qhen I lukit to haf the band subscryvit be him and his cationeris, thai returnit and offerit Sir James himself suld-subscryve it; but the cationeris culd not tak on the burthen.   Qhen I told them it wes no securitie except the cationers subscryvit, thai said, thai wold gif the father securitie during Sir James' lyftym, and so longe as he brukit the office, but no longer.   I answerit tham, the father behovit to be securit for his tym, qhither Sir James livit or deyit, and if thai fearit to bind them selfis in this sort, qhy wold not thai counsil him to end with his brother, Mr. Jhon, as thai had agreit, and Mr. Jhon wold mak his father securitie?

Finding I culd prevail nothing, nether for the fatheris securitie, nor to haif the agrement maid with his brother perfytit, I went to my Lord Secretary and cravit his advyse, schewing his Lordship the state of materis, reading your Maiesties letter, for I took that with me to him. He advysit me to requyr both parties submit tham selfis to freindis, and to me as him qhom your Maiestie had trustit with the busines.   This I did; the father wes content; only because it was not semly he suld submit with his sonne, he said Mr. Jhon suld tak burthen for him, qhiche wes thocht sufficient.   Sir James desyrit a continewatioun to the fyftent of September, and put me in hope he wald submit, and his freinds schew me the tym wes cravit only to gif sum satisfactioun to his gud-mother, that culd not be movit to agre with the decisioun of the Clerkship.   I took the submissioun subscryvit be Mr. Jhon as taking the burthen from his father, and submitting also for himself, and gaif the father to understand that Sir James wold certainly do the lyk, and that al materis suld end be decreit the fyftent of September.   Qhen the day cam, I fand the submissioun refusit in effect, for thai wold haif me try ane contract betwen the father and Archd. Jhonstoun, qhen he contractit his sonne with thair dochter, qhiche I denyit to enter into as being impertinent to me ; and yit, to se if that wold do any gud, I went to the father, and before Sir Jhon Arnot and Sir James Stewart, talkit in that purpose with him. I fand him gif satisffactioun in his answeris, so as it semit thair wes nothing to be requyret of him, qhiche he wes not willing to perform. But seing tham set only to stay the perfyting of matters agreit between Sir James and his brother, I dischargit my self of further travelling, and told tham, I would mak my report to your Maiestie, qhiche I did, thocht not in such particulars as now.

Sire, this is the true procedinge of matteris amongest them. I wes very careful to haif had tham agreit, specially to haif keipt your Maiestie from thair faschery. I piteit the estait of the aged man, qho wes brocht to the termis of hard necessitie, either be the unkyned or incircumspect dealing of his sonne. I lovit the sonne for the gud qualities I saw in him, and often bothe in privat and publick, before his freindis, entreatit him to rubbe away that blot be his father's satisfactioun, tho it wer with his worldly losse, and gaif him also lovinge and freindlie, I am sure better, counsellis, than he had from his allya. But they took no place. Sir, I know to tel the truth gettis offense, yit I fear nothing to do it, specially being commandit be your Maiestie; and voyd of al particular affectioun, inclyning to none of tham, God is my witnesse, but as I saw the matter mufit me, and to testifie as your Maiestie requyris me, on qhat syd the agreement faylit: Sir, it faylit on Sir James' parte, qho if he had stand to that qhiche wes desyrit be him self of his brother, it had been setlit, and your Maiestie not been trublit, and the blame of this lyis, and at that tym, as I understand, lay vpon his mother-in-law, qhom he fearis to displease.

I beseche your Maiestie pardon for my long and tediouse discourse, since it is maid to clear thingis to your Maiestie. Praying Almychtie God to blesse your Maiestie with al health and happiness, I humbly tak my leave.

Your Maiestie's humble and obedient servitour,

GLASGOW.

Edinburgh the 2nd of November, 1613.
  To His Most Sacred Maiestie.

2.

LETTER, SIR JOHN SKENE TO KING JAMES.

Sir,

It may pleis your Maiestie, that your vndeservit favour and beneuolence toward me hes bene so gryt and fauorable, that in all my trubillis and adversiteis I have had recourse to your Maiestie as my onlie refuge, and helper, vnder God; swa now, I have taken the baldnes, nochtwith-standing your Maiesties gryt effaires, to remember your Hienes of the lettir your Maiestie directit to my Lordis of Glasquow and Secretar, anent the office of Registration of Letteris of Hornying quhilk your Maiestie promisit to me, to cause the samyn to be given to my son, Mr. Alexander, and wes wrangouslie takin fra my son, Mr. Johne. And that thai suld deall with this Clerk of Register to that effect; quho hes done thair diligence thairanent, and desyrit the samyn mater to be referrit to thame; as Jugis Arbitratouris; quhilk I and my son readelie obeyit. Bot this Clerk of Register alluterlie refusit, and wald na wayis gif ony other answer in that mater. Swa my Son is delayit and postponit, and I am disappointit of the summe of ane thowsand markis yeirlie, qhilk my Son, obteining that office, suld pay unto me yeirlie, induring my lyftym. Quherof I dout nocht but your Maiestie will have respect on consideration, and caus direct your Hienes letter to the said Clerk of Register, commanding him to gif the said office to my said Son, conform to your Maiesties will, and promise made to me thereanent. I am assurit of your Hienes guid will in this my Petition, as I have had guid experience of your Maiesties fauour and beneuolence for my lewing and esteat; and sua committis your Maiestie to the protection of Almichtie God. From Edinburgh, the ix. day of August, 1614.

Your Maiestie's humill and obedient seruitour and subject,

S. JOHN SKENE.

To the Kingis Sacred Maiestie.

3.

LETTER, THE ARCHBISHOP OF GLASGOW AND LORD BINNING TO KING JAMES.

Most Sacred and Gratiouse Soueraigne—

The expectations we had to haif wrocht sum agrement between the Lord of Register and Sir Jhon Skein, movit us to differ the Report of our travellis in that business unto this tym. According as your Maiestie was plesit to direct us, that we suld travel to haif Maister Alexander Sken resavit in the office of hornings, or then cause sum satisffactioun be gefin him be the Clerk of Register; we urgit the first, and hafing resàvit his answer twiching the office, that he could not dispone it for dyverse reasons, we cam to the second, anent satisfactioun. The Clerk of Register offerit to submit himself to us two, in that point; only excusit, that he could not submit with Mr. Alexander Sken, as ane with qhom he had no thing to do, but with his father or brother, that had the office before, he wes willing. We bothe thocht that none of tham suld differr upon that point to agre, for if he gaif satisfactioun, it wes al one to him qho suld resaif it, if he suld be dischargit be them al. But he answerit, that he had signefeit his mynd to your Maiestie in those termis, qhiche he culd not alter without your Maiesties commandement. On the other syd we fand them noway inclynit to resaif satisfactioun, because the burthen lay upon Maister Alexander, be thair privat barganis amongst tham selfis, to mak payment to his father out of the office, yeirly, of the sowm of ane thowsand merkis Scottis, qhiche thai knew the satisfactioun that wold be modefeit suld never extend to. And so, finding these difficulties, we haif left the busines and tham to do as thai may best. Sir, this is the true account of our proceedings in that mater, qhairin, as in al things, we sal ever be careful at our possibilities to serve as your Maiestie sal pleise to command us. Praying Almychtie God to blisse your Maiestie with al happines, and many yeirs, we humbly kisse your Maiesties hands.

Your Maiesties most humble and obedient servants,

GLASGOW.
BINNING.

Edinburgh, last of September, 1614.
To his most Sacred Maiestie.

APPENDIX N^{o.} V.

PROCEEDINGS CONNECTED WITH A COMPLAINT AGAINST SIR JAMES SKENE OF CURRIEHILL, FOR NOT COMMUNICATING AT EASTER, 1619.

ACT OF PRIVY COUNCIL.

Apud Halyrudhous decimo septimo Junij 1619.
Sederunt.

Chancellair	Carnegy	Clerk of Register
Lotheane	Mr. of Elphinstoun	Aduocat
Melros	Previe Seall	Medhop
Lauderdaill	Thesaurair Depute	Mr. P. Rollok
Maxuell	Justice Clerk	Sir Andro Kerr
L. Gordoun		Sir Peter Young

Forsameikle as althocht the Kingis Maiestie, be his letters directit to the Lordis of his Maiesties Previe Counsall and Session, willed thame to have ressaueit the Communion at Easter last, with all dew reuerence, efter the maner prescryued be the ordouris and actis of the last Generall Assemblie of the Kirk haldin at Perthe, under the pane to be depoised from thair placeis in his Maiesties Counsall and Sessioun, and that, accordinglie, Sir James Skeene of Curryhill wes aduertesit to have communicat with the rest of his Maiesties Counsall and Sessioun, neuirtheles his Maiestie is crediblie informed that he not only absentit himselff frome Edinburgh at that tyme, but to the gritter contempt of his Maiestie and his authoritie, he took the Communioun in ane vther kirk, and eftir ane vther forme than was prescryued be the actis of the said Assemblie, and confermed be his Maiestie. And quhairas his Maiestie thinks it ane

A A

vnworthie pairt in ane to sit as a Judge under his Maiestie, who by his awne good example will not leade the way of dewtyfull obedience vnto others. Thairfoir the Lords of Secreit Counsall, according to his Maiesties directioun, ordanis ane messenger to pas and warne the said Sir James to compeir personallie befoir the saidis Lordis vpoun the twentie tua day of Junij instant, to ansuer to the premisses, and to hear and sie the same verifeit and provin, as accordis of the law ; And thairfor to heir and sie him suspendit from his place in his Maiesties Counsall and Sessioun till his Maiesties farder pleasour be knowin ; or ellis to schaw ane reassonabill caus quhy the samin sould not be done, with certificatioun to him, and he failzie, the saidis Lordis will suspend in maner foirsaid.

2.

Letter, the Lords of Privy Council to His Majesty King James.

Most Sacred Souerane—

According to youre Maiesteis directioun, we callit Sir James Skene of Curriehill before ws, and verie straitlie layed to his charge his dissobedience of youre Maiesties command and directioun, in not communicating with the rest of youre Maiesties Counsell and Sessioun, in the Kirk of Edinburgh, at Easter last, and for going to ane other Kirk, and ressaueing the Communioun after ane other forme then wes prescryued be the Actis of the last Generall Assemblie haldin at Perthe; and we urgeit him to cleir himsellf of thir pointis, vpoun the parrell to be suspendit from his place in Counsell and Sessioun. After that he had vtterit his greiff and sorrow for your Maiesties offence tane againis him in this particulair, quhairof he pleadit innocent, with mony protestationis that his hairt wes free frome all contempt or dissobedience of youre Maiestie, and that, in sinceritie of most loyall and dewtifull subjectioun, he had ever preast to approve him sellf your Maiesties faithfull and obedient subject, he then come to his defence againis the lybell : And tuicheing the first point thairof, for not communicating at Easter, he ansuerit, that that haill weeke he wes Ordinair in the vtter House, and Reportair, and that vpoun Satterday, quhilk wes the day for the sermone of preparatioun, his turne fell to be examinatour of the witnessis, and that he wes speciallie commandit and appoyntit to attend the same, quhairupoun he awaited frome twa of the cloke till sax of the cloke at night; and being thairby necessarlie distractit frome the sermone of preparatioun, he could not be prepairit to communicat upon the morne thairefter: And tuicheing his going to ane other Kirk to communicat, he flatlie denyit the same, affermeing constantlie, that he keipt his house that foirnoone, and that he come to the afternoones sermoun, and satt in the ordinair place with the rest of the Lordis of the Sessioun; quhilkis tua pointis, to witt, of his examinatioun of the witnesses upon Easter evin, and comeing to the afternoones sermone upoun Easter day, we can all testifie to be of trewthe; and so finding no verificatioun of the informatioun gevin to youre Maiestie in this mater, we could proceid no forder thairintill, bot hes remittit the same to youre Maiesteis princelie consideratioun, humblie beseekeing youre Maiestie not to tak in evill pairt the said Sir James his not communicatting the day foirsaid, quhilk proceidit not upoun wilfull contempt or dissobedience, but upoun the just and necessair occasioun foirsaid; and we perswade our selffis, that as he wil be cairfull to eshew all occasionis quhilkis may procure youre Maiesties iust caus of wraithe and offence againis him, so he will haif the lyke cair to approve him selff your Maiesteis faithfull and good subject. And so, with oure humble and earnist prayers vnto God for your Maiesteis long and happie reignne, we rest

Your Maiesties most humble and obedyent subjectis and servitouris,

AL. CANCELL.

LOTHIANE. MELROS.

S. W. OLIPHANT. GEORGE HAY.

KILSAYTH. CARNEGY.

A. HAY. A. M. ELPHINSTON.

Halirudhous, xxiiij Junij, 1619.

To the King his most sacred,
and excellent Maiestie.

3.

HIS MAJESTY KING JAMES TO THE LORDS OF PRIVY COUNCIL.

[James R.]

Ryght trustie and right wellbeloueit Cousens and Counsallouris, and right trustie and weilbelouit counsallouris, We greit yow weill, we haue receiued your letters of the four and twentieth of the last moneth, wherby we vnderstoode your proceedingis with Sir James Skeine, and his ansueris to suche poyntes as wer layde to his charge, and We thoght vpoun the first informatioun maid to ws, We haid verie good caus of suspitioun and pregnant presumptioun against him; yett are We glaid by your reportes to vnderstand the treuthe of his behaviour in that poynte ; and as ye have in pairt satisfeit Ws, so the only meane for him to gif Ws full satisfactioun and caus Ws reteine a goode oppinioun of him, is, if he sall with all expeditioun, at any plaice quhair the Communioun sall first be celebrated, receave the same kneilling ; and not doubting bot in the mean tyme he will approve his conformitie to the constitutionis in all vther poyntis, We bid yow fairweill.

Givin at Our Castle of Windesoir, the sixt of Julij, 1619.

APPENDIX N°. VI.

PATENT OF BARONETCY IN FAVOUR OF SIR JAMES SKENE OF CURRIEHILL, 26th JUNE, 1630.*

Oure Souerane lord with avise and consent of his Majesties rycht traist cousen and counsallour Johnne Earle of Mar lord Erskene and Gareoch etc his hienes principall thesaurer comptroller collector and thesaurer of his hienes new augmentationes of the Kingdome of Scotland   And als with avise and consent of his Majesties rycht traist cousen and counsallour Archibald lord Naper of Merchistoun his Majesties Deput in the saidis offices and of the remnant lordis of his Majesties exchequer of the said Kingdome of Scotland his Majesties commissioneris ffor propagatioun of Christian religioun within the boundis of new Scotland by and within the boundis of America (joyning to the countrey of new England thair) laitlie discoverit and surveyit be his Majesties trustie counsallour Sir Williame Alexander of Menstrie Knycht his bienes principall secritare of the said Kingdome of Scotland upoun his awin great charges and expenssis alsweill be sea and schipping as be land and now heritabill proprietar of the samen countrey and dominion and his Majesties Lievtenent and deput within the samen boundis and for the weill and furtherance of the plantation and policie of the said countrey and reducing the samen under his Majesties obedience and for gude and thankfull service done to his Majestie be Sir James Skene of Curriehill Knycht President of the College of Justice of Scotland and for divers utheris great and wechtie considerationes moving his hienes Ordines ane charter to be maid under the great seale of the said Kingdome of Scotland in dew forme Gevand Grantand and Disponand as his

---

*This is more properly the Signature for the Royal Charter, which would be in Latin, and seems to have perished in the Rubislaw charter chest.

Majestic with avise foirsaid gevis grantis and dispones to the said Sir James Skene of Curriehill Kyncht his aires male and assignais quhatsumever heritablie all and haill that pairt and portion of the saidis boundis cuntrey and dominioun of New Scotland particularlie boundit and limitat as followis To witt Beginand at the west syde of that river now callit Clyde and formerlie St. John at the north or upper end of the landis barony and regalitie of New Elphinstoun pertening heritablie to Sir Samuell Johnstoun of Elphinstoun Knycht baronet and thairfra passing northwardis up the said river thrie mylles and thairfra passing westwardis keping alwise thrie mylles in breid and the said barony of New Elphinstoun for the merche therof ay and quhile it extend to the nomber of sextine thowsand aikeris of land with castellis toures fortalices maner place houssis biggingis extructit and to be extructit yairdes orcheardis plantit and to be plantit toftis croftis parkis leasouris medowis mylnes milne-landis multures and suckin wodis fishingis alsweill of reid as quhyt fishes salmond and utheris great and small baith in salt and fresche wateris advocation and donation of benefices kirkis and chaplanris and richtis of patronages of the samen annexis connexis dependences tenentis tenandries and service of frie tennentis of the landis and otheris abonewritten Togidder with all and sindrie teindschaves and utheris teindis alsweill personage as vicarage of the landis fishingis and utheris abone specefeit includit With all and sindrie mynes minerallis vanies rockis and quarrellis theirof alsweill of metallis and minerallis regall and royall of gold and silver within the foirsaidis boundis and landis as utheris mynes of iron steill tyne lead coppar brass lattoun Toggider with all and sindrie precious stones gemmes pearles cristall alome corall and utheris And with full power privilege and jurisdiction of frie regalitie within all and haill the foirsaidis boundis and landis and all and sindrie pairtis pendiclis privileges and commodities of the samen landis and utheris abonementionat With full power and privilege to the said Sir James Skene of Curriehill his aires male and assignais foirsaidis to kid tent delve dig and search the ground of the saidis landis for the saidis mynes minerallis precious stones gemmes pearles and utheris abonewritten and to use all lawfull and ordinarie industrie for obtening and recovering therof and to win extract draw out purge fyne refyne and purifie the samen alsweill the said gold and silver as utheris mettallis precious stones pearles and utheris abonementionat and to use and convert the samen to

thair awin prapper ussis Sicklike and alsfrilie as the said Sir William
Alexander his aires and assignais mycht have done thame selffis be vertew
of his originall Infeftment maid and grantit to him therupoun quhilk is
of the dait at Windsoir the tent day of September 162j yeares or be
vertew of the infeftment grantit be his Majestie to the said Sir William
Alexander therupoun of the dait at Otlandis the xij day of July 1625
yeares   Reservand onlie to his Maiestie his aires and successouris the
tent pairt of the said royall metall commounlie callit the ure of gold and
silver to be win and gayned in all tym cuming within the saidis boundis
and landis and the remnant haill mettallis precious stones minerallis
gemmes pearles and utheris quhatsumever to pertene properlie to the
said Sir James Skene his aires males and assignais   And to be
intromittit with and remane with thame for ever to thair awin
praper uses with all praffeittis dewties and commodities theiroff
With power also to the said Sir James Skene and his foirsaidis to
carie and transport furth of the saidis boundis and countrey
to quhatsumever pairt or pairttis in all tyme cuming at thair plesour
all and quhatsumever metallis minerallis precious stones gemmes
pearles gold silver and all sortis of moneyis cunyeit and uncunyeit
quhilk salhappin ather to be win and gayned within the saidis boundis or
utherwise brocht into the samen   With power also to the said Sir James
Skene his aires male and assignes to build extract and erect within the
boundis of the samen ground and landis quhatsumever cities burghis
tounes villages burghis of baronie frie poirtis bayes harbouris heavins
and stationes for shippis within the samen castellis touris fortalices forthis
blockhoussis skonses rampires and bulwarkis within the samen haill
boundis and landis cities burghis harbouris portis and uthers places alsweill be sea and sea coist as be land gairdit and furnishit with compenies
of garrisones of men of warr and souldiouris for fortifeing strenthning
saifgard and mantenance therof   And siclike to erect and appoint faires
mercattis and mercat places within the saidis cities burghis tounes villages
and burghis of barony or within onie uther pairt off all and sindrie the
forsaidis boundis and landis ather to burgh or land to be kepit observit
and mantenit at quhatsumever speciall dayes seasones of the year places
and occasiones as the said Sir James Skene his aires male and assignais
sall think expedient and to impose uplift exact and ressave all and
quhatsumever toillis customes anchorages prymgilt doksilver and utheris

dewties of the samen cities burghis tounes villages portis harbouris faires and mercattis as the said Sir James Skene his aires male and assigneis sall think' expedient with all and sindrie privileges liberties and commodities belonging thairto   And likewise to constitute and appoint capitanes commanderis leaderis and governouris majoris officearis provestis and baillies of the foirsaidis burghis tounes villages and burghs of barony regalitie portis harbouris castellis and forthis   Togidder with Justices of peace constables utheris officearis and judges alsweill in all caussis civill as criminall for government and for dew and lawfull administration of Justice within the samen and in and throuchout the remnant boundis of the foirsaids landis boundis and coistis   And as they pleis to alter and change the samen magistrattis and officearis for the better government of the saidis boundis and to take ordour with their government as they sall think expedient   And siclike to mak set doun and establishe sick particular lawis ordinances and constitutiones within all and haill the foirsaidis boundis and landis alsweill to burgh as land as thay sall think expedient thair to be observit in all tyme cuming and the breakeris and contraveneris therof to chastise correct and punishe conform thairto And siclike to build and extruct shippis barkis and vessellis great and small alsweill for warr as merchand shippis ather within the samen dominioun of New Scotland boundis and pairttis of the foirsaidis landis speciallie designit to the said Sir James Skene his aires male and assignais or within the said Kingdome of Scotland or utheris his Majesties dominiones at all tymes convenient and to use and sayill the samen shippis barkis and vesshellis under his Majesties awin flaggis and ensegnes furnisit with skipperis pilottis marineris governouris capitanes commanderis and souldiouris to be impute therin be the said Sir James Skene his aires male and assignais with all kynd of munitioun great and small powder bullet armour harness and all weapones invasive and defensive and all uther engynes and exercise of warre and lykewise to transport thairby or be quhatsumever uther shipping to the said countrey of New Scotland and speciall boundis abone designit canonis demy cannons zetlingis and other munitioun great and small for defence saiftie and mantenance of the said countrey and likewise with expres power privilege and licence to the said Sir James Skene his aires male and assignais deputies or utheris in thair names to transport furth of the said Kingdome of Scotland or utheris his majesteis dominiones or ellisquhair at thair plesour all and quhatsumever persones souldiouris men of war labouraris artificeris wodismen or utheris of quhatsumever qualitie estait or degrie being willing to repair to the said countrie of new Scotland with thair guides geir horss nolt sheip munitioun great and small armour provisioun and victualling to the said ground and landis for the better furtherance and advancement of the said plantation and siclike to use and exerce all lawfull trade of merchandice for the better policie of the samen boundis and landis and to exclude prohibite discharge resist repell and invaid be force of armes all and quhatsumever persones intending to plant occupie or possess the foirsaidis boundis and landis or exerce and use trade and traffique within the samen without the expres avise licence and consent of the said Sir James Skene his airis male and assignais or deputies had and obtenit thairto and to confiscat intromit with detene and withhald all and sindrie thair shipping guides geir and plennising ather be sea or land usurping the contrair. And to apply the samen to the proper use utilitie and proffeit of the said Sir James Skene and his foirsaidis with express warrand and command also to all his majesties shireffis Stewartis and baillies of regalities justices of peax majores aldermen provestis baillies and magistrattis of quhatsumever boundis cities tounes villages burghs and utheris alsweill to land as burght thair officiaris serjandis constabillis and ministeris of Justice quhatsumever to concur fortifie and assist the said Sir James Skene and his foirsaidis theranent and in deu and lawfull execution of all and sindrie pointis clausses and articles of the said charter and infeftment and that they may have readie shipping at all occasiones for thair men companyes gudes geir munitioun armes armour victuall and furnissing to and fra the saidis boundis and countrey of New Scotland with thame selffis as neid beis upoun thair reasonabill chargis and expenssis as effeiris with power also to the said Sir James Skene his aires male assignais and deputies incais ony rebellioun mutinie or seditioun fall out within the saidis boundis ground and landis or in the course of thair voyages and navigationes to dissobey and withstand thair commandementis, in that caise or ony of the saidis caissis to use and exerce the power and privilege of all lawis militar aganes the delinquentis and offendaris and to punishe and correct thame thairby as they sall think expedient excluding be thir presentis his majesties said livetenent and all uther persones quhatsumever fra using and exercing ony law militar aganes the saidis persones or ony of thame within the saidis boundis or in thair saidis courssis and voyages to and fra the samen except onlie the said Sir James Skene his aires male assignais and thair deputies allanerlie and likewise his majestie for him and his successoures with avise and consent forsaid be thir presentis does exeme frie and liberat for ever the said Sir James Skene his aires male and assignais from all punishment arreist tortour and execution of militar lawis which may be usit or execute aganes thame or onie of thame be his majesties said livetenent or ony uther persone or persones quhatsumever and gif it sal happin also the forsaidis persones or ony of thame being under the charge maintenance or dependence of the said Sir James Skene and his forsaidis to abstract and withdraw thame selffis for the obedience of the said Sir James Skene and his foirsaidis or fra thair service in the said plantation and mantenance thairof ather be sea or land or in thair course or voyage to or fra the said countrey of new Scotland or to withdraw and abstract thame selffis thair guidis and geir fra the seruice and obedience of the said Sir James Skene and his foirsaidis or to remove thame selffis thair gudes and geir furth of the boundis and ground of the samen landis and sick pairttis and portiones therof as sal happin to be designit to thame or to joyne them selffis with the natives and savages of the said countrey or to inhabite onie remote or desert places of the samen countrey without the special auise licence or consent of the said Sir James Skene and his forsaidis had and obtenit thairto Than and in these caiss or ony of thame thay sall tyne and amit ipso facto all and sundrie thair landis possessiones guides and geir being within the samen boundis ground and landis And it salbe lesome to the said Sir James his aires male assignais and deputies to confiscate recognosce and posses the samen landis boundis possessiones guides and geir and apply the samen to thair awin proper uses frilie but danger of law and but onie foirder declaratour thairanent And likewise give onie barganes blokis or conditiones salbe maid betuix the said Sir James Skene his aires male assignais or deputies with quhatsumever uther persone or persones ather natives of the said cuntrey or foreyneris aliens or utheris persones qubat- sumever for transporting of onie guides geir waires merchandice muni- tioun armes victuall furnissing or utheris quhatsumever or for fulfilling of quhatsumever deid or deidis to the said Sir James Skene and his foir- saidis ather within the said countrey of New Scotland or be sea cours or passage to or fra the samen countrey under quhatsumever paines or soumes of money And sall brek and violat the samen barganes contractis bandis or conditiones or sall failzie in performing and fulfilling therof to the hurt and detriment of the said Sir James Skene and his forsaidis and to the stay and hindrance of the said plantatione and policie theirof Then and in these caissis or ather of thame it salbe lesum to the said Sir James Skene and his abonewrittin to intromit with bruik and possess the samen guides geir merchandice soumes of money and utheris to thair awin use but foirdir proces and declaratour of law And siclike with express power and privilege to the said Sir James Skene his aires male assignayis and deputies thair men tennentis and servandis within the saidis boundis and landis To hunt use and exerce trade and traffique with the natives and savages of the said countrey and to tak mak and contract peace troust and affinitie and truce with thame and to intirtaine freindship and amitie with thame and with thair leaderis governouris and commanderis And in cais of offence brek of dewtie promeis or freindschip on thair pairttis to tak and use armes in thair contrair be all hostill maner baith be sea and land with power and privilege also to the said James Skene and his foirsaidis in all tyme cuming to export out of the saidis boundis and countrey of New Scotland all waires merchandice and commodities quhatsumever and to import and inbring the samen to the said kingdome of Scotland or to quhatsumever uther pairttis at thair plessour And lykewise to export out of the said kingdome of Scotland and utheris places quhatsumever all waires merchandice and commodities quhatsumever and to inbring the samen to the saidis boundis and countrey of New Scotland for payment of five poundis Scottis money of custome for ilk hundreth pundis allenerlie without payment of onie uther custome impositione or dewtie quhatsumever To be upliftit taken or exactit thairfor be his Majestie his aires or successouris or be thair customaris deputies or officiaries or be any uther person quhatsumever ather within the said kingdome of Scotland or countrey of New Scotland Dischargeing heirby all his Majesties customaris and officearies from exacting any farder custome or imposition thereanent and of thair offices in that pairt. With power also to the said Sir James Skene and his foirsaidis be thame selffis thair deputies officearis and utheris in thair name to uplift exact and ressave from all his Majesties and his successouris subjectis quha sal happin to trade or trafficque within the saidis boundis ground and landis abone designit portis and harbouris therof fyve pundis money foirsaid of custome for ilk hundreth pundis of all guides waires merchandice or commodities ather to be importit thairto be thame or ony of thame or exportit from thence and the sowm of Ten pundis from all strangeris for ilk hundereth of all guides waires or merchandice to be exportit or importit be thame or ony of them, and that by and attour the said soum of fyve pundis dew to his Majestie and his successouris as said is. And forder his Majestic for him his aires and successouris with avise and consent abouewrittin be thir presentis Willis ordines and declaires That the said sowme of fyve pundis money foirsaid of custome appointit to be payit as said is to his Hienes his airis and successouris thair customaris and deputtis for all guides waires merchandice and commodities ather to be exportit out of the said countrey of new Scotland or importit to the samen sal be payit and deliverit to the said Sir William Alexander his aires and assignayis being his Majesties Livetenentis of the said countrey and to nanc utheris for the space of sextine yeares nixt efter the day and date abonewrittin of the said last infeftment grantit to the said Sir Williame Alexander of the samen countrey of New Scotland, and for that effect it salbe lesome to the said Sir Williame Alexander to uplift ask crave and ressave the samen acquittances and dischargeis, to give and grant therupoun quhilkis his Majestie be thir presentis for him his aires and successouris willis and declaires to be sufficient to the ressaveris of the saidis acqittances and payeris of the said sowme of fyve pundis of custome, and with power to the said Sir Williame Alexander and his foirsaidis during the said space to bestow and convert the said soume of fyve pundis for ilk hundreth sa to be upliftit to thair awin proper use and utilitie as thay sall think expedient for thair better help and mantenance of thair charges and expenssis in government of the said countrey and furthering of the said plantation. And albeit it be nawise lawfull ony nobill man or landit gentilman within the said kingdome of Scotland to pas out of the samen without his Majesties speciall licence his Majestie for him his aires and successouris Willis grantis and declaires be the tenour heirof That thir presentis ar and salbe sufficient licence and warrand in all tyme to cum to the said Sir James Skene and his foir saidis and such other persones (not being giltie of lesemajestie or utherwise being speciallie inhibite) as salbe desyrous to go with thame or ony of them or ony of thame to the saidis landis and boundis frilie to pas furth of the said kingdome of Scotland and to go and repair to the saidis boundis and countrey of New Scotland but onie danger or inconvenient to them in thair bodies landis guides or geir, Wheranent his Majestie with avise foirsaid hes dispensit and be thir presentis for him his aires and successouris dispenssis for ever. And farder geving granting and declairing lyke as be thir presentis his Majestie for him his aires and successouris with avise and consent abonewrittin gevis grantis willis declaires and ordines that all his Majesties subjectis and utheris persones quhatsumever quhilkis salbe willing to render them selffis under his Majestie his aires or successouris obedience quha sall at any time herefter go to the saidis boundis and landis heirby disponit to the said Sir James Skene and his abonewrittin and inhabit the samen or ony pairt therof with the licence consent and permission of the said Sir James Skene his aires maill assignayis or deputies, That all and everie ane of the saidis persones with thair childrene and posteritie respective sall have hold enjoy bruik and posses all and quhatsumever liberties privileges and immunities of frie and naturall subjectis of the said Kingdome of Scotland and utheris his Majesties dominiones as gif thay had bene borne and procreat within the samen kingdomes and dominiones, And for establissing of the greatter auctoritie commandement power and jurisdictioun in all tyme cuming in the persone of the said Sir James Skene his aires male assignayis and deputies in the saidis landis his Majestie for him his aires and successouris with avise and consent foirsaid hath gevin and grantit and be thir presentis gevis and grantis to the said Sir James Skene his aires male and assignayis quhatsumever heritablie the Justiciarie and Sherefschip of the saidis haill particular boundis and landis abouespecifeit and hath maid and constitute and be thir presentis makis and constitutis the said Sir James Skene his aires male and assignayis his Majesties heritabill Shereffis Justices and Justicaries heritablie for ever within all and haill the saidis particular boundis and landis abouespecifeit and speciallie designit with all and sundrie liberties privileges freedomes immunities and commodities belanging to the said Sherefschip and Justiciarie with power to the said Sir James Skene his aires male assignayis or thair deputies to sit judge cognosce and decyde in all and quhatsumever caussis alsweill civill as criminall within the saidis boundis and jurisdiction of the samen landis sicklike and als frilie

in all respectis as ony uther justice justiciarie or Sheref quhatsumever may or micht have done in ony tyme bygane or to cum   And
least any question micht arryse anent the tyme within the quhilk
the said Sir James Skene and his foirsaidis as Shereffis or Justices
may sitt cognosce and decyde in caussis criminall efter the crymes committit his Majestie for him his aires and successouris with avise and
consent foirsaid be thir presentis willis grantis and declairis That it salbe
lesum and lawfull to thame to challange and persew attaiche and arreist
quhatsumever criminall offenderis within the saidis boundis and landis
for ony crymes committit be thame, And to sitt cognosce judge and
decyde thairanent at any tyme within the space of sex monethis nixt
efter the committing of the samen crymes   During the quhilk space it
salbe lesum onlie to the said Sir James ·Skene and his foirsaidis and to
nane utheris to try cognosce judge and proceid thairanent, Excluding
during that space his Majesties Livetenent and all uther persones qubatsumever from exercing of ony judgement or jurisdiction theranent òr to
attache arreist adjournay call or convene the saidis criminall offenderis
and committeris of crymes be any maner of way providing alwise that
gif efter the said space of sex monethis beis expirit the saidis crymes and
criminall offenderis beis not judgeit or tryed be the said Sir James Skene
and his foir saidis   In that cais it salbe lesome therefter to his Majesties
said Livetenent his aires and assignayis being his Majesties saidis
Livetenentis and thair deputtis to challange attaiche arreist call and
convene the saidis persones giltie and to judge and cognosce anent the
crymes committit be thame as they sall think expedient with power also
to the said Sir James Skene and his foirsaidis notwithstanding of the
provision abonewrittin efter the expiring of the saidis six monethis at
all tymes in the absence of the said Sir Williame Alexander his aires
and assignayis being his Majesties Livetenentis and thair deputtis to
judge cognosce and decyde in all caussis criminall and to punishe all
criminall offendaris within the saidis boundis at thair plessour   And in
lyke maner in thair absence out of the said countrey ather within the
said space of sex monethis òr therefter at all tymes quhatsumever to remit
and forgive the saidis crymes and criminall offenderis within the saidis
boundis and landis upon suche reassonabill caussis and consideratione as
thay sall think expedient And farder with power to the said Sir James
Skene and his foirsaidis to sitt judge and cognosce upon all crymes and

criminall offendaris within the saidis boundis and ether to punishe remit
or forgive thair saidis crymes and criminall offendaris as thay sall
think expedient at all tymes efter the said space of sex monethis befoir
the said Sir Williame his aires and assignayis being his Majesties Livetenentis and thair deputies do provoik cite or indyte the saidis criminall
ofendaris to compeir to thair judicatorie albct thay be in the said
countrey of New Scotland for the tyme But prejudice alwise to the said
Sir William Alexander his aires and assignayis being his Majesties
Livetenentis and thair deputies being first citeris efter the said space of
sex montheis beis expirit   To sitt judge cognosce punishe or remit the
saidis crymes and criminall offendaris at thair plessour as said is   And
likewise his Majestie be thir presentis ordines that in cais it salhappin
the said Sir James Skene or his foirsaidis to for give or remit ony of the
saidis crymes or criminall offenderis as said is   That in that caiss thair
remissioun and pardoun so to be grantit salbe publist and proclamit
within the saidis boundis at the day and dait of the granting therof be sum
of thair particular officiaris to be appointit be thame to that effect   And
efter the publication therof that the samen remissioun salbe registrat in the
register of the said Sir William Alexander his aires male and assignayis
being his Majesties Livetenentis of the samen countrey within the space
of thriescoir dayss efter the publication therof, at the least that the samen
salbe offerit and presentit befoir twa famous witnessis to the keper of the
samen register give the samen register Clerk or keper therof salhappin to
be in the said countrey of New Scotland for the tyme with full power
and privilege to the said Sir James Skene his aires male and assignayis
and thair deputies for ever   To sitt fence hald or caus be haldin in thair
names Justice courttis Shereff courttis courttis of frie regalitie baroun
courttis and burrow courttis within and upoun all and haill the foirsaidis
boundis and landis abone designit to him as said is or ony pairt of the
samen at all tymes and occasiones as thay sall think expedient Clerkis
officiaris serjandis and utheris memberis of courts quhatsumever To mak
and creat unlawis and amerciamentis of court to ordane exact uplift and
ressave and apply the samen to thair awin proper use as thay sall think
expedient with all and sindrie utheris privileges liberties commodities and
casualities perteining or that may fall or pertene to the saidis offices and
jurisdictiones of Justiciarie frie regalitie and sherefship and utheris abone
expremit with full power and privilege also to the said Sir James Skene

his aires male and assignayis to sell annallie and dispone heritablie or utherwise all and haill the foirsaidis boundis and landis abone designit at thair plessour with all and sindrie liberties fredomes immunities and commodities abone and under exprest heirby grantit to him or with sa many of the saidis liberties fredomes and utheris as he or his foirsaidis sall think expedient To quhatsumever uther persone or persones thair aires or assignayis being under his Hienes obedience To be haldin of his Majestic his aires and successouris or of the said Sir James Skene his aires male and assignayis as it sall best pleis the said Sir James Skene and his foirsaidis Quhilkis landis boundis privileges and utheris abone exprest or onie pairt therof being disponit be the said Sir James Skene and his foirsaidis to ony other person or persones To be haldin of his Majestic his aires and successouris his Majestic his aires and suc- cessouris Sall ressave and admit thame and everie ane of thame as thair fric vassellis and immediat tenentis therof And sall grant unto thame and everie one of thame such sufficient infeftmentis of the samen and with the samen maner of halding as is now grantit to the said Sir James Skene his aires male and assignayis quhenever thay sall dessyr the samen With power also to the said Sir James Skene his aires male and assignayis and to all uther persone or persones being under his Majesties obedience to quhom thay salhappin to annallie and dispone ony pairt or portioun of the saidis landis To intitill and call the samen or ony pairt or portion therof be quhatsumever name or titill thay sall think expedient in all tyme cuming. As also that it salbe lesome to the aires male and successouris quhatsumever of the said Sir James Skene and his assignayis To enter thame selffis as aires to thair predicessouris to the saidis landis boundis and utheris quhatsumever grantit and dis- ponit to the said Sir James Skene or ony pairt therof be vertew of thir presentis And that ather be ordour of the chancelarie of the said King- dome of Scotland be service brevis retouris and preceptis dwell furth of the samen and be the ordour observit theranent or utherwise be the ordour of the chappell and chancelarie of the said countrey of New Scotland at the plessour and option of the aires male and successouris of the said Sir James Skene and his assignayis quhatsumever With power also to the said Sir James Skene his aires male assignayis and thair deputies in all tyme cuming To convocat all and sindrie thair men tenentis servandis and inhabitantis quhatsumever of the saidis boundis and landis

abone designit at all tymes and occasiones as thay sall think expedient
for the weill defence and mantenance of them selffis or of thair saidis
boundis and landis for resisting of forreyne enemeis repressing of inso-
lencies and ryottis of mutinous seditions or rebellious people Reducing
the natives and savages to conformitie and dew obedience and utheris
lawfull or necessarie caussis quhatsumever. And mairour Geving and
granting as be thir presentis his Majestie for him his aires and successouris with avise and consent abone writtin gevis grantis willis ordines
and declaires That the said Sir James Skene his aires male and assignayis sall in all tyme cuming have voit and voice in making of all
lawis to be maid in all tyme cuming concerning the publict weill stait
and government of the said countrey of New Scotland and in all
metingis assemblies counsallis and conventiones to be callit convenit or
haldin for that effect And that thay salbe dewlie and lawfullie warnit to
that effect and that na lawis salbe maid nor established theranent or be
valid without the avise and consent of the said Sir James Skene his aires
male and assignayis and without the avise and consent of the remanent
baronettis haveris ilk ane of thame the lyke quantitie and proportioun of
landis within the said countrey pertening heritablie to thame as is heirby
disponit to the said Sir James Skene To wit ilk ane of thame sextene
thowsand aikeris of land at the leist without the avise and consent of the
maist pairt of sa mony of thame as sall convene to gif thair voittis and
voices upoun dew and lawfull warning given to them in maner to be
condiscendit upoun and sett doun at the first meting and assemblie to be
haldin be thame and his Majesties said Livetenent his aires or assignayis
being his Majesties Livetenentis for making of lawis and ordinances of
that countrey And that na persone or persones quhatsumever and ilk
ane of them quha sall not be heritouris of sextine thowsand aikeris of
land within the said countrey sall have voit or voice of making of onie
lawis concerning the said countrey without the mutuall avise and consent
of the said Livetenent his aires and assignayis being his Majesties Livetenentis and of his aires and successouris and of the said Sir James
Skene and his foirsaidis and the remanent baronettis foirsaidis And
farder in cais the said Sir James Skene his aires male and assignayis be
not personalie present at suche metingis counsallis conventiones or
assemblies as salbe haldin callit or convenit to the effect foirsaid within
the said countrey of new Scotland In that cais thair deputies or

actornayes having thair power and authoritie and having the quantitie of ane thowsand aikeris of land pertening to them in heritage within the said countrey sall have the like voit and voice as gif thay wer personalie present Bot in cais any metingis or assemblies be haldin to that effect within the said kingdome of Scotland in that cais gif thay be personallie present for the tyme within the said kingdome thay sall have onlie voit and voice be thame selffis and not be thair deputies or actornayes having thair power and warrand Bot in cais of thair absence furth of the said kingdome at sick tymes In that cais thair deputies and actornayes having thair power and warrand sall have the lyke voit and voice as gif they wer personallie present them selffis And that the said Sir James Skene and his Majesties haill remanent subjectis and inhabitantis of that countrey of new Scotland in all tyme cuming salbe judgeit rewlit and governit in all caussis civill and criminall be the lawis of the said countrey onlie and na uther But prejudice alwise to the said Sir James Skene and his foirsaidis be themselffis and thair deputies to mak sic particular lawis constitutiones and ordinances within thair awin proper boundis particu-larlie abone designit as they sall think expedient for the better policie weill and government therof and inhabitantis of the samen and for keping of gude ordour and administration of law and justice within the samen And but prejudice to the said Sir James Skene and his foirsaidis of ony uther particular libertie privilege immunitie claus or conditioun quhatsumever abone or under exprest conceavit in thair favouris provyding alwise that all quhatsumever generall lawis to be maid and set doun in maner foirsaid concerning the publict weill stait and government of the said countrey or be the said Sir James Skene and his foirsaidis within thair awin particular boundis as said is salbe maid als conforme and aggreabill to the lawis of the said kingdome of Scotland as convenientlie may be Regaird being had to the circumstances of tyme place and distance of the said countrey and inhabitantis therof and thair conditiones and qualities And farder albeit be expres condition of the said originall Infeftment grantit to his Majesties said Livetenent It is grantit and appointit to him his aires and assignayis to convocat all and sindrie the inhabitantis of the said countrey of new Scotland be pro-clamation or utherwise in maner therein mentionat Nevirtheles his Majestie hath grantit willit and ordanit and be thir presentis for him his aires and successouris with avise and consent abonewrittin Willis grantis

declaires and ordines That it salbe nawise lesum nor lawfull to his
Majesties said Livetenent his aires successouris assignayis or ony utheris
his Majesties or his successouris officiarias quhatsumever To convocat
or convene be proclamation or utherwise the said Sir James Skene his
aires assignayis successouris deputies men tenentis servandis or inhabitantis of the said particular boundis now disponit to the said Sir James
Skene Bot upoun sick reasonabill necessar and lawfull caussis as
salbe fund fitt and expedient for the publict weill of that countrey
be the said Livetenent and his foirsaidis with 'avise and consent of
the said Sir James Skene his aires male assignayis or deputies and
the avise and consent of the remnant persones abonenominat appointit to have voit and voice in making of lawis as said is Quha
and everie ane of thame thair aires successouris assignayis deputies men
tenentis servandis and inhabitantis of thair severall boundis and landis
salbe subject to the lyke condition And likewise that it sall not be
lesum nor lawfull to the said Livetenent or his foirsaidis or ony utheris
his Majestic his aires or successouris officearis quhatsumever to exact
impose or uplift onie taxatioun or imposition fra or upoun the said
Sir James Skene his aires male assignayis deputies men tenentis servandis
or inhabitantis of the saidis boundis and landis particularlie abone
specifeit and disponit to him or upoun thair landis rentis gudes and geir
without the speciall consent of the said Sir James Skene his aires male
and assignayis notwithstanding of onie power grantit to the said Livetenent and his foirsaidis be the said originall infeftment or be vertew of
ony uther richt or title quhatsumever maid or grantit or to be maid or
grantit be his Majestie his aires or successouris to the said Livetenent
or ony uther persone quhatsumever But prejudice alwise to the said
Sir James Skene his aires male assignayis and deputies within the propper
boundis particularlie abone designit and heirby disponit to him To call
convocat and convene thair men tenentis servandis and inhabitantis at
all tymes and occasiones in maner and for the caussis abone exprest be
ane speciall claus theranent And further geving granting and disponing
as be thir presentis his Majestie for him his aires and successouris with avise
and consent foirsaid gevis grantis and dispones heritablie for ever To
the said Sir James Skene his aires male and assignayis all and
quhatsumever uther privileges liberties fredomes commodities immunities proffeittis aismentis prerogatives dignities and casualities generallie

or particularlie mentionat or exprest in the said originall infeftment grantit to the said Sir William Alexander and his forsaidis and in als full frie and and ampill forme and maner as if the samen privileges prerogatives immunities liberties fredomes dignities commodities and utheris with all claussis and conditiones theranent wer heirin and in the bodic of the said charter to be extendit heirupoun at lenth speciallie ingrost and contenit in thir presentis in sa far allanerlie as the samen may be extendit or concerne the particular boundis and landis abone designit disponit heirby to the said Sir James Skene his aires male and assignayis as heritouris therof (exceptand alwise and reservand to the said Sir Williame Alexander his aires and assignayis the Livetennandries of the said haill countrey and dominioun of New Scotland The power and privilege of striking and coyning of moneyes the office of cheif Justiciarie generall of the samen countrey in caussis criminall The office of admiralitie making of officearis of estait conferring of titillis of honour with full power and jurisdiction of frie regalitie chappell and chancellarie of the said countrey and privilege of making of lawis concerning the publict weill stait and government of the said countrey granted to him be his said originall infeftment provyding that the samen reservatioun and exception now conceavit in favoures of the said Sir William Alexander and his foirsaidis sall be nawise prejudiciall to the said Sir James Skene and his foirsaidis anent all or ony of the particular privileges fredomes liberties immunities commodities and utheris abone and under-mentionat heirby grantit to the said Sir James Skene and his foirsaidis in maner generallie and particularlie abone and under writtin Quhilkis landis boundis advocation and Donation of benefices kirkis and chaplanries and richtis of patronage therof with the teind shaves and utheris teindis parsonage and vicarage of the samen includit mynes minerallis metallis precious stones gemms pearles wodis fishingis mylnes multures offices privileges and jurisdiction of frie regalitie justice and justiciarie Shereff and Sherefschippis and all uther liberties immunities privileges conditiones fredomes customes casualities and utheris quhatsumever generallie and particularlie abone mentionat perteine heritablie of befoir to the said Sir Williame Alexander And wer dewlie and lawfullie resignit surrenderit and upgevin be him be his lawfull procuratouris in his name to that effect speciallie constitut and patent Lettres in the handis of the saidis Lordis of his Hienes Exchekquer of

the said kingdome of Scotland his Majesties Commissiounaris nominat
and appointit be his Hienes to that effect as in the handis of his Majestie
the said Sir William Alexander his immediat lawfull superiour of the
landis boundis and utheris foirsaidis purelie and simplie be staff
and bastoun as use is at Halyrudhous Togidder with all richt titill
entres and clame of richt etc   To and in favouris of the said Sir James
Skene his aires male and assignayis quhatsumever in maner and with
the provisiones limitationes exceptiones and reservationes respective
abone mentionat   And that for new heritabill infeftment to be maid
gevin and grantit be his Majestie to the said Sir James Skene his aires
male and assignayis quhatsumever   To be altogidder erectit unit
annexit and incorporat in ane haill full and frie barony and regalitie for
ever to be callit in all tyme cuming the Barony of [*sic*] To be haldin of
his Majestie his aires and successouris of the croun and kingdome of
Scotland in frie blenshe for yearlie payment of ane penny usuale money
of the said kingdome of Scotland upon the ground of the saidis landis
and boundis or ony pairt therof at the feist of the nativitie of our Lord
in name of blenshe ferme give it beis askit allanerlie with dispensation
also of the nonentrie of the samen haill landis boundis and barony
maillis fermes proffeittis and dewties therof during the samen nonentrie
And farder geving granting and disponing as be the tenour heirof his
Majestie for him his aires and successouris of his certane knawlege and
meir motive with avise and consent foirsaid and for divers gude and
thankfull services done to his Hienes be the said Sir James Skene and
utheris wechtie caussis and considerationes moving his Majestie Gevis
grantis and dispones of new to the said Sir James Skene his aires male
and assignayis heritablie for ever   All and haill the foirsaidis boundis
landis mylnes wodis fischingis advocation and donation of benefices
kirkis and chaplanries and richtis of patronages therof with the foirsaidis
teind schaves and utheris teindis personage and vicarage of the samen
includit mynes minerallis precious stones with power privilege and jurisdiction of frie regalitie offices of justiciarie and Sherefschip privileges
power and jurisdiction Justiciarie and Sherefdome in all caussis criminall
and civill Courttis unlawis amerciamentis escheattis   And all and sindrie
utheris liberties fredomes immunities customes casualities profeittis
dewties and utheris quhatsumever particularie or generallie abonexprest
Quhilkis his Majestie for him his aires and successouris with avise and

consent foirsaid be thir presentis Willis and haldis as heirin arid in thè said chárter to follow heirupoun speciallie and particularlie ingrost repeittit insert and exprest with the particular exceptiones limitationes and provisiones respective and particularlie abonewrittin and of new Erectis unittis annexis and incorporattis All and sindrie the foirsaidis landis and boundis mylnes wodis fischingis advocation and donation of benefices kirkis and chaplanries and richtis of patronage therof teind schaves and utheris teindis personage and vicarage of the samen includit mynes mettallis minerallis precious stones pearles offices regalitie justiciarie and Sherefschip liberties fredomes privileges and immunities customes proffeittis casualities dignities power jurisdiction and utheris quhàtsum-ever generallie and particularlie abonexprest quhilkis his Majestic for him and his successouris haldis as heirin and in the said charter repeittit and particularlie insert with the particular exceptiones and reservationes speciallie abone mentionat Dispensing for ever with the generalitie In all and ane full and frie Baronie and Regalitie of To be haldin and to be had be the said Sir James Skene his aires male and assignayis off our said Soverane Lord and his successouris of the said croun and kingdome of Scotland in frie heritage frie regalitie and barony for ever Be all richt meithis merchis and divisis as the samen lyes in lenth and breid in houssis biggingis mylnes multures etc with balking hunting court plent herzeld bludùite and mercheat unlawis amerciamentis and escheattis of courttis and with furk fork sok sak tholl theve vert wrack wair venyson waith pitt gallows infang theiff and outfang theif therof And with commoun pasture frie ische and entrie And all and sindrie uther commodities fredomes privileges proffeittis aismentis prero-gatives dignities and casualities grantit of befoir be his Majestic or his predicessouris to quhatsumever barone mair or les within the said kingdome of Scotland and all utheris contenit in the said originall infeftment thairanent And quhilkis his Majestie be him selff or ony utheris his maist royall progenitouris and antecessouris hes gevin grantit and disponit or may give grant and dispone be vertew of ony charteris infeftmentis lettres patentis grantis or donationes to ony his Majesties Subjectis of quhatsumever qualitie state or degrie or to quhatsumever Societies companies or utheris particular memberis therof in seiking leiding purchessing acquyring conquesing or mantayning of onie forraine landis or colonies quhatsumever with the exceptiones reservationes and provisiones speciallie abone mentionat   And in als full frie and ampill forme and maner as the samen privileges liberties commodities and immunities with all and sindrie claussis conditiones and provisiones theranent wer at lenth speciallie ingrost insert and contenit in thir presentis   Togidder with all richt titill entres and clame of richt alsweill petitor as possessour quhilk his Majestic his predicessouris or Successouris had hes or onywise may have clame or pretend thairto or to the maillis fermes proffeittis and dewties of the foirsaidis landis barony and utheris speciallie and generallie abone mentionat off quhatsumever yeares and termes preceiding for quhatsumever caus or occasioun bygane Renuncing and Dischargeing the samen with all action and instance thairanent   To and in favouris of the said Sir James Skeine his aires male and assignayis for ever alsweill for not payment of the dewtie contenit in the said originall infeftment or for not doing of dew homage conform thairto or not fulfilling of onie point of the samen originall infeftment or for committing of onie fault deid commissioun or omissioun prejudiciall thairto or quhairupoun the samen originall infeftment may be lawfullie quarrellit impugnit or drawen in questioun ony maner of way acquyting and forgiving the samen simpliciter with all action theranent competent or that may be competent to his Majestie his aires or successouris ony maner of way and renuncing the samen juri liti et cause cum pacto de non petendo   And with supplement of all faultis and defectis alsweill not namit as namit quhilkis his Majestie will have as for exprest in the foirsaid charter and infeftment following thereupoun   And forder his Majestic with avise and consent abone-writtin Willis and grantis and for his Hienes and his successouris Decernis and ordines that the landis baronie and utheris foirsaidis salbe extentit and retourit to ane twentie shilling land usuale Scottis money alsweill of new as auld extent in all tyme cuming   To the effect that retouris and preceptis of Chancelarie may be past in favouris of the aires and successouris of the said Sir James Skene aggreable to the auld forme observit in his Majesties Chancelarie of Scotland and that ather in the said kingdome of Scotland and his Majesties Chancelarie therof or in the said countrey of New Scotland and chancelarie of the samen in the option of the said Sir James Skene and his abone writtin   And in cais it sall pleis the aires and successouris foirsaidis of the said Sir James Skene to be servit retourit infeft and saisit in the landis and utheris foirsaidis within the said kingdome of Scotland In that cais his Majestie withe consent foirsaid Willis grantis decernis and ordines that the Brevis to be direct for that effect salbe direct to the Shereff of Edinburgh and his deputtis and retourit to his Majesties Chancelarie of Scotland and the preceptis of saising to be direct therupoun salbe direct to the said Shereff of Edinburgh and his deputtis and put to dew executioun be thame Quhilkis retouris preceptis and saisingis swa to be past salbe als valide effectuall and sufficient in all respectis as gif the landis and utheris foirsaidis did lye within the said Sherefdome of Edinburgh Gevand therfoir yearlie the said Sir James Skene his aires male and assignayis to our said Soverane Lord his aires and successoures of the said croun and kingdome of Scotland The foirsaid blenshe ferme dewtie of ane penny usuall monie of the said kingdome of Scotland upoun the ground of the foirsaidis landis and baronie at the feist of the nativitie of our Lord in name of blenshe ferme give it beis askit allenerlie ffor all uther dewtie question or demand that may be socht or impute upoun the saidis landis and barony And be reasoun of the great intervall and distance of the saidis boundis and countrey of New Scotland fra the said ancient kingdome of Scotland and that the samen countrey of New Scotland is yit altogidder destitute of notaris and publict Tabelliones requisite for authorizing of Saisingis and geving of infeftmentis therupoun And regairding thairwith the great and manyfold inconvenientis quhilkis may fall out in defalt of dew and tymous saising or saisingis to be taken upoun the said charter and utheris lyke charteris and infeftmentis grantit or to be grantit of the foirsaidis landis landis and baronie to the said Sir James Skene his aires male and assignayis And seing that the said countrey of New Scotland and originall infeftment of the samen is haldin in cheiff of the said ancient kingdome of Scotland and laitlie surveyit discoverit purchest and acquyred be the said Sir Williame Alexander his Majesties Livetenent thairof foirsaid and upoun his proper chargis quha is ane persone native of the said ancient kingdome of Scotland and now pairtlie plantit and to be plantit with Colonies and natives of the said kingdome and thairby callit and justly meriting the name style and titill of New Scotland Quhairthrow the samen countrey of New Scotland is and must be now reput and haldin ane pairt of the said kingdome of Scotland Thairfoir his Majestie with avise foirsaid be thir presentis decernis and declaires

and ordines that ane saising to be taken at the castell of Edinburgh as
the maist eminent and principall place of the said kingdome of Scotland
or at the plessour and option of the said Sir James Skene his aires male
and assignayis upon the ground of the foirsaidis landis and barony of
                                       or onie pairt therof is and salbe sufficient in all
tyme cuming ffor all and haill the samen landis and baronie or onie pairt
or portion therof Quhairanent his Majestie hes dispensit and be thir
presentis dispenssis for ever   And for all and sindrie the saidis privileges
and utheris speciallie and generallie abonementionat and becaus that be
the halding of the saidis landis and barony in blenshe ferme as said is
and that be defalt of the tymous and lawfull entrie of the air or aires
male of the said Sir James Skene and his assignais succeeding in the
samen baronie and utheris quhilk hardlie may be done be thame dewlie
and in tyme be occasion of the far distance therof fra the said kingdome
of Scotland quhairby the samen boundis and barony may befall and
becum in his Majesties handis or in his successouris be reasoun of
nonentrie ay and quhile the lawfull entrie of the richteous air or aires
male of the said Sir James Skene and his assignais thairto   And his
Majestie being nawise willing nor myndit that the foirsaidis landis and
barony sall at any tyme fall in nonentrie nether yit that the said Sir
James Skene his aires male and assignais salbe frustrat of the benefite
and proffeit therof in the meantyme   Therfoir his Majestie with avise
foirsaid for him and his successouris hes dispensit and be thir presentis
dispensis with the said nonentrie Renuncing the samen alluterlie and als
exonering quitclaming and dischargeing the said Sir James Skene his
aires male and assignais of the samen nonentrie simpliciter quhensoever
the foirsaidis landis and barony salhappin to fall in his Majesties handis
his aires or successouris be reasoun of nonentrie with the maillis
fermes proffeittis and dewties therof and all action and instance
theranent jure liti et cause simpliciter with all that may follow therupone
Provyding nevirtheles that the aires male of the said Sir James
Skene and his assignais sall within the space of sevin yeares efter
the deceis of thair predicessores or entrie to the possession of the
samen landis and barony do thair dew homage be them selffis
or thair lawfull procuratouris to that effect haveand thair sufficient
power thairto to our soverane Lord and his successouris of the said crown
and kingdome of Scotland And sall enter and be ressavit be his Majestie

D D

and his successouris to the samen landis barony and utheris abone mentionat in maner abone writtin. In the quhilk cais the air or aires male of the said Sir James Skene and his assignais sall have bruike and enjoy all and sindrie benefites and privileges therof Togidder with all and haill the samen landis and barony maillis fermes proffeittis and dewties therof and utheris quhatsumever generallie and speciallie abonementionat. Siclike and alsfrilie as gif the said nonentrie had nevir bene fallin And forder his Majestic considering that vertew and industrie is to be nothing moir advancit and nurished then be honour and preferment and that thairby cheiflie generous spiritis ar animat and stirit up to intend and prosequit nobill and vertuous actiones and interpryses and that all splendour and greatnes of dignitie and honour hath the beginning and incres from the King as from the fountain therof To quhais bienes and eminencie properlie belongeth to erect and institute new titillis of honour and dignitie as fra quhom the ancient first did flow And thairby willing to imitat his Majesties maist nobill progenitouris and antecessouris of royall and famous memorie quho had and did put in practise the power of creating and erecting of new dignities and degries amongst thair worthie subjectis His Majestic of his royall power and authorite hath erectit creatit maid constitute and ordanit and be thir presentis for him his aires and successouris off his speciall grace favouris certane knawledge meir motive and deliberat mynd with avise and consent foirsaid Makis erectis constitutis creattis and ordines ane certane hereditarie state degrie dignitie name ordour titill and style of Baronett To be and remane perpetuallie in all tyme cuming within the said kingdome of Scotland and countrey of New Scotland and to be had and enjoyed be such persones quhom his Majestic his aires or successouris for the weill and furtherance of the said plantatione of the said countrey of New Scotland and thair worthis and deservingis utherwise sall mak baronettis and prefer the said degrie and style and therfoir his Majestie for the help and assistance alreadie gevin be the said Sir James Skene towardis the weill and furtherance of the said plantatioun and for divers utheris gude and thankfull services done be him to his Majestic and for divers utheris gude and wechtie caussis and consideratiounes moving his Hienes his Majestie hes erectit and be thir presentis of his special grace favour certane knawledge meir motive and deliberat mynd with avise and consent foirsaid Erectis prefeiris and creattis the said Sir James Skene and his aires male qubat-

sumever from tyme to tyme perpetuallie in all tyme cuming in and
to the said hereditarie degrie state name ordour titill and style of
Baronett, with all and sindrie prerogatives privileges precedencies conditiones and utheris generallie and particularlie underwrittin and hath
maid creat and constitute and be thir presentis makis creattis and constitutis the said Sir James Skene and his aires male quhatsumcver from
tyme to tyme heritablie Baronettis for evir To have and enjoy all and
sindrie prerogatives privileges and utheris generallie and particularlie
underwrittin conceavit in thair favouris and hath gevin grantit willit
ordaint and declarit and be the tenour heirof his Majestie for him his
aires and successouris off his speciall grace favour certane knawlege
meir motive and deliberat mynd with avise and consent abonewrittin
Gevis grantis willis ordines and declaires That the said Sir James Skene
and his saidis aires male from tyme to tyme perpetuallie sall be vertew
of thir presentis and of the said degrie stait dignitie name ordour titill
and style of Baronet heirby grantit to thame Have hold tak and enjoy
in all tyme cuming efter the day and dait heirof baith in the said kingdome of Scotland countrey of New Scotland and ellis qubair place
prioritie preeminencie and precedencie in all and quhatsumever commissiones brevis lettres patentis directiones writtis appelationes nominationes
sessiones conventiones assemblies and metingis at all tymes places and
occasiones quhatsumever befoir all and quhatsumever knichtis lordis
esquyeris and gentilmen quhatsumever (excepting his Majesties said
Livetenent and the aires male discending his bodie being his Majesties
Livetenentis of the said countrey of New Scotland and na utherwise
Quhais wyffis and childrene likewise sall have and enjoy place and precedence accordinglie And lykewise excepting such knichtis banncrettis
as salhappin to be maid and knichtit be his Majestie his aires or successouris under thair standert and displayit baner in ane army royall in oppin
warre and the King personallie present and na otherwise And that
during the tyme of the lyfis of the saidis knichtis bannerettis allanerlie
and na lunger) and befoir all baronettis to be maid be his Majestie his
aires or successouris and befoir thair aires or successouris Albeit it salhappin onie uther baronet or baronettis to be maid be his Majestie
heirefter To pas and exped thair patentis of the said degrie dignitie
name ordour titill and style under the great seall of the said kingdome of
Scotland befoir the said Sir James Skene sall pas and exped thir

presentis and the charter following heirupoun under the said seale not-withstanding of ony law custome or constitution to the contrair quhat-sumever And in lykemaner his Majestie hath willit grantit declarit and ordånit and bé thir presentis for him his aires and successouris off his speciall grace favour certain knawlege meir motive and deliberat mynd with avise and consent foirsaid willis grantis appointis declaires and ordines that the wyff or wyffis of the said Sir James Skene and his saidis aires male from tyme to tyme perpetuallie sall be vertew of thir presentis and of the said degrie state and dignitie of thair husbandis have hold tak and enjoy in all tyme cuming place precedence prioritie and precedencie alsweill during thair husbandis lyftyms as therefter during thair awin lyftymes (gif they salhappin to be the langer livers) befoir the wyffis of all persones quhatsumever befoir quhom the said Sir James Skene and his saidis aires male may or sould be vertew of thir presentis or of the said degrie dignitie name ordour titill and style of Baronet now grantit to the said Sir James Skene and his saidis aires male Have hold tak and enjoy place preeminence and precedence and befoir the wyffis of the saidis knichtis bannerets aboneexceptit Becaus the said degrie of Baronet is ane hereditarie degrie in blude And likewise that the sonnes and dochteris respective of the said Sir James Skene and his saidis aires male for ever sall be vertew of thir presentis and of the said degrie and dignitie of Baronet now grantit to the said Sir James Skene and his aires male have hold tak and enjoy place and precedence befoir the sonnes and dochteris respective of all persones befoir quhom the said Sir James Skene and his aires male may or sould tak place or precedence and befoir the sonnes of the saidis knichtis bannerettis abonexceptit and likewise that the wyffis of the sones of the said Sir James Skene and his saidis aires male respective in all tyme cuming sall have hold tak and enjoy place prioritie and precedence befoir the wyffis of all persones befoir quhom thair husbandis may or sould tak place And farder his Majestie of his speciall grace favour certane knawlege meir motive and deliberat mynd be thir presentis for him his aires and successouris willis grantis ordines declaires and promeissis That at quhat tyme and seasone the eldest lawfull sone of the said Sir James Skene or the eldest appearand air male of the said Sir James Skene or of ony air male succeeding to him sall attayne to the aige of xxj yeares That thay and ilk ane of thame respective salbe knichtit be his Majestie his aires and

successouris notwithstanding that thair father be on lyff for the tyme
quhosoever thay or ony of thame sall desyre the samen without payment
of onie fynes or charges quhatsumever   And that the said Sir James
Skene and his aires male in all tyme cuming sall and may bear for ever
heirefter ather in ane contour in thair coat of armes or in ane inscutchion
at thair election the armes of the said countrey of New Scotland quhilkis
ar argent the ancient armes of Scotland on ane salturie azure supportit
be ane unicorne on the richt and ane wyld man propper on the left and
for the crist a lawrell branche and a thrissell proceding out of armed and
naikit handis conjoynit with this motto (munit hec et altera vincit)   And
that the said Sir James Skene and his saidis aires male sall in all tyme
cuming have place in the armes of his Majestie his aires or successouris
in the grosse near about the Royall Standart of his Majestie his aires
and successouris for defence of the samen   And that the said Sir James
Skene and his saidis aires male may and sall have in all tyme cuming twa
assistantis of the bodie to support a pall a principall murnour and four
assistantis to him at thair funerallis   And that the said Sir James Skene
sall in all tyme cuming be namit callit placit styllit and designit be the
name and titill of Sir James Skene knicht baronet   And that the saidis
aires male of the said Sir James Skene perpetuallie sall likewise be
namit callit styllit placit and designit be the name of Baronet   And that
the said style name and titill of Baronet salbe put to and adjoynit to the
end 'of the surnames of the said Sir James Skene and his saidis airis
male respective for ever   In all and sindrie his Majestic his aires and
successouris brevis lettres patentis and commissiones and in all and
sindrie utheris charteris paipperis deidis writtis and lettres quhatsumever
as trew lawfull and necessar addition of dignitie and that in all Scottis
speiches languages and writtis this addition (Sir) and in all uther
languages and speiches the lyke significative worde salbe premittit to the
names respective of the said Sir James Skene and his saidis aires male
for ever And that the titill name and style of Baronet, salbe adjoyned
to the end of thair surname.   And also that the wyff and wyffis of the
said Sir James Skene and his saidis aires male respective for ever sall
have use hald and enjoy for ever in all tyme cuming the style titill and
appellation of (Lady Madam and Dam) respective according to the use
and phrais of speiche and writting.   And forder his Majestic of his
speciall grace favour certane knawlege meir motive and deliberat myud

be thir presentis for him his aires and successouris, gives grantis ordines and promeissis to the said Sir James Skene and his saidis aires male respective for ever   That the number of Baronettis of the said kingdome of Scotland and countrey of New Scotland sall nether now nor at any tyme heireftcr exceid in all the number of ane hundreth and fyftie Baronettis.   And farder his Majestic of his speciall grace favour certane knawlege meir motive and deliberat mynd for him his aires and successouris be thir presentis gevis grantis declaires ordines and promeissis to the said Sir James Skene and his saidis aires male respective for ever   That nether his Majestie his aires or successouris sall or will at any tyme heirefter erect ordane mak constitute creat or appoint ony uther degrie dignitie name ordour titill or style quhatsumever nor give grant promit ordane or appoint place prioritie prceminence or precedence to onie persone or persones quhatsumever under or beneth the style dignitie and degrie of ane Lord of Parliament of the said kingdome of Scotland who sall or may be taken haldin reput usit or accomtit to be heicher befoir or equall to the said degrie stait dignitie name ordour titill and style of Baronet now presentlie gevin and grantit to the said Sir James Skene and his saidis aires male respective for ever And that the said Sir James Skene and his saidis aires male respective for ever sall and may in all tyme cuming frilie and quietlie have hold tak and enjoy all and sindrie thair saidis dignities places priorities precediencies preeminencies prerogatives and privileges befoir all uther persones quhatsumever who ar or salbe maid or appointit of onie suche degries stattis or dignities names ordouris titillis and styllis or to quhom onie suche place precedence or preeminence salbe so gevin and grantit And that the wyffis sones dochteris and sones wyffis of the said Sir James Skene and his saidis aires male respective for ever sall have hold tak and enjoy thair saidis places priorities and precedencies accordinglie And farder that na persone or persones quhatsumever at onie tyme heirefter salbe maid Barronettis of the said kingdome of Scotland and countrey of New Scotland bot such as for the weill and furtherance of the said plantatioun of the countrey of New Scotland sall first perform the conditiones appointit be his Majestic for that effect and certifie the samen to his Hienes or his commissionaris be his Majesties said Livetenent quhom his Majestic hath appointit to sie the performance therof And mairover that thir presentis salbe gude valide effectuall and sufficient in

all tyme cuming in all pointis as is abone writtin To the said Sir James
Skene and his saidis aires male respective for ever and to thair wyffis
sones dochteris and sones wyffis respective and ilk ane of thame in the
law aganes his Majestie his aires and successouris and aganes all persones
quhatsumever in all his Majesties his aires and successouris courttis and
in all places quhatsumever at all tymes and occasiones notwithstanding
of ony law custome prescriptioun use ordinance or constitution quhatsumever ather alreadie maid usit publist ordanit or providit or quhilk
heirefter salbe maid publist appointit usit ordanit or providit and notwithstanding of onie uther mater caus or occasioun quhatsumever
And finallie his Majestie for his Hienes and his successouris with
avise foirsaid Willis decernis and ordines the foirsaid charter to follow
heirupoun with all and sindrie liberties privileges claussis articles conditiones and utheris foirsaidis to be ratifeit approvin and confermit in
the nixt Parliament of the said kingdome of Scotland or onie uther
Parliament of the samen kingdome therefter at the plessour of the said
Sir James Skene and his saidis aires male and to have the strenth force
and effect of ane Decreit and sentence of that soverane and supreme
Judicatorie (Quhairanent his Majestie for his Hienes and his successouris
Willis and declaires the samen charter and claus therin contenit to be
sufficient warrand to that effect promitting the samen to be so performit
in verbo regio and to extend and inlarge the samen with all claussis neidfull in ampil forme Quhilck charter under the great Seale sall contene
therin ane precept of saising direct to the Shereff of Edinburgh and his
deputtis or to Shereffis in that pairt with ane blank for inserting of thair
names chargeing thame upoun the sicht of the said charter to be
grantit to the said Sir James Skene and his abone writtin be his
Majestie under his Hienes said great Seale of the said kingdome of
Scotland that thay or ony of thame sall incontinent herefter give
heritable stait saising and possessioun corporall actuall and reall
of all and haill the foirsaidis landis baronie and regalitie of   with
all and sindrie thair pairtis pendiclis privileges liberties commodities
and utheris quhatsumever alsweill particularlie as generallie abone
mentionat   To the said Sir James Skene or his actornay or actornayes
beararis of the said charter be deliverance of eard and stane at the
Castell of Edinburgh And that thay on nawise leave this undone The
quhilk to do his Majestie be the said charter sall give his full and irrevo-

cabill power to the saidis Shereffis in that pairt and ilk ane of thame conjunctlie and severallie as said is   The quhilk saising his Majestie with avise foirsaid willis decernis declaires and ordines be thir presentis to be als valide effectuall and sufficient in all respectis as give preceptis of saising had bene severalie and ordourlie direct furth of his Majesties Chancelarie to that effect upoun the said Charter anent the quhilk his Majestie with consent foirsaid hes dispensit and be the tenour of the said Charter for his Hienes and his successouris be thir presentis dispenssis for ever   And that preceptis etc.   At Halyrudhous the   · day of   Suprascribitur Charles R.   Et Subscribitur sic Geo. Cancell^s Mar th^{rs} Hadintoun Roxburgh Arskyne Naper Arch : Archesone

May it pleis your Lordshippis

This Signature grantit be his Majestie to Sir James Skene of Currie-hill Knycht President of the Session (wherby he is creat Knycht Barronet) is in all thingis conforme to these alreadie past the great seale of the same nature and wherupoun he hath gevin satisfactioun to Sir Williame Alexander Knycht his Majesties principall Secritarie of Scotland and Livetennent of New Scotland   Quhilk I do testifie sic subscribitur

J. SCOTTISTARVETT

Registrat 26 January 1630

APPENDIX N$^{o.}$ VII.

LETTERS FROM HUGH SKENE AND HIS WIFE, PETRONELLA VAN SORGEN, ADDRESSED TO "THE LADY HALYARDS, LIVING IN THE SKINNER'S CLOSS, EDINBURGH, NORTH BRITAIN."*

I.

Dear and Loving Mother, Sisters and Brother,—

Since it is the pleasure of the Almighty God to lay his hand on me, and by all appearance litle or no hopes of recovery, my disease being given over by all my physicians, I having taken it by a severe grave colique, which continued for some days, and at last being found that it is a putrification in my lungs, that my only recourse is to the Almighty God and my Saviour Jesus Christ, and to be in unity with all men. Soe my Dear mother, sisters and brother, wherein I have offended you, I first ask pardon of God, and then of you all, and begs earnestly off you all that if my Heavenly Father shall remove me from this world to his heavenly rest, that you will take this poor woman, my dear and Loving Wyff and children, in your motherly, sisterly, and brotherly care, for believe me wee shall never be in capacity to repay her for the care that she hath taken of me. Soe my Dear Mother, sisters and brother, this being my earnest and last desire to you all, and while I am here my prayers shall allwise be for you, recomending you all to the protection of the Almighty God, and hopping that this, my last desire, shall be granted.

I rest, Dear and Loving Mother, sisters and brother, your ever affectionate and Loving son and brother, while I am upon this side of time.

HEUGH O SKENE, his
mark. |

Tournay, Jully 23 (N. S.), 1724.

* From the Curriehill Charter Chest.

E E

Postscript—This day I have taken the last consultation of all the doctors of the town, but I am affrayed to non effect.

My wife is within two months of her time to come in childbed. Dear Mother, perform a loving mother to them. Adue. Dear brother, if you can help her to a pension from the king, I am hopfull you'l doe it.

2.

Loving Mother—

I am sorry to give you the disconsolate newes of your sones death about four weeks ago. He was taken with a violent cholick, and upon that a strong fever with stitches in his right side, so that it hes pleased the Lord to take him to himself. He departed upon Tuesday last, being the 25th (new style), with his full understanding and compleatt sences. After that the doctors had all given him over I had three severale consultationes of the best Docters in Town to see if ther was any possible remedy, but against death ther is none. He was so entirely beloved of all, that all or most of the officers in generall of the garrisone conveyed him to his buriall place (with great Lamentatione), which was in the French Church, wher he was most honorably interred, both for my own particular respect, as also of you and all his friends. I doubt not but you will sympathize with my disconsolate conditione, considering how I am stated, with a young child, and another in my belly. I know not well what to doe, only I cast myself upon God, who cares for the widow and fatherless, and upon my good friends. I shall patiently wait your answer and advice what I shall doe. Your son many times said that he had a great desire, if it had pleased God, to have seen you once more had it been possible. Be pleased to signifie his death to all our good friends with my most entire love to them all. I hope you will do your endeavour and employ our friends to see to procure me a pensione. No more, but recommending you to the care of the Almighty, I rest, Loving Mother,

Your affectionate daughter,

PIETERNELA VAN SORGEN,
WEEDCUN SKENEN.

Tournay, July 30 (New Style), 1724.

In case your son be not in toun, pray doe not fail to send the enclosed to him, by a corier, with all possible speed.

3.

Dear and Loving Mother—

After my very humble respects to you, the first October (new style), I was brought to bed of a daughter, and was called after Sister Helen. I received the 3 guineas from Mrs. Mosman, but no letter, she having lost it by the way. I am very thankful to you for your motherly care you have of me, and I shall never omitt that part of my duty to be instante with God for you that he may bless and prosper you and every thing that you take in hand. I have sent Dromondus over, according to your desire, which I am hopfull you'l be mother and father to him, he haveing no other as you, under God. I have given the woman 14 flamish gu : which is 14 pounds Scots for her journay.

It is earnestly desired that you will put George in mind of me, for you can very well think in what condition I am in. Recommending you all in the protection of the Almighty God.

Dear and Loving Mother,

Your affectionate daughter and humble servant,

(Signed)   PIETERNELA VAN SORGEN.

Tournay, Oct. 4th, 1724.

APPENDIX N⁰· VIII.

PAPERS CONNECTED WITH THE SKENES OF BELHELVIE.*

Inhibition James Arbuthnot agt. Gilbert Skene in Overhill, and others.
31 July, 1587.

JAMES be the grace of God King of Scottis To our lowittis Thomas
Maneris Messingeris our Shereffis in that part conjunctlie and severallie
speciallie constitut greting fforsamekill as it is humlie menit and schawin
to ws be our lowit James Arbuthnot of Lentusche That qubair he obtenit
decreit befoir the lordis of our counsall Aganis Thomas Ker burges of
Aberdeen Thomas Buk burges of the same bruch Gilbert Skein in Overhill John Clerk in Pottertoun George Gordoun burges of the same brugh
and George Ker of Benvellis for the wrangous violent and maisterfull
spoliatioun away taking resetting detening and withhalding be thame selffis
thair servandis complices and wtheris in thair names of thair causing command assistance and ratihabitioun fra the said complenar furth of the grund
of the landis of Overtoun of Balhelveis Murtoun Keir and Langseitt with
thair pertinentis lyand within our Sherefdome of Aberdeen and furth of
the duelling houssis thairof hallis chalmeris buithis byris and wtheris
office houssis of the same pertening to the said complenar be guid rycht
and tytill vpon the sextene day of Junij the yeir of God Jᵐ. Vᶜ. fourscoir
four yeiris of certane cornes catell hors nolt scheip insicht plenesing
wreittis obligatiounes infeftmentis abulzementis gold siluer and wtheris
guidis and geir extending to certane gryt quantateis availlis and pryces as
in the principall lybellit summondis rasit and execut at the said complenaris instance aganis thame thairwpon schawin to the lordis off our counsell

* From the Public Records.

at mair lenth is contenit and now the saidis persones perfyitlie vnder-standing that the said complenar will obtein decreit condamnatour aganis thame in the said mater that in the meintym in manifest defraud of him anent the executioun,thairof intendis as he is informit to sell annalie dispone put away and dilapidat thair landis heretages takis stedingis rowmes togidder with thair cornes cattell guidis and geir swa that the saidis persones sall mak tham selffis onabill to fulfill the said decreit to the said complenar quhairby he will be altogidder frustrat and defraudit of all executioun thairof to his gryt apperand skayth without we and the saidis lordis provyid remeid as is allegit OUR WILL IS heirfoir and we charge yow straitlie and commandis that incontinent thir our letteris sene ye pas and in our name and auctoritie fence and arrest all and sindrie the foirnamit persones cornes cattell merchandice dettis sowmes of money insicht plenesing maillis fermes and deweteis of thair landis gif thai ony have and all wtheris thair guidis and geir quhatsumevir in quhat handis or quhairevir the samyn can be apprehendit within our realme and mak Inventar to remane vnder arrestment at the said complenaris in-stance ay and quhill sufficient souertie be fundin that the samyn salbe furthcumand to him as law will And als that he in our name and auc-torite command and charge the saidis defendaris that thai on nawayis sell annalie wadsett dispone dilapidat nor putt away óny of thair landis heretages takis stedings rowmes or possessionis or yit thair cornes cattell guidis or geir in defraud off the said complenar anent the forsaid decreit to be obtenit be him aganis thame as said is And siclyk that ye mak Inhibi-tioun be oppin proclamatioun at the mercat croces off Aberdeen and wtheris places neidfull to all and sindrie our lieges and wtheris quhom it affeiris that thai nor nane off thame persew nor tak vpon hand to by tak in wadsett be assignatioun resignatioun reversioun alienatioun lang or schort takis nor ony wther maner of dispositioun quhatsumevir fra the foirnamit defendaris or ony of thair saidis landis heretagis takis stedingis rowmes or possessiones or yit thair cornes cattell guidis or geir in defraud of the said complenar, or yit to by or blok or sell with thame as said is with certificatioun to thame that dois in the contrair that all sic bying selling wadsetting be assig-natioun resignatioun reversioun alienatioun lang or short takis or ony vther maner of dispositioun quhatsumevir salbe decernit and declarit be the saidis lordis of our counsall to be of nane availl force nor effect with all that sall follow thairwpon   Becaus the saidis lordis hes sene the dependance abonewrittin according to Justice as ye will answer to ws thairwpon   The quhilk to do we commit to yow conjunctlie and severalie our full power be thir our lettres delyvering thame be yow deulie execute and indorsit agane to the berar gevin vnder our Signet at Edinburgh the tent day of Januar and of our regne the tuentie yeir 1586 yeiris.

Ex deliberatione dominorum consilij   Vpone the tuentie fyift day of July the ycir of God J^m. V^c. fourscoir sevin yeiris I Thomas Maneris messinger Sheref in that part past at the command and charge of our soverane lordis lettres to the mercat croce of Aberdeen and thair be oppin proclamatioun arrestit all the guidis and geir movabill and and vnmovabill pertening to Thomas Ker burges of Aberdeen   Thomas Buk burges of the said brugh Gilbert Skeyne in Overhill John Clerk in Pottertoun George Gordoun burges of the said brucht   To remane vnder arrestment ondisponit be thame or ony wtheris in thair names in qubat place or quhais handis the samin is fund or may be fund ay and quhill sufficient cautioun be fund to the said complenar as law will vnder all hiest pane and charge that eftir may follow conforme to thir our soverane lordis letteris in all pointis · And siclyk Inhibit all our soverane lordis lieges to have bying and selling with the saidis persones in defraud of the said complenar or ony wtherwayis be ony privat or publict actioun maid be thame thairanent   And this I did befoir thair witnessis James Cunningham servand to my lord bischop of Aberdeen Andro King burges thair and Andro Kilgour in Auld Aberdeen with wtheris dyvers And for the mair securetie to this my executioun and indorsatioun subscrivit with my hand my stampt is affixit.

Productum et registratum vt supra vltimo die mensis Julij 1587.

2.

Decreet Andro Crombie agt. David Skene, burgess of Posen.
11 November, 1596.

Vndecimo Novembris 1596

The quhilk day the lordis of counsall Advocattis the actioun and caus persewit of befoir at the instance of Andro Crambie and Mertine Howiesoun burgessis of the burgh of Abirdene allegit executouris confermit to vmquhile Thomas Crambie burges of the said burgh of Abirdene and als allegit tutouris testamentaris to Marjorie and Jeane Crambies lauchfull dochteris to the said vmquhile Thomas Aganis Dauid Skene merchand and burges of Poisnay in Poill Befoir Andro Sklatter watter baillie in Leyth Tueching the decerning of the said Dauid Skene be the said baillies decreit to content and pay to thame as allegit executouris foirsaidis the soume of aucht hundreth floranles concerning the said vmquhile Thomas part and allegit intromettit with be the said Dauid Skene in the yeir of God J^m. V^c. fourscoir aucht yeiris As at mair lenth is contenit in the pretendit principall petitioun and clame gevin in be thame aganis the said Dauid Skene To thameselffis to be proceidit befoir thame siclike and in the samin manir as micht or suld haif bene proceidit befoir the said watter baillie And thairfoir discharges the said Andro Sklatter watter baillie foirsaid of all forder proceiding in the said mater dischargeing him thairof and of his office in that part And hes assignit and assignis the last day of November instant with continewatioun of dayes to the said Dauid Skene to answer to the said principall petitioun and clame And in the menetyme hes continewet the said mater vnto the day foirsaid The said Dauid Skene compeirand be Maister Thomas Henrisoun his procuratour and the saidis Andro Crambie and Mertine Howiesoun compeirand be Maister Alexander King thair procuratour Quhilkis ar warnit heirof   Apud acta.

3.

Decreet Patrick Lord Glammis against his Tenants.   14 July, 1597.

Decimo quarto Julij 1597.

The quhilk day in the actioun and caus persewit at the instance of ane nobill and michtie lord Patrik lord Glammis Aganes Elizabeth Forbes relict of vmquhile Walter Barclay in Courtestoun and Walter Barclay his sone pretendit tennentis and occupearis of sax pleuches of land of Courtestoun with the Mylne of Auchinacher and Mylnelandis thairof Andro Halyburtoun and William Layng pretendit tennentis and occupearis of the landis of Drumgovane with the pertinentis Patrik Johnnstoun in Haltoun James Arbuthnot in Portertoun Johnn Arbuthnot in Egie Maister Thomas Gairne of Blairtoun Jeane Gordoune relict of vmquhile George Gordoun in Cragie William Gordoun hir sone Sir Johnne

Gordoun of Pitlurge Knicht Katherene Meinzeis in Horscruik Thomas Johnnstoun hir sone Dauid Arbuthnot in Lamfute Johnne Tillerie in Hilbray George Smyth in Tannareis Andro Lyoun younger in the Maynes of Ardow Dauid Lyoun thair Robert Clark thair Patrik Tailzeour in Yronruffis Paul Rae thair Johnne Beane in Eister Ardow Andro Lyoun elder thair James Smith thair Gilbert Jafray thair Gilbert Sandie in Mekle Murc   Tailzeour his mother thair Gilbert Skene in Overhill Robert Skene his sone thair Andro Tailzeour tailzeour Dauid Skene at the Mylne of Potterfeild Marjorie Baird relict of vmquhile James Lyoun in Smyddie Croft Patrik Ramsay at the Mylne of Haltoun George Clark thair Andro Mylne in Haltoun Andro Cold thair Walter Edmand thair Thomas Symesoun in Fischischillis Elizabeth Thomsoun relict of vmquhile Williame Kay in Mureburne Johnne Kay hir sone thair Patrik Leith in the Bra Johnne Clark in the Pottartoun Andro Wod thair and Gilberth Forsyth at the Mylne of Ardocht Tuitching the decerning of thame to flit and remove thame selffis thair tennentis familie subtennentis cottaris guidis and geir furth and fra all and haill the foirsaidis landis and baronie of Bahalveis with annexis connexis pairtis pendicles mylnes multuris fischingis and all and sindrie thair pertinentis ilkane of thame respectiue for thair awin pairtis safar as thay occupie thairof conforme to ane warning maid to thame to that effect befoir the feist and terme of witsonday last bipast or ellis to have allegit ane ressonabill caus quhy the samin suld not have bene done as at mair lenth is contenit in the principall summoundis raisit in the said mater Compeirit Maisteris Johnne Scharpe and William Oliphant procuratouris for the said noble and michtie lord persewar foirsaid and Maister Johnne Nicolson procuratour for the said James Arbuthnot, Johnne Arbuthnot, Katherene Meynzeis Andro Myll, as also compeirit the said George Gordoun, David Arbuthnot and Patrik Johnnstoun be Maister Alexander King thair procuratour It was allegit be the saidis Maisteris Johnne Nicolsoun and Alexander King procuratouris foirsaidis for thair clientis abonewrittin that thay aucht not be decernit to flit and remove fra the landis abonewrittin safar thairof as is occupeit be thame Becaus thay ar subtennentis to Patrik Lyoun burges of Dundie quha was heritable infeft in the foirsaidis landis lybellit the tyme of the foirsaid warning and be vertew thairof in possessioun of the samin landis lykas the saidis tennentis war in vse to pay thair maillis and dewteis to the said Patrik at the leist vtheris in his name at his command divers yeiris preceiding the said warning   And the said Patrik being infeft as said is and in possessioun in maner abonewrittin and be not warnit to flit and remove na proces of removing can be grantit at the said persewaris instance aganis the saidis persounes subtennentes to the said Patrik   To the quhilk it was answerit and replyit for the part of the said persewar be the saidis Maisteris Johnne Scharpe and William Oliphant his procuratouris foirsaidis that the said alledgeance aucht to be repellit nather can the saidis tennentis defend thameselffis be ony richt that is in the persoun of the said Patrik Lyoun thair allegit maister and that he is not warnit in this removing Becaus the said Patrik compeiris and concurris with the said persewar in persute of the said actioun of removing lykas thay compeir as procuratouris for him to that effect quhairby this proces of removing can not be hinderit or stayit throw the not warning of the said Patrik Lyoun to flit and remove as said is.   Secondlie it was answerit for the part of the said persewar that the said alledgeance aucht to be repellit nather was it necessar to the said persewar to have warnit the said Patrik Lyoun to have flittit and removit Becaus gif ony infeftment the said Patrik Lyoun haid of the foirsaidis landis the samin with all richt title of richt that he haid or mycht pretend in and to the saidis landis was renuncit be him And siklyk the saidis persounes can not be hard to stay the said proces of removing nor to cleith thame selff with ony richt in the persute of the said Patrik Lyoun thair allegit maister albeit he nather haid nor wald concur in this persute.   Thridlie answerit that the said alledgeance aucht to be repellit becaus gif ony infeftment was grantit to the said Patrik of the saidis landis the samin was simulatlie grantit in safar as it was mediatlie grantit to the said Patrik Seing that nochtwithstanding the said infeftment contenit and bur that it was grantit to the said Patrik yit the samin in verie deid is disponit and givin to the behuif and utilitie of Sir Thomas Lyoun of Auldbar Knicht quha remainit in continuall possessioun thairoff to the tyme that the said Patrik Lyoun maid renunciation of the foirsaid infeftment grantit to him of the samin Lykas he offiris him to preve that the saidis tennentis maid payment of thair maillis and dewteis of the foirsaidis landis to the said Sir Thomas Lyoun continuallie fra the said allegit infeftment grantit to the said Patrik Lyoun to the yeir of God J^m. V^c. lxxxxv yeiris And sa the infeftment grantit to the said Patrik can na wayes be presupponit to be his richt bot altogidder to be grantit to the behuif of the said Sir Thomas Lyoun Quhilk alledgance with the saidis thrie answeris maid thairto preponit for elyding thairof being at lenth hard sene and considderit The lordis of counsall be sentence interloquutour hes admittit and admittis the said exceptioun to the said excepientis probatioun nochtwithstanding the thrie said replyes abonewrittin maid thairto Quhairupon the saidis Maisteris Johnne Nicolsoun and Alexander King askit instrumentis And the saidis lordis declairis that the admissioun of the said exceptioun nochtwithstanding the saidis thrie answeris maid thairto is alwayes but prejudice of ony vther reply alreddie proponit quhilk hes ressavit na answer and of quhatsumever vther reply may be heirefter allegit for elyding of the said exceptioun as accordis of the law.

4.

Letters of Horning Gilbert Hendrie agt. David Skene, and others.
15 February, 1596-7.

JAMES be the grace of God King of Scotis to our Louitis Alexander George messinger our Sherifis in that part conjunctlie and severalie specialie constitute greiting fforsamekill as it is humlie menit and schawin to ws be our louit Gilbert Hendrie burges of Aberdeen That quhair George Clerk in Overhill of Balhelvie David Skene at the Milne of Pottertoun Gilbert Skene in Overhill of Balhelvie band and oblist thame conjunctlie and severalie be thair Lettres obligatouris to pay and delyver to the said complenar All and haill the soume of four pundis vsuall money of this realme for ilk boll of twelfscoir and ten bollis ait meill at ane certane terme alreddy bypast Lyik as the lettres obligatouris maid thairanent of the dait at Aberdeen the sevint of Junij in the yeir of God J^m. V^c. fourscoir and threttene yeiris decernit and ordanit to be insert and registrat in the buikis of our commissariot of Aberdeen with executioun to follow thairvpoun of poinding and horning on ane simpill charge of sex dayis off the dait at Aberdeen the xiij day of August the yeir of God J^m. V^c. fourscoir and sextene yeiris at mair lenth proportis Nevertheles the saidis personis refuisis postponis and deferris to pey and delyver to the said complenar the soumis of money abonwrittin inrespect quhairof the said complenar raisit our commissaris precept and thair that causit charge the said George Clerk David Skeyne and Gilbert Skeyne to mak payment to him of the soumes within ane certane space nixt efter the charge as the precept dewlie execute and indorsat and schawin to the lordis of our counsall hes testifeit   Quhilk space being bypast the saidis personis hes nawayis as yit obeyit nor will obey the command of the saidis charge without thay be forder compellit as is allegeit   Oure will is heirfoir and we charge yow straitlie and commandis that incontinent thir our Lettres sene ye pas and in our name and auctoritie command and charge the saidis George Clerk David and Gilbert Skeynes conjunctlie and severalie to mak peyment to the said complenar of the said sowme of four pundis money of our realme for ilk boll of the said tuelf scoir bollis ait meill efter the forme and tennour of the saidis Lettres obligatouris decrete of our said commissar interponit thairto and precept past thairvpoun in all pointis within sex dayis nixt efter thaj be chargeit be yow thairto vnder the pane of rebellioun and putting of thame to our horne and gif they failzie the said sex dayis being bypast that ye incontinent denunce the disobeyaris rebellis and put thame to our horne and ordane all thair movabill guidis and geir to be escheit and imbrocht to our vse for thair contemptioun and immediatlie efter your said denunceatioun that ye mak intimatioun thairof conforme to our act of parliament maid thairanent   Becaus the saidis lordis hes sene the commissaris precept deulie execute and indorsat according to Justice as ye will answer to ws thairvpoun   The quhilk to do we commit to yow conjunctlie and severalie our full power be thir our Lettres delyvering thame be yow deulie execut and indorsit agane to the berar   Givin wnder our signet at Leyth the fyftene day of Februar and of our ring the threttie yeir 1596.

Ex deliberatione Dominorum consilij.

Wpoun the aucht day of Marche the yeir of God J^m. V^c. fourscoir and sextene yeiris   I Alexander George messinger executour of our soverane Lordis lettres withinwrittin past at command thairof and commandit and chargit George Clerk in Overhill of Balhelvie David Skeyne at the Milne of Pottertoun Gilbert Skeyne in Overhill off Balhelvie all personalie aprehendit and delyverit to ilkane of thame ane auctentik copie of the withinwrittin lettres to pey and delyver to Gilbert Henrie complenar within specifeit the soume of four pundis Scotis money for ilk boll of tuelf scoir and ten bollis ait meill within sex dayis nixt efter this my charge wnder the pane of rebellioun and putting of thame to our souerane lordis horne Certefeing thame gif thaj failzeit the saidis sex dayis being bypast I wald denunce thame thairto conforme to the tennour of the saidis lettres in all pointis And this I did befoir thir witnessis respective Robert Skeyne in Overhill of Belhelvie Patrik Ramsay at the Nethir Milne callit the Denmilne of Balhelvie Alexander Henrie sone to the said Gilbert Henrie And for the mair verificatioun to this my executioun subscryvit with my hand my signet is afixit sic subscribitur Alexander George messinger with my hand Wpoun the first day of Junij the yeir of God J^m. V^c. nyntie and sevin yeiris I the said Alexander George messinger executour within constitute past at the command of the within-writtin lettres and be vertue thairof maid intimatioun to the said Gilbert Skeyne personaly aprehendit of my former charge given to him and to George Clerk now duelland in Milneden of Balhelvie at his duelling place of the Milden and David Skeyne at his duelling place of the Milne of Pottertoune becaus I could not aprehend thame personaly efter I haid knokit sex knokis at ilkane of the durris of thair saidis duellingis maid intimatioun thairat of my former charge that inrespect of thair disobedi-ence I wald denunce thame our soverane lordis rebellis and put thame to his hines horne conforme to the tennour of the withinwrittin Lettres in all pointis And this I did befoir thir witnessis Patrik Ramsay in Milneden Johne Folay servitour to me the said Alexander George And for the mair verificatioun to this my executioun subscryvit with my hand my signet is afixit sic subscribitur Alex^r George messinger And vpoun the samin first day of Junij the yeir of God foirsaid I the said Alexander George messinger executour withinconstitute past at the command of the Lettres withinwrittin to the merkat croce of the brugh of Aberdeen and thair in our Souerane Lordis name and auctoritie conforme to the tennour of the saidis Lettres lauchfullie denuncit the said George Clerk Gilbert Skeyne and David Skeyne our souerane lordis rebell and put thame to his hines horne be thre blastis as vse is and ordanit thair haill movabill guidis and geir to be escheit and imbrocht to our souerane lordis vse for thair contemptioun and that becaus thaj haid dissobeyit my former charge and intimatioun maid thairof and haid nocht maid peyment of the soumes withinspecifeit to the said complenar conforme to the saidis Lettres and charge givin thame be vertue thairof And this I did conforme to the tennour of the saidis Lettres in all pointis befoir thir witnessis Johne Irwing in Funerssy David Knollis David Ranaldsone

Johne Layng Robert Forbes eldar burgessis of Aberdeen   And for the mair verificatioun to this my executioun my signet is affixit sic sub-scribitur Alex^r George messinger with my hand.

Productum et registratum vndecimo die mensis Junij anno Domini millesimo quingentesimo nonagesimo septimo.

5.

Relaxation from Horning of David Skeyne and James Bannerman. *9 January, 1602.*

JAMES be the grace of God King of Scottis To our lovittis Johne Craü-furd messinger our Shereffis in that pairte conjunctlie and severalie specialie constitute greiting forsamekle as it is humelie menit and schawin to ws be our lovittis David Skeyne at the Mylne off Potertoun and James Banerman baxter and burges of our burghe of Aberdeen   That quhairas the said compleneris ar informeit thej ar denunceit rebellis and put to our horne be vertew of our vtheris letteris of horning raisit at the instance of the persones respective efter nameit and for the caussis vnderwrittin viz the said David Skeyn be vertew of our saidis vtheris letteris of horning raisit at the instance of Gilbert Hendrie burges of our said burgh of Aberdeen for non payment making to him of the sowme of four pundis money of our realme for ilk boll of Twelf scoir ten bollis ait meill contenit in ane obligatioun maid to him be George Clark at the Mylne of Haltoune as principall and Gilbert Skeyn in Ouertoune of Balhelvie and the said David Skeyne as souerties and full debtouris for him and with him of the dait at Aberdeen the sevinteine day of Junij the yeir of God J^m. V^c. fourscoir fourtein yeiris and registrat in our commissareis buikis of Aberdeine vpoune the fourtein day of August the yeir of God J^m. V^c. four scoir sexteine yeiris and the said James Banerman be vertew of vtheris Lettres of horning raisit at the instance of Alexander Chapman sumtyme in Blairdaff and presentlie dwelland in Sauchthyne aganes Johne Banerman in Boigfairlie as principall and the said James as cautioner and souertie for him for non payment making to the said Alexander of the sowme of four pundis money of our realme for ilk boll of certane bollis of victuall specifeit in the Lettres obligatouris maid be thame to him thairanent maist wrangouslie and injustlie considering it is of veritie that the saidis compleneris and ilkane of thame haif maid compleit payment to the saidis persones and ather of thame of the forsaidis haill sowmes of money respective abonewrittin and hes reportit thair severall acquittance thairvpoune nocht onlie grantand the resset of the saidis sowmes ilkane of thame for thair awin pairtes of the samen and dischargeing the saidis compleneris and ather of thame respective thairof bot als renunceing and dischargeing all lettres of horning poynding and captioune and vtheris quhatsumever raisit at ony of thair instances thairvpoune as the saidis acquittances schawin to the lordis of our counsall hes testifiet and thairfoir our saidis vtheris lettres of horning raisit and execute aganes the saidis compleneris and ather of thame at the instance of ilkane of the saidis persones and effectis thairoff aucht and suld be suspendit vpoune the saidis compleneris and thaj and ilkane of thame simpliciter relaxt fra the proces of horning respective execute aganes thame be vertew thairof namelie   In respect that thej haiff alreddie interponit with our thesaurer for the gift of thair escheitis and hes satisfiet him thairfoir as the contract of the gift grantit thairvpoun lyikwayis schawin to the saidis lordis of our counsall beiris   Oure Will is heirfoir and we charge yow that ye lauchfullie summond warne and charge the saidis Gilbert Hendrie and Alexander Chapman pairties forsaidis To compeir befoir ws and the lordis of our counsall at Edinburgh or quhair it sall hapine ws to be for the tyme the Twentie fourt day of Januar instant in the hour of caus with continewatioun of dayis bringand with thame the forsaidis registrat obligatiounes and our saidis vtheris lettres of hornings respective raisit at ather of thair instances thairvpoun with the execu- tiounes thairof to be seine and considerit be the lordis of our counsall and to heir and sie the samen lettres effect thairoff and horning contenit thairintill susspendit vpoune the saidis compleneris and thaj simpliciter relaxt fra the proces of horning execute aganes thame and ather of thame be vertew thairof in all tymes cuming for the caussis forsaid Atour we and the saidis lordis of our counsall in our name be the tenore heirof suspendis our forsaidis vther lettres of horning raisit and execute at the instance of ather of the saidis persones effectis thairof and horning contenit thairin and discharges all our officiaris of puting of the samen to ony forder executioune vpone the saidis compleneris or ony of thame and of thair office in that pairte And als that he in our name and auctoritie relax the said David Skeyne and James Banerman and ilkane of thame fra the forsaidis proces of hornings respective abone reherseit execute aganes thame at the instance of ather of the forsaidis persones in maner abone mentiounat receave thame to our peace and delyver to thame or ony vtheris in thair names the wand thairoff quhill the last day of the samen moneth becaus the saidis lordis hes seine the discharges and gift of escheit abonewrittin According to justice as ye will answer to ws thairvpoune The quhilk to do we commit to yow conjunctlie and severalie our full power be thir our Lettres delyvering thame be yow dewlie execute and indorsate agane to the berar Givein vnder our signet at Edinburgh the nyint day of Januar and of our regne the xxxv yeir 1602 Ex. deliberatione dominorum consilij. Wpone the sevinteine day of Februar the yeir of God J^m. sex hundreth and twa yeiris I Johne Craufurd messinger shereff in that pairte within constitute past to the marcat croce of the burghe of Aberdeine and thairat be vertew and command of thir our souerane lordis lettres withinwrittin be opine proclamatioun and reiding of the saidis lettres in his bienes name and auctoritie relaxt David Skeyne of Potertoun and James Banerman baxter and burgeis of Aberdeine fra the proces of horne respective as is within reherseit quhilk was execute aganes thame at the instance of Gilbert Hendrie and Alexander Chapman resaveit the saidis David Skeyne and James Banerman to our Souerane lordis peace and delyverit in signe the wand thairof to the foirnameit David Skeyne and the said James Banerman baith personalie present And this I did conforme to this our souerane lordis lettres withinwrittin in all poyntes quhairof I left and affixt ane copie on the said cros Befoir thir witnessis Patrik Leslie William Leyth Robert Alschoner James King Johne Kempt burgessis of Aberdeine and for the mair verificatioun heirof to this executioun writtin and subscryvit with my hand my stampt is affixt heirto sic subscribitur Johne Craufurd messinger with my hand.

Apud Aberdeen primo die mensis Marcij anno Dominj milesimo sexcentesimo secundo Productum per Magistrum Joanem Leyth advocatum et registratum in libro registrj vicecomitatus de Aberdeen per me Magistrum Gulihelum Andersone notarium publicum scribam ejusdem subscriptum secundum tenorem actj parliamentj sic subscribitur M^r. W^m. Andersone.

APPENDIX N⁰· IX.

Renunciation of Sins by Sir George Skene of Rubislaw. *

A Solemn Renunciation, Ane Holy Divorce of all and every Sin and of my sins in a special manner from this day hencefurth and forever.

Aug. 24, 1684.

O Eternal, Heart-searching, Sin-Pardoning, Lord God! I come unto thee this day, under a deep sense of my many heinous provocatiouns, desyring to humble myself in the dust before thee, acknowledging I am unworthy to lift up mine eyes to thy Heavens or to trade thy earth. That I have deserved thy eternal wrath and the hidings of thy face through eternitie. But thou spares when nothing is deserved but wrath. Thou art a God, mercifull, and gracious, yea, thou invites us to come to thee, though we have played the harlot with many lovers. Thou hast also promised whoso confesseth and forsaketh his sins shall find mercy.

Upon which promise I lay hold, and I, Geo. Skene, do incall the Almighty, dreadfull Jehovah, God, the Father, Sone, and Holy Ghost, to whom I., G. S., appeal the sinceritie of my heart, that its the grief of my soul that ever I should have greeved thy blessed Majesty, and that I should have offended so oft tymes past number, and more especially that ever my idol lust should have prevailed so much over me, and that its my greatest grief I did not divorce them long ere now And therfor I call heaven and earth to record this day that I, G. S., do give ane everlasting divorce to all and everie known sin, and that from henceforth I renounce my dearest lust, even to the end of my lyfe, and that it shall

* From the Rubislaw Charter Chest.

be my greatest care never to fall into any sin any more, promising and vowing unto thee, the searcher of hearts, that if I have done iniquity that I shall do so no more.

Only, Lord, lett not unallowed failings make void this everlasting divorce betuixt sin and my soul.

Almighty God, since I am unable of my self to resist sin for one moment, I therefore vow to perform, through thy strength alone and desayre wholly to rely upon thee, O God never leave me nor forsake me.

And now I, Geo. Sk., again incall the Almighty, dreadfull Jehovah, God the Father, Sone, and Holy Ghost, that this is the fixt resolution of my soul never to fall into any known sin, and more particularly to guard against any idol sin, never to give it a kyndly look any more. And now, Almighty, all-seeing Lord, what is done on earth let it be ratified in heaven (even so help me God).

(Signed)   GEO. SKEYNE.

In confirmatioune whereof I seal it with my hand and wished to doe it with my blood, upon the bended knee both of soul and body.

A SOLEMNE VOW AND COVENANT BETWIXT THE ALMIGHTY LORD GOD OF HOSTS AND GEORGE SKENE, FROM THIS DAY FROM HENCEFORTH AND FOREVER.

Augt. 24, 1684.

O ALMIGHTY, Dreadful, Covenant-keeping Lord, who searches the heart and tryes the reines, I have run farr away from thee, I have sind against heaven and in thy sight, and am no more worthy to be called thy sone, O that thou woldst make me as the meanest of thy servants, yet since of thy infinit mercy thou hast provided mercy to all that turn in unto thee, I desayre trembling to come and fall down before thee, to through away all the weapons of my rebellion, and wholly to submitt myself to thy laws.

And since thou hast promised to all such as forsake their evil ways and turn to thee with their whole heart, that thou wilt be their God, and they shall be thy people,

G G

I, Geo. Skene, do her take heaven and earth to record that I take the great God, Father, Sone, and Holy Ghost, for my portion and chief good, and do give up myself, soul and body, wholly to thy service, and to strengthen thus my resolution, I promise to vow and forsake all that is dear unto me in a world, rather than to forsake thee, and that no temptation to sin shall withdraw me from thy service, promising and vowing to serve thee in holiness and righteousness all the days of my life.

And since thou hast appointed Christ as the only way for lost sinners to come to thee, I doe here, upon the bended knees, of my soul and body accept of Christ, as the only way by which I, ane lost, undone wretch, may have access unto thee, and do here solemnly joyn myself in a marriage covenant to be his for ever, to take him as my alon Lord and Saviour, without whom I am undone through eternity. I hear take him for my head and husband, to be ruled and governed by him, and that I do take my lott with him, come what will come. I'll never forsake him, verily, supposing that neither death nor lyfe shall separate me from the love of God in Jesus Christ.

Onely Lord let not unallowed misscarriages make void this everlasting covenant betwixt thee and my soul.

And since O Lord, I am unable of myself to think a good thought, much less to keep closs with the throughout my lyf, therefore I vow to perform only through the assistance of thy spirit ; never leave me, therefor, nor forsake me, for if thou leave me I cannot stand one moment. Now, I, G. S., again call thee to witness the sinceritie of my heart, and that I doe it without any grudge, solemnly promising and vowing to own the for my Lord, and live to thee so long as I have a breathing tyme here (even so help me God), and now what is done on earth, lett it be ratified in heaven.

(Signed)   GEO. SKENE.

In confirmation whereof I seal it with my hand, and wish I could doe it with my blood, upon the bended knees both of my soul and body.

APPENDIX N^{o.} X.

INTRODUCTION TO CANTO FOURTH OF MARMION.

TO JAMES SKENE, ESQ.

Ashestiel, Ettrick Forest.

AN ancient Minstrel sagely said,
" Wherè is the life which late we led ? "
That motley clown in Arden wood,
Whom humorous Jaques with envy view'd.
Not even that clown could amplify,
On this trite text, so long as I.
Eleven years we now may tell,
Since we have known each other well ;
Since, riding side by side, our hand
First drew the voluntary brand ;
And sure, through many a varied scene,
Unkindness never came between.
Away these winged years have flown,
To join the mass of ages gone ;
And though deep mark'd, like all below,
With chequer'd shades of joy and woe ;
Though thou o'er realms and seas hast ranged,
Mark'd cities lost, and empires-changed,
While here, at home, my narrower ken
Somewhat of manners saw, and men ;
Though varying wishes, hopes, and fears
Fever'd the progress of these years,

Yet now, days, weeks, and months but seem
The recollection of a dream,
So still we glide down to the sea
Of fathomless eternity.

Even now it scarcely seems a day,
Since first I tun'd this idle lay;
A task so often thrown aside,
When leisure graver cares denied,
That now, November's dreary gale,
Whose voice inspir'd my opening tale,
That same November gale once more
Whirls the dry leaves on Yarrow shore.
Their vex'd boughs streaming to the sky,
Once more our naked birches sigh,
And Blackhouse heights, and Ettrick Pen,
Have donn'd their wintry shrouds again:
And mountain dark, and flooded mead,
Bid us forsake the banks of Tweed:
Earlier than wont along the sky,
Mix'd with the rack, the snow mists fly.
The shepherd, who in summer sun,
Had something of our envy won,
As thou with pencil, I with pen,
The features traced of hill and glen;
He who, outstretch'd the livelong day,
At ease among the heath-flowers lay,
View'd the light clouds with vacant look,
Or slumber'd o'er his tattered book,
Or idly busied him to guide
His angle o'er the lessen'd tide;—
At midnight now, the snowy plain
Finds sterner labour for the swain.

When red hath set the beamless sun,
Through heavy vapours dark and dun;

When the tired ploughman, dry and warm,
Hears half-asleep, the rising storm
Hurling the hail, and sleeted rain,
Against the casement's tinkling pane;
The sounds that drive wild deer, and fox,
To shelter in the brake and rocks,
Are warnings which the shepherd ask
To dismal and to dangerous task.
Oft he looks forth, and hopes, in vain,
The blast may sink in mellowing rain;
Till, dark above, and white below,
Decided drives the flaky snow,
And forth the hardy swain must go.
Long, with dejected look and whine,
To leave the hearth his dogs repine;
Whistling and cheering them to aid,
Around his back he wreathes the plaid:
His flock he gathers, and he guides,
To open downs, and mountain-sides,
Where fiercest though the tempest blow,
Least deeply lies the drift below.
The blast, that whistles o'er the fells,
Stiffens his locks to icicles;
Oft he looks back, while streaming far,
His cottage window seems a star,—
Loses its feeble gleam,—and then
Turns patient to the blast again,
And, facing to the tempest's sweep,
Drives through the gloom his lagging sheep.
If fails his heart, if his limbs fail,
Benumbing death is in the gale:
His paths, his landmarks, all unknown,
Close to the hut no more his own,
Close to the aid he sought in vain,
The morn may find the stiffen'd swain:
The widow sees, at dawning pale,
His orphans raise their feeble wail;

And, close beside him, in the snow,
Poor Yarrow, partner of their woe,
Couches upon his master's breast,
And licks his cheeks to break his rest.

Who envies now the shepherd's lot,
His healthy fare, his rural cot,
His summer couch by greenwood tree,
His rustic kirn's* loud revelry,
His native hill notes tuned on high,
To Marion of the blithesome eye ;
His crook, his scrip, his oaten reed,
And all Arcadia's golden creed ?

Changes not so with us, my Skene,
Of human life the varying scene ?
Our youthful summer oft we see
Dance by on wings of game and glee,
While the dark storm reserves its rage,
Against the winter of our age :
As he, the ancient Chief of Troy,
His manhood spent in peace and joy ;
But Grecian fires, and loud alarms,
Call'd ancient Priam forth to arms.
Then happy those, since each must drain
His share of pleasure, share of pain,—
Then happy those, beloved of Heaven,
To whom the mingled cup is given ;
Whose lenient sorrows find relief,
Whose joys are chasten'd by their grief.
And such a lot, my Skene, was thine,
When thou, of late, wert doom'd to twine,—
Just when thy bridal hour was by,—
The cypress with the myrtle tie.
Just on thy bride her Sire had smiled,
And bless'd the union of his child,

* The Scottish Harvest Home._ Note by the Author.

When love must change its joyous cheer
And wipe affection's filial tear. ·
Nor did the actions next his end,
Speak more the father than the friend :
Scarce had lamented Forbes paid
The tribute to his Minstrel's shade ;
The tale of friendship scarce was told,
Ere the narrator's heart was cold—*
Far may we search before we find
A heart so manly and so kind!
But not around his honour'd urn,
Shall friends alone and kindred mourn
The thousand eyes his care had dried,
Pour at his name a bitter tide;
And frequent falls the grateful dew,
For benefits the world ne'er knew.
If mortal charity dare claim ·
The Almighty's attributed name,
Inscribe above his mouldering clay,
" The widow's shield, the orphan's stay."
Nor, though it wake thy sorrow, deem
My verse intrudes on this sad theme;
For sacred was the pen that wrote,
" Thy father's friend forget thou not:"
And grateful title may I plead,
For many a kindly word and deed,
To bring my tribute to his grave:—
Tis little—but 'tis all I have.

To thee, perchance, this rambling strain
Recalls our summer walks again;
When, doing nought,—and, to speak true,
Not anxious to find aught to do,—

---

* These lines allude to Sir William Forbes of Pitsligo, having died shortly after his daughter's marriage to Mr. Skene, and after he had completed his life of Dr. Beattie, author of "The Minstrel."

The wild unbounded hills we ranged
While oft our talk its topic changed
And, desultory as our way,
Ranged, unconfined, from grave to gay.
Even when it flagg'd, as oft will chance
No effort made to break its trance,
We could right pleasantly pursue
Our sports in social silence too;
Thou gravely labouring to pourtray
The blighted oak's fantastic spray;
I spelling o'er, with much delight,
The legend of that antique knight,
Tirante by name, yclep'd the White.
At cither's feet a trusty squire,
Pandour and Camp,* with eyes of fire,
Jealous, each other's motions view'd,
And scarce suppress'd their ancient feud.
The laverock whistled from the cloud;
The stream was lively, but not loud;
From the white thorn the May-flower shed
Its dewy fragrance round our head:
Not Ariel lived more merrily
Under the blossom'd bough than we.

And blithesome nights, too, have been ours,
When Winter stript the summer's bowers. ·
Careless we heard, what now I hear,
The wild blast sighing deep and drear,
When fires were bright, and lamps beam'd gay,
And ladies tuned the lovely lay.
And he was held a laggard soul,
Who shunn'd to quaff the sparkling bowl.
Then he whose absence we deplore,
Who breathes the gales of Devon's shore,
The longer miss'd bewail'd the more ;

* Pandour was a fine wolf hound Mr. Skene had brought from the Continent.   Camp
is one of the dogs in Raeburn's portrait of Sir Walter Scott.

And thou, and I, and dear-loved Rae,*
And one whose name I may not say,—†
For not Mimosa's tender tree
Shrinks sooner from the touch than he,—
In merry chorus well combinèd,
With laughter drown'd the whistling wind.
Mirth was within ; and Care without
Might gnaw her nails to hear our shout.
Not but amid the buxom scene
Some grave discourse might intervene—
Of the good horse that bore him best,
His shoulder, hoof, and arching crest :
For, like mad Tom's,‡ our chiefest care,
Was horse to ride, and weapon wear.
Such nights we've had ; and, though the game
Of manhood be more sober tame,
And though the field-day, or the drill
Seem less important now—yet still
Such may we hope to share again.§
The sprightly thought inspires my strain !
And mark, how like a horseman true,
Lord Marmion's march I thus renew.

* Sir William Rae of St. Catharines, Bart.
† I believe, Colin Mackenzie of Portmore.
‡ See King Lear.   Author's Note.
§ Both Sir Walter Scott and Mr. Skene belonged to the troop of Yeomanry Cavalry.

H H

Arms of John Skene of Halyards in Fife, from a Stone at Halyards Castle.

INDEX.

* The references in a heavier type are to pages on which members of the different branches of the family in direct line of descent are given under separate headings.

PRINTED BY MILNE AND HUTCHISON, ABERDEEN.

ERRATA.

Page 61, line 13, *for* Emily Raitt *read* Lucy, daughter of Peter Hay of Leys.
Page 63, line 2 from foot, *for* Sarina *read* Lorina.

New Spalding Club.

REPORTS OF COMMITTEES.

1887.

RESOLUTIONS ADOPTED BY THE COUNCIL, 25th NOVEMBER, 1886.

That the following gentlemen be appointed an Acting Committee, to manage the finance and general business of the Club, to make arrangements for the printing and distribution of the works to be issued, and to receive and deal with the Reports from the Special Committees : with power to add to their number : three to be a quorum. *Mr. Ferguson*, Convener ; *Dr. Francis Edmond, Mr. Alexander Walker, Mr. George Walker, Dr. Webster ;* the Conveners of the Special Committees ; the Secretary and the Treasurer. [*Principal Geddes*, added 12th January, 1887 ; *Rev. Mr. Gammack*, added 26th January.]

That the following gentlemen be appointed a Special Committee to determine on the works to be issued by the Club, and to select the editors: with directions to report to the Acting Committee as often as requisite : with power, &c., as above. *Mr. Dalrymple*, Convener ; *Dr. Alexander, Principal Geddes, Dr. Grub, Mr. Moir.* [The Secretary, added 19th May, 1887.]

That the following gentlemen be appointed a Special Committee to investigate the contents of charter chests and other family and territorial records within the North-Eastern Counties of Scotland, or relating thereto : with directions, &c., as above. *Colonel Allardyce*, Convener ; *Mr.*

Dalrymple, Mr. A. Davidson, Mr. C. B. Davidson, Mr. Ferguson, Mr. J. M. Garden, Mr. Wolrige Gordon, Mr. Morice; the Treasurer.

That the following gentlemen be appointed a Special Committee to investigate the municipal, judicial, and commercial records of the N. E. Counties: with directions, &c., as above. *Mr. Cran,* Convener; *Dr. Davidson,* Inverurie, *Lord Provost Henderson, Mr. Kemlo, Mr. Littlejohn, Mr. Matthews, Sheriff Rampini,* Elgin, *Mr. Ramsay,* Banff, *Sheriff Dove Wilson.*

That the following gentlemen be appointed a Special Committee to investigate the ecclesiastical and educational records of the N. E. Counties, and the records of Scottish educational institutions at home and abroad: with directions, &c., as above. *Mr. Moir,* Convener; *Rev. Mr. Cooper, Mr. J. P. Edmond, Rev. Mr. Gammack, Principal Geddes, Rev. Dr. Gregor, Dr. Grub, Major Ramsay.* [*Mr. Robert Walker,* added 7th January, 1887.]

That the following gentlemen be appointed a Special Committee to investigate the place-names, folk-lore, and general topography and archaeology of the N. E..Counties : with directions, &c., as above. *Rev. Dr. Gregor,* Convener; *Dr. Alexander, Mr. Crombie, Mr. Ferguson, Colonel Ross King, Rev. Mr. Michie, Mr. Moir, Mr. Robertson.* [*Rev. Mr. Temple,* added 17th March, 1887.]

REPORT BY THE EDITORIAL COMMITTEE

(approved at the Meeting of the Acting Committee on Wednesday, 12th January, 1887).

THE EDITORIAL COMMITTEE are glad to report that they have received from gentlemen in various parts of the country a number of offers to edit works of interest and importance. These offers they have carefully considered, and they now beg to recommend the following works as the first issues of the Club.

1st. The Rev. James Cooper, Aberdeen, has undertaken to edit for the Club THE CHARTULARY OF THE COLLEGIATE CHURCH OF SAINT NICHOLAS. This was one of the works contemplated by the Spalding Club, and there seems a peculiar fitness in its receiving precedence and priority among the works to be issued by the new Club. Your Committee recommend that the Text of the Chartulary should be printed and distributed first, and that Mr. Cooper's Prefatory Notes on the Chartulary, and Materials for a History of the Church of Saint Nicholas, should follow as a separate issue, to be afterwards prefixed to the Text. Mr. Cooper proposes to incorporate in his Notes the substance of a monograph on the Church, by the late Mr. James Logan, an interesting work in manuscript, containing a number of coloured illustrations. Your Committee have to acknowledge the courtesy of the Society of Advocates in placing at their service Mr. Logan's volume, and also a transcript of the Chartulary, the possession of which will enable the printing of the work to proceed without delay.

2nd. Dr. W. F. Skene, Historiographer Royal for Scotland, has kindly consented to edit for the Club a HISTORY OF THE FAMILY OF SKENE (based on four old manuscript Histories), similar to "Ane Account of the Familie of Innes," edited for the Spalding Club by Mr. Cosmo Innes. Your Committee gladly accepted an offer from an antiquary so distinguished, and they feel assured that his contribution to the works of the Club will be most acceptable to the Acting Committee. It is confidently hoped that this volume will be issued within the first year, as Dr. Skene expects to be able to put the manuscript into the printer's hands in about three months.

3rd. The Secretary, Mr. P. J. Anderson, has in preparation SELECTIONS FROM THE RECORDS OF MARISCHAL COLLEGE AND UNIVERSITY, and your Committee look forward to obtaining, in the course of the second year, a part of his work. This work when completed will form, it is hoped, a companion volume to the "Fasti Aberdonenses.'

4th. The Rev. James Gammack, Aberdeen, has undertaken to compile for the Club, COLLECTIONS FOR THE HISTORY OF ANGUS AND THE MEARNS, similar to the Collections printed by the Spalding Club for the History of the Counties of Aberdeen and Banff.

Your Committee have been in communication with Mr. William Troup, Bridge of Allan, relative to a "History of the

Family of Forbes," on which that gentleman has bestowed much labour, and which he is willing to submit for examination by the Committee.

Your Committee have also considered the propriety of printing under the auspices of the Club the recently discovered "Lives of the Saints" attributed to Barbour. They were favoured with the views of Professor Masson on this subject. That eminent scholar is of opinion that the "Lives of the Saints" in its entirety naturally falls to be edited by the Scottish Text Society, but that a volume of " Barbouriana," containing all that is known about Barbour from documents, or that can be gathered from his writings, would be a very suitable work for the Club to take up—the life of Saint Machar, the local saint, forming a nucleus. If a competent editor can be found for such a work, your Committee would heartily recommend it.

Among other works which have been mentioned, but regarding which no exact information is as yet before the Committee, are "The Book of Banff," by Mr. W. Cramond, Cullen, and a new edition of "The Book of Bon-Accord," by Mr. A. Kemlo, Aberdeen.

WM. D. GEDDES, *pro C.*

REPORT BY COMMITTEE ON BURGH AND JUDICIAL RECORDS

(approved at the Meeting of the Acting Committee on Wednesday, 12th January, 1887).

I.—Documents in the Charter Room, Town House.

Your Committee beg to report on the various documents in the Burgh Charter Room as follows :—

1. *Burgh Charters.*—There is a large number of Royal and other Charters of an interesting nature in the possession of the Town, the printing of which has been undertaken by the Town Council, apart from the Club. These Charters are at present in process of being translated and prepared for the press by the Secretary of the Club.

2. *Council Registers.*—With the exception of a single volume the series is complete from 1398 to 1883 (when the Minutes began to be printed), and consists of 118 volumes. Four volumes of extracts from the Registers have been printed: two by the Spalding Club, embracing the period from 1398 to 1624, and two by the Burgh Record Society, continuing the selection from the last date down to 1747. It would be desirable to have a complete index of subjects, names of persons and places : and Mr. Anderson, when reporting to the Town Council on the matter, in April of last year, estimated that by adopting certain conditions the bulk of the index matter might be condensed into three volumes of 1000 to 1200 pages each.

3. *Sasine Registers or Protocol Books.*—This series commences in 1484, and is complete to the present time. The period from 1484 to 1800 occupies 83 volumes. Your Committee are confident that material suitable for the Club's publications can be obtained from these volumes, but would defer reporting more fully upon them at present.

4. *Correspondence, &c.*—A collection of " Letters," covering the period from 1552 to 1800, is contained in 20 volumes, having an average of 400 letters each, or 8000 in all. Besides letters received there are also copies of letters sent, copies of instructions to the Burgh representatives at the Convention of Burghs, receipts and memoranda of a miscellaneous character, connected with the business of the Burgh during the period indicated. The Council Registers also will furnish copies of letters received before the commencement of this collection, chiefly Royal and Privy Council Missives. There is likewise a series of " Letters sent," beginning in 1729, and comprising about 1600 letters from that period till 1800. As the two series are of considerable historical importance, a Calendar of all the letters would doubtless prove interesting to the members of the Club, while some of the more important letters might be printed *in extenso*.

5. *Register of Deeds, Bonds, Contracts, &c.*—This series is complete from 1569 to 1710, and embraces 15 volumes. The Contracts from the latter date to 1809 are not bound in volumes, but arranged in bundles, and are not so accessible. The Contracts, Deeds, &c., recorded in this Register are of a very interesting nature, comprising contracts of marriage, wadsets of County and Burgh properties, agreements between heirs-portioners, and such like. A comprehensive Calendar of these Deeds might be prepared, and where of general interest the Deeds might subsequently be printed in full.

6. *Propinquity Books.*—This series comprises four volumes, and embraces the period from 1637 to 1797. Previous to 1637 it would appear

that the Birth Brieves were recorded in the Council Registers, and an examination of these would carry the period of commencement back to a much earlier date than the first recorded in this series. Specimens of these Birth Brieves, from the first volume of the series, have been printed in the 5th volume of the Miscellany of the Spalding Club.

7. *Accounts.*—The importance of Accounts in illustrating contemporaneous events is well known, and it may be proper to keep in mind that the archives of the Town contain the following sets of Accounts :—

Treasurer's Accounts, 1569-1800. 9 vols. A few extracts are printed in volume V. of the Spalding Club Miscellany, from the Council Registers, in which the earlier Accounts are engrossed.

Guildry Accounts, 1453-1800. 8 vols. A large number of extracts from these Accounts is given in the volume above referred to.

Shore Work Accounts, 1596-1800. 4 vols.

Kirk and Bridge Work Accounts, 1571-1800. 8 vols. Your Committee beg to draw the attention of the Family History Committee to the very complete lists contained in this series of Accounts, of Interments in St. Nicholas Churchyard, from 1571 downwards.

Hospital Accounts, 1607-1800. 6 vols.

Mortification Accounts, 1615-1800. 12 vols.

II.—Sheriff Clerk's Records.

There are in the custody of the Clerk of Supply 21 MS. volumes of Extracts made by the late Mr. John Grant Leslie, Sheriff Clerk Depute, some of which are said to have been prepared with a view to publication by the Spalding Club. They consist of a Report on the State of the Parochial Registers of the

County of Aberdeen, now in the General Register House, Edinburgh; copies of services of heirs; copies of proceedings at Head Courts of the County and in the Sheriff Court, &c., &c.

Your Committee have appointed a Sub-Committee of their number to examine and report on these volumes, and generally as to the Records under the charge of the Sheriff Clerk.

After full consideration your Committee are of opinion that as a first instalment of the matter above referred to, a Calendar of the Correspondence should be prepared, and a number of the most interesting and important letters printed, and they accordingly beg to recommend the General Committee to remit to the Editorial Committee to report on the desirability of this being carried out by the Club. They further recommend that the work of calendaring should be entrusted to Mr. Alex. M. Munro, who has expressed his willingness to undertake it.

P. M. CRAN, *C.*

REPORT BY THE COMMITTEE ON ECCLESIASTICAL AND EDUCATIONAL RECORDS

(approved at the Meeting of the Acting Committee on Wednesday, 12th January, 1887).

YOUR Committee are glad to learn that the Rev. James Cooper has undertaken to edit for the Club the St. Nicholas Chartulary, and that the Secretary, Mr. Anderson, is engaged on the Fasti of Marischal College, both of which works have been approved by the Editorial Committee.

There is also some prospect of an interesting monograph on the emblazoned ceiling of St. Machar's Cathedral being submitted to the Club. Principal Geddes has kindly offered to furnish the historical part of the work, and Mr. Peter Duguid, Advocate, is willing to undertake the elucidation of the heraldic portion, embracing the Forty-Eight Shields represented on the roof of the Cathedral.

A reference to the Reports of the Royal Commission on Historical Manuscripts will show that there is a wide field of investigation open to your Committee. The collection of manuscripts belonging to the late Bishop Kyle, and now preserved at Buckie, includes an immense mass of letters and papers connected with the Ecclesiastical History of Scotland (chiefly of the Northern District), from about 1597; as well as seventy-two original letters of Mary Queen of Scots. This collection also contains ample materials for the history of the Scots

Colleges at Valladolid, Ratisbon, and Rome. Bishop Macdonald has courteously promised to use his influence to obtain for the Club's editorial staff full access to these, as well as to the Collection at Blair's College, which includes, among other interesting material, a History of the Scottish Benedictine Monastery of St. James at Ratisbon from the earliest times, and copies of bulls, charters, &c., relative to the Scots College at Ratisbon. There are also said to be at Blairs many papers and books which belonged to the Scots College at Paris. This statement alone would justify an enquiry into the contents of this interesting library.

Other Ecclesiastical documents connected with the district and still unedited are :—

The Charters of the Maturin, Dominican, Carmelite and Franciscan Friars of Aberdeen, 1211-1560. (Mr. Anderson looks forward to edit these.)

The Charters of the Priory of Restennet in Angus. (It is understood that the late Dr. John Stuart made some progress in preparing these for publication.)

The "Martyrologium Secundum usum Ecclesiae Aberdonensis," which lies in the Library of Edinburgh University.

The Kalendar of the Præmonstratensian House of Fearn, which is preserved in the Library at Dunrobin Castle.

With regard to Ecclesiastical Records generally, your Committee propose as a preliminary course to send out a series of queries, addressed to Synod, Presbytery, and Session Clerks, Parish Clergymen, Town Clerks, and others, resident within the five Counties which form the more immediate field of the Club's operations, asking for information as to the Records in their possession, the dates of the commencement of these Records, the nature of their contents, references to Educational and Social Questions, &c. Your Committee request that you will grant them authority to incur the necessary expenses.

Apart from the Secretary's promised " Fasti," nothing has as yet been done in connection with Educational Records. It is felt that until the Ecclesiastical and Town Council Records have been thoroughly explored, any broad treatment of the History of Education in the district will be impossible.

Your Committee would hope that by the publication of the History of the Scots Colleges at Ratisbon, Valladolid, Paris and Rome, much information would be gained regarding the " Scot abroad." The printing of the " Register of Propinquities," preserved in the Town House Charter Room, would throw much light on the origin of the Scots who visited the Continent ; but a recommendation having this object in view might come more appropriately from the Committee on Burgh Records.

JAMES MOIR, C.

REPORT BY THE COMMITTEE ON FAMILY HISTORY

(approved at the Meeting of the Acting Committee on Wednesday,
26th January, 1887).

YOUR Committee beg to report that they have sent letters of
enquiry to a number of parties within the area embraced in the
operations of the Club, who are supposed to have material that
is suitable for historical and genealogical purposes. They have
received very favourable replies regarding the amount of material
and the willingness of owners to co-operate in the work before
the Club. The Committee must particularly acknowledge the
generous offers of the use of documents and special information from their own collections or from those under their
charge, made to the Committee by, amongst others, the Marquis
of Huntly, the Earls of Southesk, Northesk, and Aberdeen,
Lord Forbes, the Lyon King of Arms, and Mr. Dickson,
Curator of the Historical Department in H.M. Register House,
Edinburgh.

In estimating the work that comes naturally before this
Committee and the amount of documentary material that is
likely to be found in the north-east of Scotland, or can be drawn
from other quarters in order to illustrate its history, the Committee
turned first to the published Reports of the Royal Commission
on Historical Manuscripts, in so far as they relate to the district,
and then to the sources from which the Spalding Club obtained
both charter evidence and other contributions. For convenience
in preparing the Report, the plan is here adopted of dividing,

by the general line of the Dee, the ground to be specially investigated.

I. ELGIN, BANFF, AND ABERDEEN.—In the counties of Elgin, Banff, and Aberdeen, the following Charter-chests and Libraries have been examined and reported upon by the Historical MSS. Commissioners with more or less of fulness :—Gordon Castle, Burgh Records and Registers of Aberdeen, Aboyne Castle, Dunecht, Castle Forbes, Crathes Castle, Drum Castle, Whitehaugh, Aberdeen University, Cullen House, Duff House, Auchmacoy, Invercauld, Haddo House, Craigievar and Fintray, Fyvie Castle, and Gordonstone. Of these, the following have contributed special articles to the Spalding Club Miscellany, besides many illustrative charters : Gordon Castle, Burgh Records &c. of Aberdeen, Crathes Castle, Drum Castle, Whitehaugh, Auchmacoy, and Aberdeen University. But while the Collections at Gordon Castle, Aberdeen Burgh Registers &c., Castle Forbes, Aberdeen University, Cullen House, Auchmacoy, Invercauld, Haddo House, Craigievar and Fintray, Fyvie Castle, and Gordonstone appear to be reported upon with considerable minuteness and care by the Royal Commissioners, there is evidently much that remains to be done at Aboyne Castle, Dunecht, Crathes Castle, Drum Castle, Whitehaugh, and Duff House. Some of these are reported to be peculiarly rich in material for the history and pedigrees of Scotch families : such are the Collections at Gordon Castle, Aboyne Castle, Castle Forbes, Crathes Castle, Whitehaugh, Cullen House, Duff House, Invercauld, Haddo House, Craigievar and Fintray, Fyvie Castle, and Gordonstone.

There are many other valuable repositories within the Northern counties that should still yield a rich harvest, although some of them have already provided selections to the Spalding Club. In Aberdeenshire may be mentioned the Collections at Slains Castle, Keith-hall, Philorth, Monymusk, Castle Fraser, Leith Hall, Craigston, Meldrum,

Druminnor, Fetternear, Pittodrie, Cluny Castle, Strichen, Straloch, Brucklay, Parkhill, Wardhouse, &c.; in Banffshire, at Forglen House, Montblairy, Troup, Ballindalloch, Park and Drummuir, Kinninvie, Letterfourie, Edingight, &c.; and in Elgin, at Darnaway, Brodie, Dunphail, Duffus, Altyre, Gordonstone, &c. This list is far from exhaustive, and there are many others that will come into view as time permits investigations to be made.

II. KINCARDINE AND FORFAR.—Keeping in view the compilation of COLLECTIONS FOR THE HISTORY OF ANGUS AND THE MEARNS, undertaken by the Rev. James Gammack, Aberdeen, and sanctioned by the Editorial and Acting Committees, your Committee have carefully enquired into the documentary resources of these counties. The following Charter-chests and Libraries have been examined and reported upon by the Historical MSS. Commissioners:—Panmure House, Brechin Castle, Glamis Castle, Cortachy Castle, Guthrie Castle, Blairs College, Montrose Burgh Records, Monboddo, House of Dun, Kinnaird Castle, and Arbuthnott House. To this may be added a reference to the papers at Buchanan Castle and at Ochtertyre, which are also reported upon, and contain numerous documents that bear upon the families connected with the Lindsays and the Keiths-Marischal : the Collection belonging to Mrs. Barclay Allardice is most valuable for many Kincardineshire families. The Spalding Club has published contributions, obtained from the following Houses :—Panmure House, Brechin Castle, Cortachy Castle, House of Dun, and Arbuthnott. The owners of these and others are willing to allow the Committee to use whatever is suitable among their muniments, and means will be adopted for definitely bringing the wants of this Special Committee before them.

There is evidently an abundant supply of illustrative documents in the Collections already named, as well as in many old family Houses throughout the two counties, such as Aldbar, Airlie Castle, Balnamoon, Fotheringham, Guynd, Baldovan, Tealing, Anniston, Fettercairn, Fasque,

Thornton, Dunninald, Brotherton, Usan, &c. The Town Records of Montrose, Brechin, Forfar, Arbroath, and Dundee are practically untouched for this purpose, while in the Public Offices in Edinburgh there must be unlimited stores.

From the enquiries made, as described above, the Committee are fully convinced of the existence of a very large amount of most interesting and valuable information, suitable for the compilation of Volumes either as Antiquities or as Miscellanies. At the same time, however, it may be mentioned that, both south and north of the Dee, the ground has already been gone over for works now published by other literary clubs, though these works are more connected with Ecclesiastical objects than with those of Family History. Of such a character are the *Registrum Episcopatus Aberdonensis, Registrum Episcopatus Moraviensis, Liber Pluscardensis,* and *Records of the Monastery of Kinloss,* belonging to the three northern counties ; and the *Registrum Episcopatus Brechinensis, Registrum de Aberbrothoc, Registrum Prioratus S^{ti} Andree, Registrum de Panmure, Chartulary of Cupar Abbey,* and *History of the Carnegies, Earls of Southesk,* for the two southern. But these have not exhausted the field, especially in the direction that is contemplated by this Committee.

J. ALLARDYCE, C.

SECOND REPORT BY THE EDITORIAL COMMITTEE

(approved at the Meeting of the Acting Committee on Tuesday, 5th July, 1887).

THE EDITORIAL COMMITTEE, believing that it would interest the members of the Acting Committee, and of the New Spalding Club generally, to learn what further works, suitable for issue by the Club, are in progress, or are likely to be placed at their disposal, have pleasure in submitting the following Report :—

5th. The Committee have gladly accepted the offer of a Monograph on the EMBLAZONED CEILING OF ST. MACHAR'S CATHEDRAL, ABERDEEN, the historical and literary part of which will be contributed by Principal Geddes, and the heraldic by Mr. Peter Duguid, Advocate. In connection with this, the Principal reports that the trustees of the late Mr. Andrew Gibb have offered to afford the Club the use of a volume of illuminations, executed by Mr. Gibb, containing the complete series of escutcheons on the ceiling, on certain terms and conditions, which appear to be very moderate and reasonable. The Editors wish to have the proposed book illustrated by reproductions in colour of these beautiful drawings ; also by sketches of the Cathedral as it now is ; of the ground plan ; of the heraldic ceiling as a whole ; of the fretwork connecting the roof with the walls ; and of the tomb of Bishop Gavin Dunbar, erector of the heraldic ceiling ; also by a photogravure of his portrait in the possession of the University. We cordially adopt these proposed additions to the volume, which bids fair, with such illustrations, to form one of the most attractive ever issued by any Book-Society; and we hope that the Acting Committee may be able, when the time comes, to find that the finances of the Club admit of the work being brought out as soon as it is reported to be ready for the press, which is expected to be early next year.

6th. We have also much satisfaction in announcing that the Rev. Walter Gregor, LL.D., Pitsligo, has in preparation a work on the PLACE-NAMES AND FOLK-LORE OF NORTH-EASTERN SCOTLAND, which he has placed at the disposal of the Club, and which we, as Editorial Committee, gladly accept. We consider that the Club is to be congratulated on the prospect of possessing a book which, there can be no doubt, judging by other work coming from the same source, will gain a permanent and even European reputation.

7th. Mr. George Burnett, LL.D., Lyon King-of-Arms, has consented to compile for the Club a volume on the ancient baronial FAMILY OF BURNETT OF LEYS, amplified and illustrated by materials of great interest, existing in this country and on the Continent. Sir Robert Burnett, in the most liberal and gratifying manner, has consented to give the Lyon unreserved access to his family papers. At the hands of the last-named gentleman, as Editor, we need scarcely point out that we may look for a work peculiarly acceptable to our members. Mr. Burnett's letter will be before the Acting Committee, and we have no doubt that the very reasonable stipulations made by him will meet with their cordial sanction and approval.

8th. We have, further, the pleasure to announce that Monsignor Campbell—who is one of our members—has consented to edit for the Club the REGISTER OF THE SCOTS COLLEGE AT ROME, of which ancient institution he is the Rector and Head, illustrated by historical and biographical notes, which Dr. Campbell is in all respects peculiarly well qualified to give. This work, we feel every confidence, will prove to be of no common interest, throwing light, as it cannot fail to do, not only on the lives of many distinguished men of Scottish origin, but on what is of high importance, historically, the intercourse between this country and the Papal See throughout the Middle Ages. From the cordial and courteous manner in which we have been met by those dignitaries of the Roman Catholic Church with whom we have been in communication, we are led to hope that, in the future, other volumes drawn from materials existing in this country—notably (as reported by our Ecclesiastical and Educational Committee in their Report of 12th January last) those deposited at Blairs, Buckie, and Edinburgh—may be brought out by the Club, illustrative of the history of the other Scottish Religious Houses of the Continent. The national origin of some of these has, we know, been matter of dispute ; but, though no doubt some were of Hiberno-Scotic foundation, they all, without exception, became Scottish—in the modern sense of the word—early in the Middle Ages. And among the recluses who found a home at Ratisbon and Paris, at Douai, Madrid, Valladolid, and other such retreats, we know that not a few had made their way, at one period or another of their lives, from North-Eastern Scotland, and also that among them were some who left names eminent in Religion, and not unknown in the Literature of their time.

9th. It was recommended by the Committee on Burgh and Judicial Records, in their Report of 12th January last, that the first work to be taken up within their province should be a CALENDAR OF THE LETTERS IN THE ABERDEEN TOWN HOUSE, 1433-1800, to be accompanied by a selection of the more interesting and important letters. They further recommended that the work of Calendaring should be entrusted to Mr. A. M. Munro. We willingly approve of both suggestions, and shall be glad to have the Calendar placed in our hands as soon as completed, with a view to the selection of the letters to be printed.

We find that Mr. W. Cramond of Cullen will be unable to have the manuscript of the work on which he is engaged—" The Annals of Banff"—in readiness for the consideration of the Committee before September of next year. Mr. Cramond expresses his strong sense of the courtesy which has accorded him access to the muniments at Duff House. He reports that a complete Calendar exists of the Charters, &c., &c., which form the extensive and multifarious collection there. It is worthy of consideration whether, with the permission of the Earl of Fife, a copy of that Calendar should not be obtained for the Club. As a work of reference, it might be both convenient and valuable.

Communications have been before the Committee from the Rev. James Cooper, Dr. W. F. Skene, and Mr. P. J. Anderson, requesting its approval of certain illustrations to the books on which, under the sanction conveyed in our First Report, they are now engaged. The desired illustrations are :—For the "St. Nicholas Chartulary, Part I."—Sketches of the interior of Colli-son's Aisle ; of the boss of St. Nicholas ; of the ornamentation on the old bells ; of the exterior of the church prior to 1835 ; of the ground plan prior to 1750 ; of the old city seals ; and of a page of the Chartulary. For the "Skene History"—Sketches by Mr. James Skene, of the houses of Skene, Halyards in Fife, Halyards in Lothian, and Rubislaw, and of Sir George Skene's house in the Guestrow; also of the "Skein" or dirk. For the "Marischal College Fasti, Part I."—Photogravures from por-traits of George, fifth Earl Marischal, by Jamesone ; of William, sixth Earl Marischal, by Jamesone ; of Principal Patrick Dun, by Jamesone ; and of Mr. Secretary Reid ; all four connected with the *incunabula* of the College, temp. Jac. VI : also a map, shewing those portions of the town of Aberdeen that are built on the crofts of the Grey, the Black, and the White Friars, which came into possession of the College. These applications had also been before the Acting Committee ; but such details being connected with works to be issued, certainly fall to be decided on by the Editorial Committee. We, however, willingly agree to them, as proposed. Principal Geddes states that the Senatus have consented to allow the portraits in their possession to be photographed. He was, however, not able to report that the Senatus could contribute, at all events at the present stage, to the expense of such reproductions.

As regards the printing of the Chartulary, we regret to have to state that the Transcript which was made in 1846 for the

Spalding Club, and on which the Editor relied as his principal guide, has been found to be so imperfect and inaccurate as to ne-cessitate much unexpected labour in its collation with the original. This, unfortunately, will postpone the completion of the work for sometime. How long, we are scarcely, at present, able to say. We find also that from various causes Dr. Skene's volume will not be completed in so short a time as, at the outset, we were encouraged to hope. Both works are, however, making steady progress, and are being sent to the press as fast as portions of the manuscripts are ready.

We have been in communication with the Rev. Mr. Temple, St. Margaret's, Forgue, with reference to his work on the District of Formartine, which that gentleman had very oblig-ingly placed at the disposal of the Club. As, however, this work brings the history of Formartine down to the present time, and as the modern portion would be unsuitable for us to issue, Mr. Temple has elected to withdraw his offer, and to publish the book in the ordinary way, as he had originally intended. It would certainly have been unfair to expect that he should curtail or mutilate a book, the result of great industry and research, and one which will be of much interest to the general reader, merely in order to bring it within the limits suitable for the purposes of our Society. We must, at the same time, express our sense of the considerate and courteous tone in which Mr. Temple has conducted the negotiations with us.

It will interest the members to learn that Mr. Lowe, the "Times" correspondent at Berlin, who has presented to the Club a copy of the brief sketch of Field-Marshal Keith by the

German writer, Varnhagen von Ense, informs the Secretary that manuscripts exist in the Royal archives at Berlin which would be of service in the compilation of an exhaustive biography of that distinguished son of North-Eastern Scotland. He suggests that such a work would be peculiarly appropriate as one to be undertaken by the New Spalding Club. The same idea had occurred to several of our members, and the Rev. Andrew Chalmers, Wakefield, calls our attention to similar material preserved in the Library of the University of Berlin. It is to be hoped that this proposal may bear fruit, and that a suitable editor may be found for a volume dealing not merely with the life of James Keith, but with the almost equally interesting though less-known career of his elder brother, George, the last of the Earls Marischal. Indeed a history of the Keith Family generally, giving authentic accounts of its many members who have gained distinction in different spheres of public life, would be singularly attractive in itself, and, we cannot doubt, would be received with much acceptance by our members.

C. ELPHINSTONE DALRYMPLE, C.

REPORT BY THE COMMITTEE ON TOPOGRAPHY AND ARCHÆOLOGY

(approved at the Meeting of the Acting Committee on Tuesday, 5th July, 1887).

CONSIDERABLE delay has occurred in presenting a Report on the work of the Topographical and Archæological Committee. This delay has arisen from the difficulty of devising a feasible plan for collecting material necessary for carrying out the work entrusted to the Committee. The other Committees have material in existence for the accomplishment of much of the work committed to them. This Committee has to collect the greater part of the material necessary for its work. The issue, as a Club publication, of a Handbook, in the form of a series of questions on the different subjects coming within the Committee's province, was at one time thought of. This plan, after mature deliberation, was considered not adapted to bring about the wished for end. The Committee would now desire to place in short form before the members of the Club, and others that take an interest in the various questions under charge of the Committee, the kind of information needed, and to ask their help in collecting such.

The attention of the Committee is directed chiefly to Topography and Folk-lore.

The main object of Topography is a collection of the names of all places (within the bounds embraced by the Club), viz. :— provinces, parishes, mountains, hills, moors, mosses, farms, fields, forests, caves, lakes, rivers, streams, wells, fords, bridges, roads, villages, churches, castles, old buildings, &c. Connected with many of these are legends and rhymes which should be carefully chronicled.

The branches of Folk-lore are numerous. Some of them are Superstitions, connected with great natural objects, as the Heavenly bodies, the Earth, the Sea; with Trees and Plants; with Animals: with Goblins; with Witches: Leechcraft; Magic and Divination; Customs, both festival and ceremonial, *e.g.*, Christmas and New-Year customs; Birth, Marriage and Burial customs; Games of all kinds, with their rhymes, if any; Nursery tales; Ballads and Songs; Jingles, Nursery rhymes, and Riddles; Proverbs and Sayings.

The smallest scrap of information on any of these subjects is of value. Each one who knows, it may be but a single rhyme or riddle, is earnestly asked to commit it to writing, and send it to the Convener of the Committee. In writing out tales, rhymes, jingles, &c., the greatest care must be taken to give them in the exact words of the speaker. At the same time, the speaker's age, with place of birth and education, should be noted. All variants, however slight, should be collected.

When received, each item will be assigned to its proper section, and when enough material has been collected, it will be carefully digested with a view to being issued as a volume or volumes to the members of the Club; such a work having received the hearty approval of the Editorial Committee. Material has been already gathered relating to several of the subjects enumerated, but not sufficient to warrant the issue of an exhaustive volume on any one subject.

As having an important bearing on the other or Archæological side of the Committee's duties, and on the primary object of the New Spalding Club—"to promote the study of the History of the North-Eastern Counties of Scotland"—it is desirable to obtain as complete a bibliography as possible of the materials in or relating to the district under survey, which are in any way calculated to elucidate and enrich its history. For this purpose, two things in particular have to be kept in view.

In the first place, it is necessary to repair as far as is yet possible the oversight of our predecessors in failing to preserve, systematically, contemporaneous documents. As materials for history these are much more trustworthy and satisfactory than oral traditions, or histories compiled some time after the events. In the second place, it is necessary that, with regard to the events of our own time, steps be taken to provide the future historical student with such full and faithful materials as can be procured.

In carrying out the former of these objects, the effort should be to obtain the co-operation of as many workers as possible scattered over the length and breadth of the district, who may be willing to hunt up, and if possible secure, such written or printed documents, bearing on the history of our region, as have survived the accidents of time and the ignorance or indifference of their possessors. If this were done on an extensive and systematic scale, and especially if attention were directed to the repositories of old family houses and farm-houses, there is reason to think that the results might be surprisingly satisfactory, and that documents of historical value, whose very existence is at present unknown, or little more than known, might be brought to light; while, with regard to others, fuller and more accurate information might now be obtained. Should this fortunately prove to be the case, there can be little doubt that the possessors of such works will be ready to second the Club in its endeavour to have them duly recorded, and if possible placed where they can be easily accessible to present and future students. , In the case where for any reason the owners are unwilling to part with their property, it would be desirable to have, along with the strict bibliographical account of the works, an intimation of the owners' names, and such information respecting the works and their authors as can be gleaned.

In carrying out the second object above mentioned, the aim in the first place should be to encourage the preservation of local publications which have just ceased to be of present value and use, but as yet have not passed into the state of venerable dignity and worth. This is the crucial stage in the history of all published works, and in their passage through it many a volume disappears, of which the historical student has to mourn the loss. In the next place, in furtherance of the same object, a systematic effort should be made to record the current publications of the day which have any literary or historic connection with the district. Under this designation are included not only books and pamphlets printed and published in it, or written by natives of it, though printed elsewhere; but also such publications as playbills, programmes of public ceremonies, civic and political squibs, and similar productions which are generally held to have only an ephemeral interest, but which, systematically collected and arranged, will be greatly valued by our successors for the interesting and valuable light they shed on the ideas, manners, and life of the day.

It is an essential part of the scheme now proposed that a suitable repository be provided for the safe custody and convenient exhibition of books or documents of the kind just mentioned. Fortunately on this score there need be no difficulty, the establishment of a Public Library in the City of Aberdeen at once suggesting an appropriate and easily accessible home. Indeed, one of the objects which the Public Library Committee has in view is a collection of literature of the very kind now suggested, and it is gratifying to know that for that purpose it has already received several valuable gifts. For its successful building up, however, the sustained and united efforts of an organised body are required, and by none other could these be more appropriately supplied than by the New Spalding Club.

Should the proposal now made meet with the desired support, there is reason to believe that, with time, sufficient material would be gathered to justify the publication of a Bibliography of the district within the view of the Club. This is a work which the Committee believes would have a permanent interest and value, and accordingly it begs to recommend that the Acting Committee should remit to the Editorial Committee to report on the desirability of such a book being included among the publications contemplated by the Club. In the event of this recommendation being approved of, Mr. A. W. Robertson, Librarian of the Public Library of Aberdeen, has kindly offered to undertake the compilation of the work. To him, accordingly, all documents or other communications bearing on the subject should meanwhile be addressed, and the Committee trusts that a liberal response will be made by members of the Club and others.

WALTER GREGOR, *C.*

REPORT BY THE COUNCIL

(approved at the First Annual General Meeting of the Club, on Thursday, 27th October, 1887).

THE COUNCIL have much pleasure in reporting that the affairs of the New Spalding Club are in a satisfactory state, and that its prospects are encouraging.

Considering the short time the Society has existed, the number of applications for admission has been large, affording gratifying evidence that the taste for such objects as it was formed to encourage is very widely diffused.

It will be in the recollection of members that, at the meeting on the 11th November, 1886, at which the Club was constituted, the number of members was fixed at 400. That limit was reached within twenty-four hours afterwards,—and the applications came in so fast that another meeting of the Club was called, for the 16th December following, to consider whether the membership might not be extended. It was then, after full discussion, fixed at 500. By the 22nd of December that further limit had been reached, and it may be noted that 61 members of the old Club, 19 of them original members, are of the number. There are now upwards of 40 candidates waiting for admission, who will come in according to priority of application.

It will, we feel assured, give much satisfaction to the members to learn that Her Majesty the Queen has intimated that she "will be happy to become the Patroness of the New Spalding Club." Her Majesty also becomes a subscriber.

A list of the members will be given in one of the first volumes issued.

The district over which the operations of the Club are to extend includes, primarily, the Shires of Angus, the Mearns, Aberdeen, Banff, Moray, and Nairn ; but, should suitable matter offer for volumes illustrating other portions of Northern Scotland, such material will not be rejected, if the acceptance thereof in no way interferes with the work of other Societies.

On November 25th, the Council elected by the Club met to consider the future action of the Society, and six Committees were appointed to carry on different branches of the proposed work.

No. I.—A Committee to manage the finance and general business of the Club ; to make arrangements for the printing and distribution of the works to be issued; and to receive, and deal with, the reports from the other Committees.

No. II.—A Committee to determine on the works to be issued by the Club, and to select the Editors.

No. III.—A Committee to investigate the contents of Charter Chests, and other family and territorial records.

No. IV.—A Committee to investigate the Municipal and Judicial Records of the North-Eastern Counties.

No. V.—A Committee to investigate the Ecclesiastical and Educational Records of the N.E. Counties, also the records of Scottish Educational and Ecclesiastical Institutions at home and abroad.

No. VI.—A Committee to investigate the Place-names, Folk-lore and general Topography and Archæology of the N.E. Counties.

The Committees have held several meetings since their appointment. It is proposed to print their reports, and to bind them with one of the first volumes issued by the Club. It is desirable that these Committees, whose duties have been generally indicated above, should as a matter of convenience be henceforth designated by the following shorter titles: No. I. Business Committee; No. II. Editorial Committee; No. III. Committee on Family History; No. IV. Committee on Burgh Records; No. V. Committee on Church Records; No. VI. Committee on Archæology.

The Committee on Burgh Records have in preparation an inventory of the documents under the charge of Town Clerks and Sheriff Clerks throughout the district. The Committee on Church Records propose to compile a similar list of the volumes in the hands of Synod, Presbytery, and Kirk Session Clerks.

The Council wish to express their sense of the courteous and obliging manner in which the Society of Advocates have afforded within their premises a room, in which the meetings of the Council and its Committees are held, and where the books and papers of the Club can find accommodation. This arrangement is one of very great convenience to the Club, and, the Council feel sure, will be duly appreciated by the members, whose thanks the Council would be glad to have authority to convey to the Society of Advocates.

It has been arranged to exchange copies of the works issued by the New Spalding Club for those of the Antiquarian Societies

of Scotland, Denmark, Sweden, and Norway,—also of the
Scottish History Society.

The Council would here offer to the Club their opinion
that a select library of reference, for the use of the editors of
their works, and of the members generally, to be composed
of books bearing on subjects within the scope of its operations,
would be a desirable addition to the working resources of the
Society; but this would, of course, entirely depend for its progress
on our financial position, from time to time.

A statement of that position, as it stands at present, will be
submitted by the Treasurer, and will be seen to justify the issue
of two volumes at an early date, in return for the first year's
subscription.*

I.—The first of these will be Vol. I. of the CHARTULARY OF
ST. NICHOLAS, edited by the Rev. James Cooper, which,
had our anticipations been realised, would have been
delivered to members before this time. Reliance had been
placed on a transcript of the Chartulary in the possession of
the Society of Advocates, but, on examination, this transcript
proved to be so full of errors that considerable delay in the
issue of the book became unavoidable. This first volume will
give the original text of the Charters, &c., and will probably
be ready in January next. The second volume, to be issued
in a subsequent year, will give a summary, or abstract, of
each document, in English, with an historical introduction,

* [The printing of a financial statement is deferred until payments shall have been made on
account of the two volumes now passing through the press. The Treasurer reports that the
amount of the first year's subscription has been received from every member on the roll, with
two exceptions.]

in which will be embodied some very interesting notes and sketches by the late Mr. James Logan, contained in a volume also belonging to the Society of Advocates : a full index to the whole work will be appended.

II.—MEMORIALS OF THE FAMILY OF SKENE, by the venerable Historiographer Royal of Scotland, William Forbes Skene, D.C.L., LL.D., will also, it is hoped, be issued early in the course of next year. Causes which could not be foreseen have, we regret to say, been the means of delaying this book also.

Other works which are now in hand, and which, it is hoped, will carry on satisfactorily the sequence of our issues during the second year, are :—

III.—A monograph on the emblazoned ceiling of St. Machar's Cathedral, Old Aberdeen ; the historical and literary portion to be contributed by Principal Geddes, LL.D., and the heraldic by Mr. Peter Duguid, Advocate, Aberdeen. This work will be illustrated by fac-similes of very beautiful illuminations by the late Mr. Andrew Gibb.

IV.—The "Fasti" of Marischal College, being selections from the records of the College, with reproductions of portraits in the possession of the Senatus and others ; to be edited by our secretary, Mr. P. J. Anderson.

There are also in reserve for future issue, and already commenced, several works which promise to be of very considerable interest. They are :—

V.—Collections for a History of the Shires of Angus and the Mearns, by the Rev. James Gammack, LL.D.

VI.—The Folk-lore and Place-names of the North-Eastern Province, with notes thereon, by the Rev. Walter Gregor, LL.D.

VII.—A History of the Family of Burnett, by George Burnett, LL.D., Lyon-King-of-Arms.

VIII.—The Register of the Scots College at Rome, edited by Monsignor Campbell, D.D., Rector of the College.

IX.—A Calendar of the Correspondence (which is very voluminous) in the Town House of Aberdeen, with selections therefrom, by Mr. A. M. Munro.

Other works to which the Council look forward as possible issues of the Club (to be edited by the gentlemen whose names are appended) are :—

X.—The Annals of Banff, by Mr. William Cramond.

XI.—A History of the Family of Forbes, by Mr. William Troup.

XII.—The Book of Bon-Accord, revised and enlarged, by Mr. Alexander Kemlo.

XIII.—A Bibliography of the Shires of Aberdeen, Banff, and Kincardine, by Mr. A. W. Robertson.

Several further books are under consideration, *e.g.*, Barbouriana ; Histories of the Families of Keith, Irvine, Gordon ; Muniments of the Friars of Aberdeen, &c. ; and others prospectively mentioned in the reports of the different Committees. .

'The various processes by which portraits, architectural drawings, &c., can now be reproduced, whether by permanent photography or photo-gravure, will render it possible to illustrate the works issued by the Club in a manner which the Council feel considerable confidence will prove satisfactory to the members, while the moderate expense will not press unduly on our finances.

The Council continue to receive very gratifying assurances of assistance from those owners of important collections of historical and family papers to whom application has been made.

GEORGE GRUB, C.

PRINTED BY MILNE AND HUTCHISON,
70 NETHER-KIRKGATE,
ABERDEEN.

CPSIA information can be obtained
at www.ICGtesting.com
Printed in the USA
BVOW06s2322171117
500675BV00017B/458/P